fakebook

fakebook

A TRUE STORY. BASED ON ACTUAL LIES.

Dave Cicirelli

This book is a memoir. It reflects the author's present recollections of his experiences over a period of years. Some names and characteristics have been changed, some events have been compressed, and some dialogue has been re-created.

Published by Sourcebooks, Inc.
P.O. Box 4410, Naperville, Illinois 60567-4410
(630) 961-3900
Fax: (630) 961-2168
www.sourcebooks.com

Library of Congress Cataloging-in-Publication Data

Cicirelli, Dave.
Fakebook : a true story based on actual lies / by Dave Cicirelli.
pages cm
1. Facebook (Electronic resource)—Humor. 2. Online social networks—Humor. I. Title.
PN6231.F24C53 2013
818'.602—dc23

2013011541

Printed and bound in the United States of America.
VP 10 9 8 7 6 5 4 3 2 1

To whoever said, "Honesty is the best policy,"
you are a wonderful liar.

contents

disclaimer

The events in *Fakebook* took place between September 2009 and April 2010. It was a wonderful time for online pranksters when cell phone cameras were still pathetically bad and "checking in" was something your mother did when you hadn't called for over a week.

This book is a true story—but life doesn't always conform to story structure. For the sake of the reading experience and the wishes of people involved, some events have been streamlined and certain names have been changed.

This is a book about how I lie a lot, so don't look so surprised.

introduction

"Thank god, Phyllis left," Netti confided to my Aunt Cathy. "I was mortified. I could barely say hello or good-bye."

"I noticed you were avoiding her. What's going on?"

"You don't know?"

"Know what? Is something wrong with my sister?"

"It's not Phyllis, though my heart breaks for her. Has she told you anything at all? Maybe she's in denial…"

"Netti." Cathy was getting impatient. "Just say what you want to say."

"I'm not sure it's my place. I could be crossing the line even talking to you…" There was a pause. She knew things about me. Sensational things. "It's about your nephew, David."

Netti's my second cousin, first cousin to my mother, Phyllis. For months, she'd been watching my life unravel, but this wake for my Great-Aunt Stella was the first time she'd come face-to-face with my immediate family since it all began.

A few years ago, none of this would have been possible—my mother had always been the main artery for news about the Cicirelli boys, and without her involvement, second cousins like Netti and I would only know each other from polite exchanges at the occasional wedding. But now Netti knew—firsthand and in startling detail—the trials and tribulations of her cousin's children.

"What about David?" Cathy asked.

With wide eyes, Netti whispered, "He ran away from home and is now hitchhiking across the country with some…some young Amish girl."

"*What?*" Cathy's voice rose above the murmur of the funeral home.

Netti felt the sweet relief of confession and continued, "He had a breakdown, quit his job, and started walking west. His father begs him to come home, pleading and bribing, even offering to bring him home-cooked meals out on the highway, but Dave won't listen to reason. It's heartbreaking."

"Where does he think he's going?"

"He won't say, but his last stop was Pennsylvania Dutch country. He walked all the way there just so he could…toilet paper an Amish farmhouse. He even got their horse and buggy! It was so cruel to that horse…"

"I've heard of a sixteen-year-old doing something like that," Netti's husband suddenly chimed in from out of nowhere, "but a twenty-six-year-old? That's very immature. Very immature."

"David was even arrested for it! Because they were Amish, he was charged with a hate crime! And now he's on the lam with his Amish girlfriend, and his friends are cheering him on! Can you believe it?"

"I'm dumbfounded," Aunt Cathy said in a daze. "Where on earth did you hear about this?"

"I saw it all on Facebook."

1 log-in

My phone and desktop chimed simultaneously.

SENDER: Christine@HandlerPR.com

SUBJECT: FW: Wine & Cheese Fries Tasting Event—Invitation Artwork-R3

The artwork is not approved. Any photography used can show a consumer holding wine, pouring wine for a guest (but not for themselves), or having the wine sit on the table, but in no way can it show a consumer drinking it. Our marketing materials should not create the impression that we are promoting excessive drinking.

I began to write back: *Then perhaps you should stop selling your wine in five-liter boxes.*

But I didn't actually hit Send—I never do.

"Hey, Dave." Christine, the account executive for the project, popped into the graphics bullpen. She was wearing a thin, gray penny coat, her purse strap carefully balanced on the edge of her shoulder. A perfect picture of typical fall New York fashion. "Just wanted to make sure you're still here. Did you get my email?"

"The one you sent, like"—I looked at the time signature of her message—"forty-seven seconds ago?"

"Yeah, we need to send these invites out ASAP, so if you could send me the revised artwork before you leave tonight, that'd be great. It should be just swapping a photo."

"I had a feeling Legal might push back. She's not really drinking the wine, though. The glass is just perched on her lips. It's really evocative."

"I hear you, but we're out of time," Christine said. "Let's just play it safe."

"Sure. It's still going to take a little bit of time to do it right. Can it wait until tomorrow?"

"Well...the event is in eight days, and it has to go through Legal again." She put her hand on my arm. "I'd really appreciate it."

I tensed up. After five years of working in a mostly female office in an industry full of charming people, I'd developed a Pavlovian response to flirty gestures. It's a real liability on first dates.

"I'll get it done," I grumbled.

"You're the best! I owe you a box of wine."

"So my overtime rate is pretty cheap, huh?"

Christine laughed as she headed for the door, and I spun my chair back toward my screen and opened the working file for the invitation. I looked at it for a moment. I was proud of it, but it didn't matter. Another good design and another night sacrificed at the altar of Legal.

I get it. You can't expect to be paid to do what you want all day. I was providing a service for a client, and revisions are part of the deal. But it still stings to have your work discarded so casually. To paraphrase legendary ad man David Ogilvy, "When a client changes the design, I get angry—because I took a lot of trouble designing it, and what I designed, I designed on purpose."[1]

I needed a moment to grieve. So I stepped out of the design department bullpen and into the cubicle-rich main office. The

---

[1]The original quote is: "If the client changes the copy, I get angry—because I took a lot of trouble writing it, and what I wrote I wrote on purpose." I recognize the irony that I did, in fact, change his copy.

bones of Handler PR are like any other office space—fluorescent lights, white walls, and gray carpeting. But everyone's workspace is a collage of client products—from stacks of action figures to top-shelf whiskey to prepackaged pastries (actually, a pretty accurate timeline of my life's vices).

Public relations is an interesting field and a little harder to understand than its sister discipline, advertising. Everyone gets advertising because you notice it. Your television show or your magazine is interrupted for a commercial break, where a brand has purchased the opportunity to evangelize on its own behalf.

PR is more subtle. Rather than interrupt the show, PR works to get the show itself to talk about your brand. A holiday gifts segment on the *Today Show*, any time you see someone holding a giant check on the news, a celebrity spotted at a sponsored event—those are all the work of a PR agency making its clients "newsworthy" to consumers. When done well, the "earned media" of PR is cheaper and more effective than the "purchased media" of advertising. People trust a third party. "It's the difference," our credentials presentation states, "between saying you're a good kisser and having your ex-girlfriend say, 'Trust me, he's a good kisser.'"

So if the account staff's job is to create a campaign that will call attention to the client, then it's my job, as a graphic designer, to call attention to that campaign with promotional packaging, logos, event invitations, sweepstakes—anything at all.

I made it to the water cooler, filled the Handler PR branded glass (that I'm pretty sure I branded), and took a sip. I wondered if Poland Spring would allow me to be photographed in such a compromising position. Then I caught myself feeling bitter. As far as gigs went, it could be a lot worse. "Get people talking." That was what PR is about. Sometimes it was an exciting challenge.

But sometimes it was like tonight—arbitrary and fickle. Sometimes it reminded you that you were in a support role, a service to another service industry, and that you ultimately had no voice in a process that has too many voices. Sometimes, I reminded myself, being a professional simply boiled down to doing what you're told.

"Do what you're told." The phrase jumped out at me whenever I heard it and had always rubbed me the wrong way. Along with "just the way it is," and a half-dozen others, it's simply a hollow argument ender. It asks someone to place blind obedience to authority ahead of reason, and that had always bothered me a bit.

At that moment, I felt a weird little itch as a slightly unprofessional but irresistible idea that had been lingering in the back of my mind for weeks slid to the forefront. It was a silly, immature, and completely absurd thought. Yet I hadn't been able to let go of it—not since the Labor Day weekend when it was conceived.

Sandy Hook, New Jersey, is an odd little sandbar that juts ten miles off the northernmost tip of the Jersey Shore, pointing toward the Manhattan skyline. Its National Park status makes it home to a lot of little curiosities—things like decommissioned World War II naval barracks, a marine-biology-focused high school, and a disappointing stretch of nude beach. (I once saw an octogenarian there wearing nothing but a knee brace.) Compared to the more commercially developed beach towns to the south, it's a truly unique place.

I sat on the beach there, facing the pink and orange sunset and completely satisfied with that morning's snap decision to spend the Labor Day weekend at my parents'. I was totally decompressed, like I'd hit a reset button on all the stresses that life in New York City can bring—with the only reminder being my new email-enabled iPhone.

Part communicator, part toy, and part office leash, the iPhone had a strange hold on me and had quickly become my go-to distraction during any moment of downtime, whether I was waiting for the ATM or waiting for the sun to set.

So as nature put on a brilliant performance in the vast vista in front of me, my eyes still wandered toward the five-inch screen. I opened Facebook.

Ted Kaiser
In Red Bank. At the Dub.
Like · Comment

It had been a while since I'd seen Ted—six months, maybe. He was a good guy, if a little predictable. He liked watching sports and bullshitting, not a whole lot else. But I hadn't left Manhattan to find adventure, and the prospect of catching up with a friend was an appealing one.

I drove along Navesink River Road, treating myself to an evening glimpse of the riverside mansions I'd spent my high school summers landscaping, and soon crossed the bridge into Red Bank. Its old, pretty downtown is lined with nineteenth-century three-story brick buildings and lit with wrought-iron fixtures. It's easy to imagine horse-drawn carriages going up and down the streets more than a century ago.

I parked my parents' Saturn between a sports car and a pickup truck and cut through the back entrance to the Dublin House. Passing through the main bar, I took a quick look in the adjacent living room, with its leather chairs circled around a big fireplace. I walked past the main staircase, then out the front door, and was instantly reminded why I liked coming here. Manhattan has almost every kind of bar, but it doesn't have a bar in a house.

I saw Ted sitting with Steve at a table on the brick patio.

"Teddy-K. Steve."

"Cicirelli. I didn't know you were around," Steve said as he signaled for another beer. "Still in the city doing the art thing?"

Steve Cuchinello was usually part of the group I saw when I was in town—our nearly identical last names had given us a half decade of homeroom together.

“Yeah, still there doing the art thing…sort of, I guess. I’m doing promotional marketing, like press kits and stuff—client work.” I instinctively reached for my phone and its inbox before I caught myself. “I don’t really want to think about work right now, though. I’m in town to take it easy.”

“You know,” Ted said, “my dad used to say September was his favorite month. I never understood it, but now I get it.”

I nodded. “It used to have this stigma of school starting—but now it’s just really nice weather. The shore trash goes home, and it’s just locals.”

“Locals? Hey, BENNY, go home!” Steve shouted, referencing the (BE) Bergen County, (N) Newark, and (NY) New York City residents who spend their summer weekends “down the shore,” supporting our local economy and ruining our reputation.

“Hey man, don’t lump me in with those Staten Italians! I’m grandfathered in, and I really do miss it sometimes…though sometimes I think I just miss going to the beach and having my mom cook me dinner. I think I just want summer vacation.”

“Yeah, that’d be nice,” Ted said.

“You are on summer vacation, Ted,” I retorted.

Ted had started an import-export business out of his house. He spent his days…setting his fantasy lineups? No one understood what he did, so we just insisted he didn’t do anything.

“I have a real job!” Ted protested. He probably did, but in our defense, it had been a long time since we’d seen him answer his door in anything other than mesh basketball shorts.

“Yeah, yeah, yeah.” I accidentally looked at my phone—it had become a habit even during conversation. There was only an email about routine building maintenance, but it was enough to return some of that anxiety I'd shed by the ocean. "You know what I do miss? I miss the lack of responsibility. I miss being immature."

"What do you mean?" Steve asked.

"Like...remember when Chris Wasco sold his prayers on eBay?"

"Yeah, of course," Ted answered. "That was classic."

"Nothing was better, though," Steve interjected, "than the time the track team took John Randell's Christmas display and decorated the front of the high school with it."

"Exactly!" I said, leaning forward. "I miss that. I miss being able to do something dumb and irreverent just because it's funny. That kind of 'what the hell' attitude we used to have. Everyone's so cautious now—everything has stakes."

Steve raised his eyebrows knowingly and asked, "Looking to pick another fight with the Amish?"

I had a respectable track record of unorthodox mischief, going all the way back to an unsanctioned comic-book art business I'd operated out of the stairwells of River Plaza Elementary School, although that was ultimately shut down by the infamous Safety Patrol sting operation of '94. But the weird high school feud I'd started with a menacing Amish webmaster was my signature piece.

As a high school junior, I'd discovered a handful of Amish web pages. Struck by the brazen hypocrisy and absurdity of the concept, I started an email feud with an Amish webmaster. Suffice it to say, things got heated, and the whole episode captured the imagination of my classmates for months. I found myself at the center of at least a dozen Amish-themed pranks.

"Ha! I don't know...maybe? I haven't been as proud of a project as that one in a long time."

"Speaking of, can you believe I have to start planning our ten-year reunion soon?" Ted interjected.

"Who cares about high school reunions?" Steve replied. "I have Facebook. I already know how fat and bald everyone got. The only reason I log in is to see how I'm doing. 'Beating you, beating you, beating you…huh, Johnny from third-grade soccer camp has a really hot wife and a sweet car? You're blocked!'"

"Yikes. Guess I better start getting ready," I said with a laugh. "I mean, Steve raises a good point—I really want to win this reunion."

"You better get on the ball. Designing press kits for fabric softeners doesn't exactly stack up to John McLaughlin practicing international law in Brussels with some hot Belgian chick and a Mercedes SLS."

"McLaughlin? He seemed like the kind of guy who'd need a lawyer before being one."

"I guess he switched sides of the bench," Steve joked.

"Well, I could always cheat," I said. "I mean, I've got Photoshop—I can post just about anything on Facebook. A hotter wife, a better car…It's like plugging into *The Matrix*!"

We all laughed and exchanged glances, suddenly excited by a shared epiphany—this joke on Facebook could possibly work! There was no reason my Facebook friends wouldn't believe it. After all, what exactly were Facebook friends? I might know lots of minutiae about their day—but what did I really know about them as people? I mean, I knew from Facebook that Debbie from fifth grade had just sold her fake cows on FarmVille. If I then found out that FarmVille Debbie had murdered someone, I'd be shocked… but I'd believe it. For all of Facebook's transparency, it's still fairly opaque. We know only what people care to share. So what was to stop me from sharing complete nonsense?

Without skipping a beat, Ted, Steve, and I began the gleeful work of creating as many premises for my "Fakebook" life as possible.

I could join Cirque du Soleil. I could become a Tony Robbins–style self-help guru, offering terrible, unsolicited advice to the fringes of my Facebook friend base. I could win the lottery and pull increasingly eccentric stunts with my newfound cash, culminating in a Somali pirate hostage situation. I could be a royal food tester, a professional wrestler, the first male Rockette—I had lived a hundred faux lives by the end of the conversation.

But as the long weekend ended and real life resumed, not only did the idea stay with me, but it blossomed. Watching a baseball game made me want to fake a life as the guy in the Mr. Met costume. A full moon made me want to pretend to be bitten by a werewolf. And on and on it went as I found myself filling my sketchbook with every funny premise that crossed my mind. I was completely inspired—and ensnared. I was viewing the world through the lens of the countless lives I could pretend to live.

If only I were still sixteen, I thought, I might actually do this.

I finished my water and put the glass in the sink of Handler PR's kitchen. Maybe this notion of creating a Fakebook on Facebook would join the pile of ideas I'd never followed through on. Or maybe I'd do it. I wasn't sure. But right now, there was a real job to do.

The tasting event invitation awaited, so I walked back to my desk and spent the next hour digging around stock photography until I found a picture I liked. It was of a woman raising her glass in front of a brick wall, smiling at nothing in particular in that plastic stock-photography way. I added the copy from my previous draft, and with some minor adjustments, it created the appearance of the woman toasting the words. It wasn't a bad start, but the tone was off.

The wine we were promoting had an old-fashioned charm, appealing for its ties to a bygone era of Sunday dinners. So I evened out the levels of light and dark and added a sepia wash to give the scene a vintage feel. I added a texture to the entire image to make it look as if age had chipped away at the finish—as if it had spent decades hanging on Grandma's wall.

Now it was time for the little details. I masked out the woman's jewelry, her painted nails, and her lipstick. I adjusted the colors into the burgundy red of our client's logo. It was subtle, but it made a random photograph into a cohesive, branded image.

I could have stopped there, but I decided it needed one final touch—the glass of wine.

Everything I had done to the photo, I now undid with the glass of wine—masking out the dust and scratches, the color adjustments, the yellow sepia tone. I took it further and pushed the colors in the opposite direction, with the blacks running deep and the red a vivid, lush hue.

The wine now commanded your attention. It was a timeless, immortal glass that deserved a place on your table—just as it had fifty years ago, just as it would fifty years from now. This was a wine to share with friends and family. This was a wine that would never go out of style.

This was a wine that, above all else, was not being enjoyed by anyone in the photo.

I was restless that night, lying in my secondhand bed. I clicked on my light—a photographer's studio lamp clamped to my window grate—and sat up, resting my back against the bare wall that served as my headboard.

To anyone but New Yorkers, I lived in a criminally expensive 250-square-foot space under a bridge—but finding a one-bedroom in the Lower East Side that I could (just barely) afford was the fruit of a four-month crusade and the accomplishment of my life.

That was three years ago, though, and by now my IKEA furniture was beginning to fall apart—which, I believe, signals the official end of early adulthood.

I looked at the stack of books next to my bed. There were four different titles on four different topics, all half read. I shuffled through them and put them down one by one. Then I looked straight ahead at the large, unfinished, and flawed charcoal figure drawing on the wall, and my drawing supplies scattered on the surface of the particleboard dresser with the drawer that didn't quite close.

I stumbled out of bed and logged on to Facebook, looking for that subdued thrill of seeing a notification—of being virtually acknowledged.

I'd been tagged in a photo from a party I'd gone to. I saw a version of myself. A guy who was doing it, making the most of being young and living in New York. He was dressed well, holding out a full drink, arms around the shoulders of a bunch of other New Yorkers who were also living exciting lives. We were partying like we were extras in a rap video.

It was a good photo. It told a good story.

But that's all it was doing, telling a story. And by just showing those posed moments where everyone was smiling—omitting the dresser drawer that didn't quite close or the frustrating notes from Legal—Facebook struck me as just another form of marketing, essentially selling a shiny version of our lives to ourselves and to others. We courted people's attention and then tried to control how we're seen. Voyeurism and narcissism—in that moment, that's all Facebook was to me.

Suddenly, my Fakebook idea felt urgent. Everybody's profile was already a little bit fiction. I could make mine completely false. Facebook seemed ripe for something like this. It felt inevitable. But I had to do it now, before this moment passed.

I grabbed my sketchbook, thumbed through it, and found a premise I'd written down a week earlier. It was perfect—believable enough to be accepted, sensational enough to be noticed, and open ended enough to accommodate whatever whims I might come up with. It was the perfect template for a social media soap opera—a premise that could court people's voyeurism.

And when they looked at the new me, who would they see? If I made myself a hero, I'd just be another person using Facebook to flatter himself. No...this had to be the opposite of all other pages. This had to be a parody of Facebook. I couldn't be heroic. Instead, I'd play the fool—the butt of the joke. Someone spiteful, arrogant, and deserving of his own unraveling.

The idea made even more sense to me as I scrolled down my news feed, looking at each new party pic, each new self-aggrandizing statement, each new humblebrag...it added to the sense that this was something I needed to do.

This scheme couldn't wait, or else I'd start thinking of all the reasons why I shouldn't do it. And there were plenty. It was lying, for one. It would be incredibly time consuming, for another. It would be also a pretty fucking weird thing to do. If I had a legal department, they'd certainly forbid it.

But for once, I didn't need anyone's approval. It was just me, sitting alone in my apartment, staring at the status box's open-ended question:

Update Status

"What's on your mind?"

So I opened the Note feature in Facebook and began to write.

IMPORTANT ANNOUNCEMENT

I'm going to start with the shocking stuff just so you read the rest.

I'm quitting my job and walking across America. Maybe the world. And I'm going to post updates, here, on Facebook. Why am I doing this? I've been in a rut.

Life is nothing, if not time. None of us know how much we

have, but we know there's a limit. For the past several years, I've been wasting my time on "repeat," playing the same song on loop over and over again. That's fine for some, but not for me. I want to switch to "shuffle," not knowing what the next day will hold.

The times I feel most alive are when I'm struck by some bizarre, impossible-to-predict possibility. But these experiences are rarely born out of routine. I need to engage life again by uprooting myself from everything that's made me comfortable and complacent.

I've been feeling this way for a while, but I'm making this decision rather abruptly. I don't want time to be talked out of it. These types of decisions are best made by your gut, not your head.

So I'm attempting a grand experiment. I don't have a real plan or a real destination, I'm just moving west and letting destiny guide me. Well, I do know my first destination. Lancaster County. I'm heading to Amish country. It's a nod to my first adventure from way back in high school. From there…who knows.

I'm traveling light, but I'm bringing my laptop and my iPhone. I've set my phone bill to autopay, and I'm leaving my credit cards at home. It's just the supplies on my back, and the cash in my pockets. I'll be chronicling my travels via Facebook, so you'll all be in the loop.

And away we go…

But I didn't go…not yet. I sat there with my cursor hovering over the Submit button and my index finger over the Enter key.

It was a feeling I'd soon be familiar with, but would never get used to. The event I'd just scripted was floating in limbo—it both had already happened and was still to come. There was something unsettling about that.

I had no idea what would happen if I hit Enter, if I gave those words life and allowed Fakebook to broadcast to the news feeds of an unsuspecting audience. I had no notion of the consequences. I didn't think about the people I'd have to avoid or the feelings I'd hurt. I didn't consider the places I could no longer go to, the events I couldn't take part in. I didn't consider the many hours a week I might have to devote to my second life, or how I'd have to be ever vigilant of exposure.

I was completely ignorant about how intertwined my real life and my online persona could become—how much of what was on that screen was actually a part of me. I didn't realize how doing this might complicate old relationships or prevent new ones.

And I certainly never imagined it could change anyone's life.

Instead, I felt excitement swelling. A sort of wry anticipation. It's true that I wanted to explore an interesting, complicated idea, to take a step out of my routine. But there was also a part of me that still liked to push boundaries. That liked mischief. That liked pretending. A part of me that liked crafting something unusual and seeing how far I could take it.

That night, the thought of whether I should do it lost out to the realization that I could. Facebook, a community of nearly a billion users, is run entirely on the honor system. To a guy like me, an insight like that is just a giant red button marked "Do Not Push."

So I pushed it.

2 | like this

That morning, I woke up with a stranger in my bed, and it was me.

Maybe that's a bit dramatic, but I did feel peculiar. It was almost like that disorienting feeling of momentarily forgetting where you are as you wake up in a hotel—only more personal. But I didn't have time to dwell on philosophical questions of self. My practical considerations were far more pressing. All the details I hadn't considered the night before, when Fakebook was still hypothetical, suddenly came rushing back in a rapid series of "oh shit" moments.

Oh shit. I needed to tell my parents.

Oh shit. I didn't have any photos planned.

Oh shit. I didn't know how long it takes to get to Lancaster County on foot.

Oh shit. I had way too much work to do before work.

It was only 6:00 a.m., but I jumped out of bed in a mild panic. My laptop was still on, the note I'd written last night still front and center. It was just as I had left it. Except that by now, people had seen it.

Pete Garra please tell me you're going to amish country for blood.

about an hour ago via mobile · Like

Elizabeth Lee Good luck! P.S. Saw your Aunt at a wedding on Saturday!

55 minutes ago · Like

Brian Eckhoff Right on. Say hi to my fam when you're in Amish country.

48 minutes ago · Like

Michael Raisch Wow, Here's to your cause...
32 minutes ago via mobile · Like

Honey Valentine Hey! I guess this means you won't be watching "Pauly Shore is Dead" with me this week?
29 minutes ago via mobile · Like

Catharine Moore Dave you are truly awesome and I wish you luck and safe travels. Can't wait for the updates! If you should need anything of course don't hesitate...
17 minutes ago via mobile · Like

Mary Carroll I love that you're starting your trip in Amish country...revenge!
less than a minute ago · Like

Matt Riggio Sounds great. Stop by Buffalo, if you're on your way west!
less than a minute ago via mobile · Like

Brendan McDermott Tell the Amish to pay their stupid taxes Dave!
just now via mobile · Like

Oh shit! I went straight onto Google Maps and plotted a course to Lancaster County. A pace of about twenty miles a day would put me in Amish country in ten days. I could stop off in Philly first in just under a week. I hit Print and began running around my apartment, filling my hiking pack full of whatever crap I haphazardly decided my other self would theoretically need. I strapped it on, complete with my sleeping bag and tent tied on top, set my camera on a timer, and posed.

I paused for a moment to plot out my new self's next steps. Crossing the George Washington Bridge into New Jersey felt like a moment worth documenting.

I uploaded my camera and dug up pictures online. I frantically found images of the bridge. Over the next couple of hours,

I stitched together an image with none of the finesse and care I'd used on the "Wine & Cheese Fries" invitation the night before.

It was almost nine. I couldn't work on this photo anymore, so I uploaded it onto my iPhone, tossed my hiking gear into my closet, threw my laptop in my work bag, and headed out the door.

If part of the joke was how ill-prepared I was for a cross-country trek, then I was off to a great start.

On the walk to the F train, I found myself refreshing Facebook at every street corner, constantly reloading to see new comments. Each new "like" was a burst of excitement—confirmation that this was really happening.

On the train, my Internet mercifully cut out and I began to settle down—but I still had enough nervous energy to tear the edges of my Google Map printout to shreds.

I started staring at the routes, plotting out again and again where I should go, when I should get there, what could happen along the way. Should I stick to highways, or would that encourage someone to try to find me? How long before I hitchhiked? Should I find ways to reach out to truck drivers so I could tag us together in photos?

I just kept staring at the map, feeling nervous. Over and over I looked at the same path and the same city names, as if the next time they'd reveal something new.

I felt like a tourist. Or like my teenage self from the suburbs of New Jersey.

As a high schooler growing up in commuter town, casual familiarity with "The City" was a point of pride—it distinguished you from your more comfortably suburban classmates. It was important to neither be intimidated nor impressed by the ins and outs of New York, and lunch-table stories about the weekend were incomplete without casually including how you "took the 6 train down to Bleecker." You'd never admit to triple-checking your foldout subway map after every stop, or the sense or relief you got when you did, in fact, successfully get off at Bleecker.

It was, of course, all bluster. Every trip was laced with the quiet but unshakable suspicion that we were about to take the wrong turn and fall off the island of Manhattan. We didn't belong. We were suburban posers—glorified tourists.

Throughout my teenage years, even as I got more comfortable with mass transit, New York remained an intimidating place. I was still aware that I was never more than just a suburban poser. Every place I'd been to was public—a shop with an open door, a stadium where anyone with a ticket could walk right in.

So much of New York was roped off. I mean, I'd never even been in a skyscraper. Office buildings aren't for suburban tourists. They only let you in if you have a legitimate reason to be there. Or in my case, an illegitimate reason.

I was nineteen years old when I first walked into the lobby of the Viacom Building, on a mission to falsely convince MTV that I was a Limp Bizkit super-fan.

I had no desire to be an MTV personality—hell, I didn't even have cable. And as far as I could tell, I wasn't pregnant or sixteen enough to qualify for most of their shows. But because I'd sign anything for a free T-shirt, I was on the "MTV casting" mailing list.

I usually just let their emails pile up in my inbox, but the opportunity to star in a fan-hosted Limp Bizkit special jumped out at me. I didn't really know Limp Bizkit, but I knew plenty of their fans. The thought of depriving one of those mouth-breathers a slot on the show really appealed to me.

So I fired up Photoshop and turned a picture of my bedroom into a shrine to Limp Bizkit's poorly played Partycore, then sent it to casting. It caught their eye.

"I'm here for my audition," I told the guard at the security desk. I pensively waited as he looked up my name. He checked my ID and took my picture. It all seemed so serious—so official.

"Fortieth floor," he said as he handed me my guest pass, barely looking up. This was routine to him, but it was epic for me. As with Fakebook years later, I'd made a bit of nonsense and thrown it out into the world—compelled to see where it would take me. It took me all the way to the fortieth floor. I was behind the velvet rope—a suburban intruder who had broken into New York's skyline.

I'll never forget the feeling of stepping into that elevator. I was excited, nervous, amused, and a little outside of myself but also totally engaged. It was a feeling I can't quite name.

Seven years later, I was once again riding an elevator up a Manhattan high-rise. By then, however, I wasn't an intruder. I was a New Yorker, and going up skyscrapers was routine. I had a security card. The doormen knew my name. I was supposed to be there.

Except I wasn't supposed to be there.

The night before, I'd told the world that I was on the move—going anywhere but here. Once again, I didn't belong. And that feeling I'd felt all those years ago when I invaded MTV…boy, I sure did feel it again.

"Dude!" I heard as I exited the elevator. "I thought you quit!"

Joe Moscone, one of the account leads and a drinking buddy, was walking toward me, sporting an ear-to-ear grin and wide eyes. He's a big guy with a linebacker build—the type of guy that wouldn't look right without a beard.

"Oh shit…" I instantly snapped out of my prankster euphoria as the reality of Fakebook started to sink in. "People here saw that, huh?"

When I'd faked Limp Bizkit super-fandom, I'd had a less

complicated life. My "profession" was cleaning the municipal pool. Expectations were decidedly lower.

I looked at the clock and saw that it was well past nine. "Oh shit."

As I hurried down the hallway, I explained to Joe what I was up to. He was a receptive audience and no stranger to making up elaborate and funny lies. In fact, a bar in Hoboken stopped serving test tube shots on the grounds that "Test Tube Joe," the first test tube baby, found them demeaning.

"That's tremendous! What do you have planned for this?"

"It'll be a parody—the hike isn't going to go well. I didn't pack a winter coat, shit like that. If you want to play along, leave some comments. Feel free to criticize. I want it to be a farce—the plan is to make my online self kind of an idiot."

Joe's eyes lit up. "Yeah, I definitely think I can pretend you didn't think this through. By the way, good luck telling the office you still work here." He laughed with his full body.

"Now seems as good a time as any to post my next update." I shrugged and smiled.

Dave Cicirelli

Goodbye Delancey Street.

This is taking hella long, my back hurts, and listening to music has drained my battery...But I'm officially on the Jersey side of the GW bridge. I'm starting to wish I hadn't given my keys to a homeless guy.

Like · Comment · Share

Ara Arnn Dude! Where are you going??
55 minutes ago via mobile · Like

Dave Cicirelli Wherever the road takes me.
54 minutes ago via mobile · Like

Ara Arnn So wait, Amish country? Safe travels dude.
52 minutes ago via mobile · Like

Anthony Brent Word, either way, whatever the move, you might not wanna watch the Devils this year, cause it might be a long season for us buddy.
32 minutes ago via mobile · Like

Dave Cicirelli I know…before I dropped everything I bought the internet hockey package. It blocks out local games, so if I hurry I can be out of market by the All Star break…
28 minutes ago via mobile · Like

Joe Moscone If you're heading down the turnpike, last weekend I tossed a half full bottle of diet coke from my car just south of the Vince Lombardi Rest Area, on the southbound side. It should serve as a nice energy boost. Enjoy!
12 minutes ago via mobile · Like

Dave Cicirelli I'll miss you too.
less than a minute ago via mobile · Like

"To a lot of people," I told Joe, "that just happened."

He just walked away, shaking his head.

"That just happened," I said again, this time to myself. It sort of gave me a chill to realize I was now in two places at once. I felt like I was at the center of one of those philosophy questions about perception. How do I know China exists if I've never been there? People have told me it exists, and I've seen pictures—but I've simply taken it on faith. In my own world, China isn't a place; it's simply a composite of secondhand knowledge. My Facebook friends had no idea that the version of me they saw wasn't me anymore.

I was greeted at my desk by a blinking light on my office phone. As my computer powered up, I took a deep breath and checked Facebook on my phone.

In the handful of minutes since I'd posted the photo of my apartment, I'd gotten three new likes and one new comment. I'd also received a personal message:

Anne DuMont ➡ Dave Cicirelli

Subject: Good Luck

Hi Dave. All I can say is wow.

I totally understand how it is to be stuck in a rut and it seems like life is just passing you by. I want you to know if you need any support I am here, and I mean if you need a ride, new shoes, food, money, MapQuest research…anything. I have family and friends all over Pennsylvania and Ohio. Let me know if they can be of help on your travels. Maybe I can visit and bring you whatever you need. I hope you got yourself some decent walking shoes, keep hydrated, rest when you need to, and write everything down. Wish you the best on this journey and that it may be awesome and safe.

I know you don't know me that well but honestly I really want to help.

Huh.

I'd planned on creating something harmless—something that, at most, would poke fun at the superficiality Facebook encouraged. It hadn't occurred to me that I might also exploit people's longings and elicit their empathy and support. I wasn't really prepared for that, and I wasn't ready to confront it. So I ignored it and put my phone away.

When I opened my inbox I saw a dozen emails from coworkers, all with subject lines to the tune of "WTF?"

Crap. I really hadn't thought this through. I immediately started typing an all-staff email, one that would explain, in as professional a way as possible, that my employment was now a secret.

A few days later, my computer screen caught the eye of another customer at the coffee shop.

Both the girl and the Cake Shop reflected the atmosphere of the Lower East Side—curated grit. That's not to say either lacked authenticity, just that there was obviously a fair amount of deliberation behind how they presented themselves—unpretentious, if not a little too hip. It was definitely a contrast to the Starbucks-like "business casual" ensemble I was still sporting from my work day.

"Can I ask," she said, flipping back her long black bangs with a tattooed arm (in a way that was totally working for me), "what you're doing?"

I should have been able to answer her, but instead I gave her a blank stare. In the week since Fakebook started, I'd had plenty of practice explaining myself at work, but the reactions always threw me for a loop. Some people, like Joe, got it and loved it. To others, the idea of willfully detonating my own reputation was mystifying. It wore me out, like rolling the dice every time I answered.

I looked down at my table, suddenly self-conscious of my weekly planner with scribbled in plot points, all corresponding to a Google Maps printout, and the laptop screen split between Photoshop and a five-day forecast. One of the ironies of pretending to live as a bohemian, I'd quickly learned, was all the planning it required.

Overall, the week had been an emotional roller coaster. I

was shell-shocked by the genuine support I was receiving from Fakebook's unwitting audience, and Anne's note was only the beginning. My Facebook inbox filled up with notes I couldn't even bring myself to read—messages with subject lines like "You're So Brave" and "Thank You."

I couldn't wrap my head around it. I mean, the whole thing was designed to make me look like a fool. Hadn't these people played *Oregon Trail*? You *never* start in October, like I had. I was living in fear that I'd inspire some fool to follow in my fake footsteps.

Even worse, the word "fraud" hadn't occurred to me when I'd conceived of the idea, but if people's opinions of me were improving solely because of a lie I was telling, what else could I call it? Whenever I gave it some thought, I felt like I was a terrible person—so I tried not to think about it.

But while the support from everyone outside the joke was crippling, the support from the insiders was intoxicating. Most of the people who knew what I was actually doing—Ted, Steve, Joe—loved it. They celebrated it. They admired it. And when I asked them to pitch in, they jumped at the chance. I needed critics to counteract all the good vibes people were sending me, and giving my oldest friends permission to make fun of me—without consequence—was an opportunity they relished.[2]

Even my bizarre all-staff email to a largely confused office bore some fruit. One senior staff member really got into the hoax. In fact, her fake Facebook reprimand added a certain credibility to the project:

---

[2]My rules were simple: you can have whatever opinion you'd like about the events, but you cannot create the events themselves. You only can react to things on the Facebook page. I needed to be the only author of the actual plot. Otherwise it would have been far too easy to contradict myself.

Claire Burke ➡ Dave Cicirelli

I thought this whole trek thing was a joke, but I called into the senior staff meeting today and they told me you're really gone. What the hell?!

So unprofessional. I have FIVE projects I was waiting on you for. Now I find out that the rest of the team are scrambling to make up for the work you just dropped. Not cool, Dave. You know we appreciate the whole artistic and creative mojo stuff—that's why we hired you—but you can't just decide to leave one day and...really leave!

Come back to NY ASAP and we'll figure something out. I'll work with the partners to present a case of stress-related something-or-other and you'll get your job back. Maybe we can work out a sabbatical next summer or something. I mean, really. You should have told me about this before you just flew the coop. Call me!!

Gina Lopez ➡ Mary Carroll

I just realized Dave seriously just packed his crap and left. I thought he was joking. My favorite post was the lady he worked with yelling at him on his wall lol. Get him on Nancy Grace or something already!

My audience's respect for what I'd claimed to do was crashing into my collaborators' respect for my claiming to have done it. I was barely able to contain the weird mixture of excitement, amusement, guilt, fear, embarrassment, and uncertainty I felt, and I found it difficult to explain myself to anyone, let alone a complete stranger in a coffee shop.

"Oh, this..." I stammered. "I'm photoshopping a drunk girl passed out at the feet of Ben Franklin."

She looked totally baffled.

"…Why?"

"Because it's funny?"

She didn't quite give me the fawning reaction I'd hoped for, so I tried again. "I'm doing this thing on Facebook—like, I'm pretending to live another life, and I have people believing it's true, and…" I was talking faster and faster, simultaneously manic and meek, unable to communicate the emotional and intellectual depth of this half-finished photo of an inebriated barfly at the feet of a founding father. I could see her eyes start to shift from curiosity to discomfort, as each attempt at clarity made me sound more and more mentally unstable.

Fortunately, my phone rang.

"I have to take this…" I didn't have to. "Do you mind just keeping an eye on my stuff while I step outside? I don't want to be 'that guy on his cell phone,' you know?"

"Sure, no problem." As I walked out onto Ludlow Street, she went back to her table and sat down with the latest issue of *BUST* Magazine, facing my table full of nonsense. I leaned up against the Cake Shop's large storefront window, sandwiched between the door and a freestanding ATM.

"Hey, Dad."

"Is this a bad time?"

"Nah…just blowing my shot with a girl Mom wouldn't approve of. What's up?"

"So I'm delivering you meatballs every night?"

Dave Cicirelli

My dad found me, and he's not happy. "Get in the car, get in the car!" haha. Sorry Ralph. Gotta see this through.

Ps. Thanks for bringing me meatballs from mom.

Like · Comment · Share

Matt Riggio I'm going to really look forward to these updates. This is great. Makes me want to do it too.
14 minutes ago · Like

Joe Moscone Those meatballs likely have a high bartering value with street people. You can probably score a lightly urine-stained bed cushion for two or three.
less than a minute ago via mobile · Like

Dave Cicirelli I know you're just being an ass but I'd kill for a mattress.
just now via mobile · Like

I started to laugh uncontrollably. When I turned around to check on my stuff, I saw the raised eyebrow of the girl watching my stuff. I responded with a poorly advised wink and faced forward again.

"It's all right that I used your picture, right?" I asked my dad.

"Yeah, it's fine. I'm too old to get Facebook…but if you're going to involve me, I want you to stop rejecting my friend requests."

"Dad, we've been over this. It's like you used to tell me, 'I'm your father, not your friend.'"

"Hey, Phil!" Ralph screamed to my mother, Phyllis. "Your son is using my words against me!" Judging by the time (7:45 p.m. on a Thursday), she was almost definitely in the family room in her pajamas, watching *Wheel of Fortune* with a cup of decaffeinated tea.

Judging by the yell, my dad was upstairs on the family computer, forwarding jokes written in multicolored Comic Sans font. If you'd read the thread of forwarded addresses, you'd have found your 1998 AOL account.

But I was actually touched that he wanted to be involved, and saw potential in adding a family dynamic to a story all about flaking out on responsibilities. After all, the antagonism of my coworker Joe and company had already turned into a perfect improv theater built around each new post.

Dave Cicirelli

Today is crazy crazy windy. It's as if the power of my Sicilian mother knows no bounds and she's commanding nature to send me home.

On that note, Taco Bell was a horrible choice for lunch and I'm 7 miles to the next rest stop/exit…

Not loving my options here…

Like · Comment

Terrance J Riley it's still crazy windy!!!

6 minutes ago · Like

Deana Rubin never mess with the sicilian mama

6 minutes ago via mobile · Like

Joe Moscone Maybe you should've checked out the AccuWeather forecast before hitting the streets.

3 minutes ago via mobile · Like

Dave Cicirelli Give me a break, Joe. This isn't easy. Did you know it's illegal to set up a tent outside a highway exit? Well, I found that out last night. Did you know that if you don't have it staked into the ground really well, and it's windy out, it collapses on you, and you're stuck trying to escape your own tent, completely blind and terrified that you've wandered into an intersection? Show a little empathy.

less than a minute ago via mobile · Like

Joe Moscone That attitude will get you nowhere.
less than a minute ago via mobile · Like

Dave Cicirelli That attitude liberated me. I'm a citizen of the road now. I live for the possibilities that await me around the next bend…which aren't rest stops often enough.
just now via mobile · Like

It was one thing to have my friends stir up trouble, but my father? The opportunity was too good to refuse. And fortunately, I come from a long line of ballbusters and envelope pushers—from my grandfather, who never used a front door in his life, to my father, whose Catholic school career lasted for all of one morning. Whether it's part of our wiring or something we teach every new generation, Cicirellis have an innate skepticism about authority and structure. We take it as a challenge when we're told not to do something.

"All right, Ralph. You can be a part of this, but you've got to play it a certain way. I want you to react as if this were actually happening."

"So I should say things like, 'Be brave, stay safe, your family loves you'?"

"You'd be that supportive?" I asked. "I'm glad to hear that, because I've actually been thinking about doing something like this for real."

"Don't be stupid," Ralph responded sternly.

"Yeah! Exactly! That kind of stuff, like how I should think about my future, act responsible…"

"You *should* be thinking about your future! I'm serious. Maybe it's time you at least look into getting your teacher degree—for the benefits. And then maybe consider getting yourself a nicer place to live."

I'd accidentally triggered an argument we'd been through a hundred times. I felt myself getting fired up, but then I remembered the coffee shop girl, who was probably still inside watching me. "All right." I took a deep breath. "This is good stuff, but let's save it for Facebook."

"Yeah, sounds good. Love you, Son."

"Love you too, Pops."

I walked back into the Cake Shop and started packing up.

"If you're interested in checking it out," I said as I walked past the girl, "you should friend me on Facebook."

"Oh, I totally would," she replied, looking back down at her coffee, "but I don't do Facebook. Good luck!"

How hip, I thought, and shrugged. So I'd made a mild fool of myself—good practice for Fakebook's inevitable self-destruction. I had no idea what was going to happen next. Fortunately, my dad had a few thoughts on the subject.

Recent Activity

Dave Cicirelli and Ralph Cicirelli are now friends.

Ralph Cicirelli Dave, Please answer your phone when I call. We need to talk. This idea is over the top. PS Your mother is worried sick. She will make some lasagna if you come home now.

yesterday · Like

Dave Cicirelli Calm down Ralph. I'm in a coffee shop now, relaxing before the second leg of my daily hike. A couple of things:

First, stop leaving 13 minute long messages. They are draining my battery.

Second, I'm not answering the phone because we'll just talk in circles. Ralph…I'm an artist, and my life has gone stale.

We artists feast on experiences. 401ks and dental plans and living in the box that society puts you in may be fine for some...no judgment here...but the life of a bohemian is what I want.

I've already written three poems.
yesterday via mobile · Like

Ralph Cicirelli Dave, I won't stop calling until you answer the damn phone! Your mother is beside herself. Neither of us buy into this bohemian BS.

Being a vagabond doesn't liberate you from the "box." It just puts you in a different "box" that you may never be able to get out of. Don't waste a promising future.
22 hours ago via mobile · Like

Dave Cicirelli I'm not going to spend my youth living for old age.

I'm going to start calling you Mime from now on. You're always trapping yourself and others in boxes that aren't there, man! You can call me Houdini, because I'm an artist who just escaped. Escape artist. Get it? See, I'm already getting my creative juices back.
21 hours ago via mobile · Like

Ralph Cicirelli You may think you're an escape artist but you're really a BS artist.

In 1972, when I was your age, I just got out of the Army, was married and was looking for a job to put some distance between me and poverty. If I was an "escape artist" you wouldn't have had the opportunities you had. Time is fleeting and you'll be where I am much sooner than you can imagine. Prepare for your future now. Don't waste time kidding yourself that you're liberated.

PS. If you come home next week, we can go to "Coffee Sunday" at St. Leo's.
less than a minute ago via mobile · Like

Even more important than my father's involvement was his blessing. On some level, I felt like I'd been given permission to keep Fakebook running, like I was off the hook for the moral ambiguity

I'd been struggling with. If my parents thought it was harmless, maybe I wasn't such a horrible person after all.

Maybe.

I opened my phone and looked at my growing list of unread Facebook messages. I sighed, put the phone back into my pocket, and walked home.

Christine sat down across from me the next day at Handler. "Dave, I can't believe people are falling for your crazy thing."

"You mean you don't believe I'm in front of that furniture store?"

Dave Cicirelli
I can't believe the furniture store let me sleep for four hours before they insisted I leave.

Like · Comment · Share

Justin Marshall Did you give anyone a dutch oven while you were there...?
29 minutes ago via mobile · Like

Dave Cicirelli The future owner of that couch will need a priest to undo the horror he'll be bringing into his home.
27 minutes ago via mobile · Like

Matt Riggio Did you pack a small pillow or anything? jesus...
18 minutes ago via mobile · Like

Dave Cicirelli And yeah, I packed a pillow. I'm not an idiot.
16 minutes ago via mobile · Like

Matt Campbell Dave…I follow your daily posts like a junkie seeking a fix. Rest easy knowing that you're helping my work days go much faster. I'm one of those stuck in the box…and the best I can do is support your journey by keeping abreast of it.
just now via mobile · Like

"Of course not. The pictures are terrible."

"I know, but no one seems to notice, as long as I make it blurry. It makes me question why I spend so much time on your projects."

"Very funny. But I like what you're doing. It's sort of a social experiment. You're testing what people are willing to believe."

I wished I had thought of putting it that way in the coffee shop.

"Yeah, I think it'll work as long as it stays on the rails. But I'm going to make this thing nuts." I grabbed a weekly planner from my desk and showed her the next three months. "I got a head start on some of the Photoshop—I'm arriving in Philadelphia tomorrow, and I have most of it made."

She thumbed through the calendar and shook her head. "Oh Dave…no one is going to believe this."

"Well, that's kind of the point. I want to see how far I can push this. It's comedy, mostly."

"Right, but Dave—you're in Mexico in time for the Day of the Dead festival? That's in like, two weeks! You're on a shipping boat to China in the middle of November after you accidentally kill a drug lord? You join the North Korean circus? This is too much. You're not going to prove anything."

"Let me show you what's going up tomorrow night in Philadelphia." I was getting defensive. I opened my phone and showed her what lay in the future.

POST 1

Dave Cicirelli
I totally just ran into a Ben Franklin impersonator and am getting a beer with him.
Like · Comment

POST 2—two hours later:

Dave Cicirelli
Ok, we've had like 7 beers. He's awsome. We're pregramming at his place, and as you can tell he doesn't fuck around.

Like · Comment · Share

POST 3—one hour later:

Dave Cicirelli
Benn insists on wearing th eoutfit. Says its gonna get him laid!!?!
Like · Comment

POST 4—half hour later:

Dave Cicirelli
the MANN!!!

Like · Comment · Share

POST 5—half hour later:

Dave Cicirelli

I said we should fly a kite…The guy sobered up instantly. I've neverr seen anyone so focused.

Like · Comment · Share

"Sorry, Dave, but this is terrible. I get that you want to push it, but wait until you're out in the middle of nowhere. People know Philadelphia. It's too soon for this sort of thing."

"Too soon?"

Christine paused and collected her thoughts.

"It's like when we launch a campaign," she said. "You can't just launch it; you need to prepare people for it. It's like a long lead. You start to build an audience slowly at first with smaller activations, smaller programs—build equity. That way people will already be looking when you do something big.

"You need people to find this, to get a foundation of followers. Take a month of just walking along—let people still be excited by the fact that you quit your job before you start pushing it. If you're going to Philly, do the Rocky steps, visit friends, things like that. Make it uneventful, because if you go through with this like it is now, you're going to blow it."

"I'll have to think about it."

I walked home, kicking Christine's advice around in my head. I wanted to push this thing as far as I could as quickly as possible, but she was right—the initial shock of walking out on my life was enough to sustain people's interest for more than just a few days.

I'd been thinking of Facebook as this big, dumb thing that served no purpose other than showing me pictures of the burrito someone I barely remembered from high school was about to eat. My aim was to take something strange and then make it stranger—to confound and, really, to entertain.

But there were those notes I was still avoiding—those messages that showed me that Facebook was something more than just absurd. What I was pretending to do out on the road mattered to people, and it was getting harder and harder to ignore that.

The loose approach I'd originally envisioned—the rapid-fire sensationalism, the increasingly unlikely events—wasn't the right approach anymore. I was going about it all wrong. Fakebook was only a week old and I needed to adjust.

I thought back again to my MTV misadventure and how much I'd had to scramble to take that as far as I could.

"Hey, is this Dave…Sicker…ell…ee?"

"Cicirelli," I said into the phone in my kitchen. "It rhymes with 'sister-smelly.' Who is this?"

"Hey! This is Kadisha, from MTV." She sounded beautiful and cool, and her call filled me with dread.

"...Yeah?"

"We got your email. We love your look. We love your style. Any chance you could come in and audition for the show tomorrow?"

I was more than a little stunned. I'd had no inkling that my hoax would ever work, and now I was panicking. I'd been called out on a lie before, but never by a major media conglomerate.

"...Uh, sure."

"Great! See you then, 10:00 a.m.! Oh, one more thing," Kadisha said. "We need you to record a tape of you at home. Be sure to use all those Limp Bizkit posters as a backdrop!"

Uh oh...those posters didn't exist. They were just images I'd grabbed off eBay and photoshopped in.

"Hey, I just remembered. I have an exam tomorrow. Can we do it Thursday instead?"

"No problem. See you then!"

The next day I skipped class and crisscrossed the state, going from Spencer Gifts to Spencer Gifts, until I had bought up every Limp Bizkit poster in New Jersey. All the while I had my Discman playing through the car's cassette deck, blasting a newly purchased *Chocolate Starfish* at top volume as I repeatedly yelled, "I LOVE LIMP BIZKIT. FRED DURST IS THE GREATEST POET OF OUR TIME."

I stayed up all night and crammed—making probably the world's first Limp Bizkit flash cards. I hopped on every message board and every fan page I could find. I read through hundreds of pages of horrendous grammar until I started to absorb the conversation, until I began to believe those opinions were mine. Until I believed in Limp Bizkit.

The email to MTV had started as a goof, just like my email to the Amish webmaster a couple years earlier. All of a sudden the goof became a challenge. And I almost made it happen. I got all the way to the final round of casting before I lost out to some dude with a very new-looking Fred Durst tattoo.

Now Fakebook was a challenge just like those, and I didn't want to come up short again. But it was different than the close call with MTV. It was much bigger, much more complex, and it had the potential to be…well, I wasn't exactly sure what yet. I just knew that I was on to something. Something that might have been right and might have been wrong, but no matter what, it wasn't something small.

To do this right, I needed to understand it. I had to dive in and understand what exactly it was that I'd stumbled into. I looked at my personal messages, finally ready to confront them.

Matt Campbell was a Facebook friend. In other words, he wasn't really a friend at all.

Sure, we were classmates once upon a time. But years later? He was just another piece of my news feed—part of that abstract mass of real-time minutiae.

Facebook friends didn't count. That's what I kept telling myself. The people I cared about, I kept in touch with, right? So those I didn't keep in touch with didn't really mean anything. Which meant it didn't matter what I pretended to do. To them I wasn't even real anymore; I was just a particular arrangement of pixels on a screen. It was all entertainment, and I was providing it.

At least that's what I'd assumed when I started this—and it was an assumption that gave me permission to do Fakebook with a clear conscience. But now I was ready to have that assumption challenged. I logged on to Facebook and read Matt's message to me.

Matt Campbell ➡ Dave Cicirelli

Subject: Godspeed, Friend.

I just suggested a bunch of friends that I know would love to follow your travels. Many of them are out around the country and may be valuable assets in your journey. I'm sure many of them will watch, and offer any help (tips or otherwise…lots of campers and outdoorsmen) or just support.

I must say, I really admire what you're doing. It is very "John Galt" and a huge life experience that some people never get to have. I am envious of your fortitude and newfound freedom…a word that many will never get to fully experience, so thank you.

Also, if Ohio comes across your path, my wife knows TONS of really good, down to earth people much like yourself that would love, if nothing else, to just sit down for a couple beers one night and hear the tales of your trip so far.

I will conclude with saying that it is a weird feeling to be almost emotionally attached to your venture. Like a "Truman Show" only with someone I knew while growing up (dating back to teasing Kelly in 7th grade). Your travels, in a small way, amount to my freedom as well.

Godspeed friend.

He was taking this so seriously. He seemed almost startled by how important my page was to him. To him, my Facebook page wasn't a frivolous thing, but an inspiring and powerful experience that he felt like he was a part of.

He was wrong. Facebook was stupid.

I switched windows to Photoshop and looked at Party Ben Franklin. The photos were funny, and I wanted to make people laugh, dammit. The absurdity of all this was why I wanted to do Fakebook in the first place. That's what had captured our imagination at the Dublin House over Labor Day weekend.

Posting the Ben Franklin images would be taking a stand—staying true to my belief that Facebook was just a silly diversion, something that deserved to be seen for how superficial it really was. I wasn't going to be pressured by Christine's criticism or Matt Campbell's support.

I switched back to Facebook to upload the first picture.

But in that split second I inadvertently reread the line about "teasing Kelly in the seventh grade."

I used to have a crush on Kelly, who used to live next door to Matt. I'd almost forgotten all about that.

I sat back in a room illuminated only by backlit words of support from someone I barely knew, but knew well enough to spark a fifteen-year-old memory that had all but faded away. He'd written a sentence that only had meaning between him and me.

It suddenly occurred to me that Facebook isn't just a website. It's an experience, and a deeply strange, deeply personal one. It involves almost everyone you know and everyone you once knew.

Updates posted by ex-girlfriends living on the other side of the world, your own mother commenting on photos of last night's debauchery, a real-time review of a McDonald's McGriddle from your tenth-grade lab partner—it's laughable on the surface. But it's also hard to ignore the feelings stirred by an ex-girlfriend's update, how much this new transparency has changed your relationship with Mom, how that review keeps an old friend from fading out of memory. The relationships may not have evolved in years, but with Facebook, they haven't disappeared either. It's the cold storage unit of friendships, keeping them on hold, just one compelling post away from revival.

I'd decided to fake my profile because I was looking at Facebook as a whole, but that was a mistake. Everything looks smooth from a distance. But I was tapping into something much less frivolous and much more personal than I'd thought. It was morally complex but also irresistibly compelling. I didn't know what I was on to, exactly…but I knew I was on to something.

Christine was right. Bar crawling with Ben Franklin was too much. It could destroy the project before I even had a chance to understand it. And I wasn't quite willing to have Fakebook fall apart over something this silly, at least not yet.

So instead, my Facebook profile had a pleasant, uneventful few days in Philadelphia, enjoying the virtual hospitality of a friend and keeping Fakebook in a holding pattern.

Dave Cicirelli

Chillin In Philla—after finally having a night's sleep with a roof over my head. Thanks so much Jen.

Like · Comment · Share

Jennifer Morton Good to have you here Dave, you really do need to shower more often while on the road though.

less than a minute ago via mobile · Like

Dave Cicirelli

Thanks Christine for putting me in touch with your lovely mother Siobhan at the library. I'm going to spend the rest of the day reading about other journeys out west.

Here's a book on the Donner Party. That worked out, right?

—with **Siobhan O'Loughlin Reardon**.

Like · Comment · Share

Christine Reardon So glad you guys were able to meet up!

4 hours ago via mobile · Like

Joe Moscone I like that Christine's mom looks younger than her. (Burn!)

3 hours ago via mobile · Like

Marc Flanagan He's joking, Christine. You look at least 3 years younger than your mom.

3 hours ago · Like

Christine Reardon Uhh thanks, Marc?? Haha. You boys are just HILarious.

2 hours ago via mobile · Like

Dave Cicirelli What an awkward thing to read next to Siobhan.

less than a minute ago via mobile · Like

Siobhan O'Loughlin Reardon It was nice to have met you Dave. Come again.

less than a minute ago · Like

Dave Cicirelli It definitely was! Thanks so much.

just now via mobile · Like

Dave Cicirelli

Leaving the city of brotherly love…Which I got none of from my actual brothers. The family is pissed…

Oh, and I was planning on staying longer, but then shit went down. See I was in west philadelphia, on the

playground is where I spent most of my days. I was just, you know, chillin' out maxin' relaxin' all cool. Shootin some b-ball outside of the school. But then...

Like · Comment · Share

Jennifer Davis ...a couple of guys they were up to no good started making trouble in your neighborhood. You got in one little fight and your mom got scared she said...

2 hours ago via mobile · Like

Ralph Cicirelli Dave, Your Mom said "COME HOME. You're being an idiot. I'll make you Lasagna."

2 hours ago · Like

Joe Moscone You were better off avoiding that shithole of a city entirely; it's America's equivalent to Mogadishu.

2 hours ago via mobile · Like

Kaedi Flanagan Joe, I can always count on a good laugh from you on these Dave posts. Keep 'em coming! Oh, and Dave, your updates are hilarious, too.

about an hour ago via mobile · Like

Dave Cicirelli No, Joe...That was Camden. That's the place I didn't hike through...I ran through it. Haha.

about an hour ago via mobile · Like

Mark Cicirelli Bro, you've got to earn this love. By the way, word of advice: don't steal Mike Tyson's tiger. It's just going to end badly. Trust me.

about an hour ago via mobile · Like

Dave Cicirelli And Mark, as always you give sound advice. I'm not doing this for your approval, but perhaps, when I return one day you'll be able to say a kind word to me without guarding it with sarcasm.

It's not easy being the artist of the family.

45 minutes ago via mobile · Like

Joe Moscone Oh for Christ's sake, Dave. Maybe you can take a waaambulance cross country?

32 minutes ago via mobile · Like

Dave Cicirelli What is it Joe? Is it that you have no depth, or is it that you only pretend to have no depth. I can't tell.

less than a minute ago via mobile · Like

With this, I was ready to figure out exactly what it was I'd started. I began to see Fakebook as a real-time, virtual *On the Road* in the form of a twenty-first-century "War of the Worlds" broadcast. It was an entirely new medium of storytelling—a medium meant to capture your passing thoughts as they happened—to an audience that didn't know it was an audience.

But this new medium needed different rules and different goals than a movie or a novel. I wanted to push my story into strange, impossible-to-believe places. To do that required a longer, more disciplined approach, and I needed to respect the timeline of actual events.

Six months, I decided. Fakebook would go on for six months, giving me the chance to end it on April Fools' Day. It was enough time for my online persona to start living a different life. We needed to be different people.

And to write a different person, I needed to get inside my protagonist's head and acknowledge the realities of his life. I needed to start treating the situations, as absurd as I was going to make them, as real events happening to a real person.

It had been fourteen years since I'd created my first online persona—back when AOL CD-ROMs were growing the Internet a hundred free trial hours at a time, and "GarbageM0n" navigated a dozen open Instant Messenger chats like a twelve-year-old day trader. I thought it was appropriate to write Fakebook that way—like an insecure, emotional teenager in search of meaning and afraid of screwing up.

After all, this Fake Dave walked down the road every day, getting closer and closer to Amish country, less and less sure about what he'd do once he got there, straying from a plan that no longer mattered. He was cut off from his friends and family—misunderstood by some, supported by others, but still terribly alone—and stubbornly clinging to an ideal of independence while unable to cut Facebook's tether to his old life.

I listened to the storm outside my window in New York City. It was a heavy rain, and it was almost certainly raining in Philadelphia as well. My online persona and I had parted ways, but he hadn't traveled far. I was under a warm blanket on my couch. Where was he?

OCTOBER 15: A BEAUTIFUL MELANCHOLY

I'm sitting under an overhang on a rainy night.

Originally I was going to make my second extended post from Independence Hall. It seemed appropriate, at least in name. But it wasn't in spirit. It's odd, in Philly I had a hard time writing. Maybe it's because I was in a city. Maybe it's because I was distracted with friends. Maybe it's because I was only $18 and a two-hour bus ride from Chinatown. It felt like a vacation more than an adventure. I'm not exactly sure what was going on.

But I'm back on the road tonight, and suddenly I can write again.

I'm approaching two weeks, and I still feel my old life like a phantom limb. Sometimes I wake up, and for a moment I forget I'm in a tent on the side of a highway. It's unusual, a little frightening and a little exhilarating.

I'm writing from the steps of a school, where I set up camp in the playground tonight. It's a good little find, because it has ample power outlets and WiFi. It's raining fairly hard, and it's... brisk out, to say the least.

But there's something about listening to the rain, you know? It's a beautiful melancholy. Today was hard. It rained a lot, I was cold, and my feet are getting worse...but I'm here, on these steps, listening to the rain, and I'm at peace.

There, I gave my online persona a dose of sensitivity, but that's not to say I made him any smarter.

Dave Cicirelli
As it turns out, camping in an elementary school's playground was not the best idea I've ever had. Still, I want to thank Officer Jim Anderson for being so cool about this misunderstanding.

Like · Comment · Share

Pete Garra haha amazing.
about an hour ago via mobile · Like

Chris Mitarotondo Camping out in a high school would have made much more sense.
45 minutes ago · Like

Katia Tron Wow. lol
39 minutes ago via mobile · Like

Elliott Askew You know…Had you actually ended up on the Megan's law list…we might have been able to track your movements using an iPhone App…So… yeah…Thanks for letting us down.
32 minutes ago via mobile · Like

Catherine Millar You live and learn I guess. lol.
12 minutes ago via mobile · Like

Dave Cicirelli The rules of the road are different. I've done things that would never be done in my old life. Things no man would be proud of.
just now via mobile · Like

True enough, Fake Dave. True enough.

3 | farmville

New York loves Halloween, and I love Halloween in New York.

I love how New Yorkers—no matter what they're wearing—still walk like New Yorkers. Seeing a wolf-man booking it down Fifth Avenue with a "Time is money" stride is surreal, just like the October 31 subway platform, with Ninja Turtles, ironic news parodies, and sexy nurses all elbowing for position. It's a citywide performance art project, an absurd spectacle, and an extremely good time.

For kids or adults, the whole of October moves to the beat of anticipation for the night when millions of people are freed from being themselves. For the twenty-something single New Yorkers like me, it's a chance to throw caution to the wind. Talking to strangers—hell, even accepting candy from strangers—is encouraged. Why not? It's Halloween, and you are not you.

But I was already not me. And maybe that's why I was feeling slightly out of step. For me, it was Mischief Night hanging in the crisp fall air, but my alter ego—the unassuming hero of Fakebook, designed to be the perfect practical joke—was living an entirely unmischievous life.

I was twenty days into the sham and just getting over the initial learning curve. Like all storytelling media, Facebook had its own strengths and limitations. The most jarring was that it made for completely decompressed storytelling. A moment was a moment, now was now—there'd be no skipping over the boring parts. My audience was living their lives in parallel with my protagonist, so not only was Fakebook going to take six months to write, it would take six months to read, too. This was a long con, and as practical jokes go, it would be a *slow* burn.

Still, I'd made the right decision to abandon the early sensationalism and stick to more plausible mini-adventures and funny banter about life on the road. Patience and restraint, especially in the beginning, were crucial. I needed people to invest in the authenticity of the story before I started stretching it.

But while I figured out how to not screw Fakebook up, I was stumbling in my ability to push it forward. Ultimately, I knew that every post was a gamble, so before long, I caught myself relying on the safe bets—living two cautious lives. I even considered a plot in which I became a midlevel manager at an Olive Garden in Pittsburgh. It'd be an easy scenario to create: my flawless pronunciation of "gnocchi" would have put me on the fast track there. But it's one thing to settle in real life—I refused to settle in my fictional life, too.

I needed to remind myself why I was doing this in the first place: games like FarmVille and its mind-numbingly boring posts from Facebook friends.

For the uninitiated, FarmVille is a social media game. Essentially, all that means is that via wall posts, players get to waste your time in addition to wasting their own. In the game, people raise ducks and cows or something. I don't really know how it's played. I just knew, judging by my news feed, that I was the only one not playing it.

It's a feeling I'm familiar with. Growing up, other than watching my friends help me "get past that one tricky part," I was on the outside of my generation's shared experience with Sega and Nintendo. The only video-game system allowed in the Cicirelli household was an Atari 2600—a product of my eldest brother's masterfully leveraged late '70s bout with appendicitis.

Any upgrade was a closed issue. In my mother's eyes, which were blind to the wonders of the sixteen-bit processor, a video-game system was a singular and static thing that we already had one of, so we didn't need another. Besides, she wasn't thrilled about the hospital bed compromise that had ushered the games into her house in the first place. Her motto? Don't do drugs, and don't be a vidiot.

Naturally, I experimented in college. Coming from such a sheltered environment—frozen in an era where game titles were just a general description of the activity—the leap up from *Adventure* and *Combat* to *Grand Theft Auto III* was monumental. I was hooked...until I faced *The Sims*.

In *The Sims*, you create a character, put him in a house...and then clean the house. It's oddly compelling. Soon I found myself consumed and blowing off real obligations just to make sure Sim Dave had a well-balanced life. (In light of Fakebook, I realize there may be a pattern emerging.) I compulsively made sure that my little Sim guy cleaned his Sim apartment, cooked some Sim dinner, went to the Sim toilet, and scored a date with his sexy Sim neighbor.

It was a striking moment of clarity when I realized all this was happening while I sat in a dirty dorm room, hungry, holding it in, and completely alone. At that moment, the walls came crashing down, and suddenly, video games—every one of them—became fool's gold, filling me with a false sense of accomplishment. Mom was right, and I've been off them ever since.

That said, I'm no snob. If people want to spend their time raising a fake pig on FarmVille or cooking a fake ham in *The Sims*, by all means, go ahead. Far be it from me to judge their fantasy lives—I just want them to leave me out of it. And that's what is so infuriating about FarmVille. While it is surprisingly touching to see sonograms from Johnny-from-third-grade-soccer-camp's wife on my news feed, it's maddening to have to watch him try to unload a crop of virtual corn there that he spent a week not growing.

As I developed and experimented with Fakebook in the first few weeks, I wanted it to be a counterpoint to the mundane updates of FarmVille. I didn't want to play games on Facebook; I wanted to play games *with* Facebook. To inject a healthy bit of misinformation into the Information Age.

Every day, more and more people were paying attention to Fakebook and believing the lie. But to what end? Every mischief-maker knows that the power of your thrill is directly related to your daring. The more brazen you are, the bigger the kick. Besides, roadside witticisms and comment-section banter had reached their peak the moment I arrived in Intercourse, Pennsylvania.

Dave Cicirelli

I'm about to enjoy Intercourse. I'm going to be expected to spend the night, aren't I? Well, at least it's a short walk of shame to Amish country now.

Ok. Feel free to fill in any jokes I may have missed. If I'm silent for a while it's because I'm really trying to concentrate. But I swear I'll call you tomorrow.

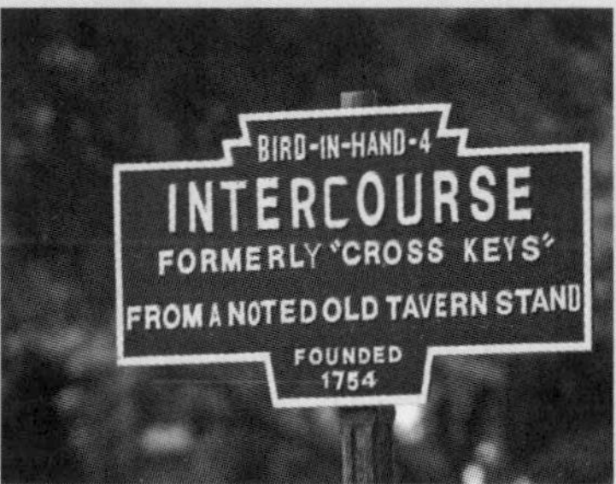

BIRD-IN-HAND-4
INTERCOURSE
FORMERLY "CROSS KEYS"
FROM A NOTED OLD TAVERN STAND
FOUNDED
1754

Like · Comment · Share

Ted Kaiser You should go to the Intercourse Pretzel Factory...I'll let you find out if it's really pretzels.

about an hour ago · Like

Dave Cicirelli It's funny, after about twenty minutes of Intercourse, all I want to do is fall asleep.

55 minutes ago via mobile · Like

Steve Cuchinello The sun was setting on intercourse for you years ago.
40 minutes ago · Like

Dave Cicirelli Nailed it!
40 minutes ago via mobile · Like

Steve Cuchinello Stuck the landing. Now go land an Amish girl.
39 minutes ago · Like

Dave Cicirelli Yikes…I gotta remember the rules. Twenty-one, single, and four kids in NY means she's easy. Twenty-one, single, and four kids in Amish country means she's a widow.
38 minutes ago via mobile · Like

Honey Valentine Next stop, Blue Balls, PA
3 minutes ago via mobile · Like

Daniel Timek Did you insert yourself into the local population?
less than a minute ago via mobile · Like

Dave Cicirelli Winner.
just now via mobile · Like

Dave Cicirelli

Like · Comment · Share

It was time to push Fakebook to its limits, and that meant taking stock of my advantages.

The biggest was the complete lack of precedent. As far as I knew, no one had flipped the switch as I had and become a work of fiction. The Fakebook idea wasn't in the ether yet, and I was dealing with innocent, uncritical eyes.

Next up was the nebulous space in which Facebook friendships exist. To many of our Facebook friends, we're nothing more than pixels on a screen, public figures projected onto one another's news feeds. Facebook is the *TMZ* and *Us Weekly* for our own little worlds—and it's just as unreliable.

So I was hoping that if something out of left field struck on Fakebook…well…I guessed that people would react to it the same way they do to celebrity scandals. As with any sensational news, it would simply be evidence of the unreliable nature of public personas (Tiger Woods, anyone?). In the end, people would shake their heads, but they wouldn't scrutinize the credibility of the report.

Besides, my chips were already on the table. I'd set things in motion the night before by posting a recap of an incident from my past, a true story that would serve as the perfect foundation for fiction…my feud with the Amish.

OCTOBER 20: THE AMISH…

I'm sitting in a coffee shop in Intercourse. Rather than make more puns, I thought I'd take a moment to reflect on what got me here.

The Amish and I have issues, and I'm here to settle them.

Turn the clock back to February 3rd, 2001. It was a more innocent time. The dangers of Y2K had passed, and the future looked bright to all who gazed ahead. How could I not be optimistic about life? I was 17 years old and the most popular and handsome senior in Middletown South.

It wasn't just my husky frame and great comic book collection that made me popular—it was also the award winning graphic design work I did for the school paper. It brought me the respect of the men, and the affection of the women. I truly knew nothing but wild success.

That all changed the night of February 3rd. It started as a celebration. It was the inaugural game of the XFL. Yes, the XFL. The short-lived football league that first brought Ron "He Hate Me" Smart onto our televisions and into our hearts…

While I watched history unfold, something arrived in my inbox… the end of my innocence. A few days earlier, I'd discovered that the Amish don't have to pay all of their taxes. I'd long suspected that their "cash only" policy was just a ploy to keep their furniture-making income off the books…but this was different.

It turns out they have special exemptions on whatever fraction of their income they choose to report…they exploit the very religious freedoms won by the very wars they're exempt from fighting!

This felt like an injustice. Their beliefs were being held to a different standard than yours and mine. I was blinded by rage and determined to catch these hypocrites in the act. And I did—on the internet.

They use websites like Amish.net and AmishHeartland.com to sell their wicker baskets and home-made candles, and to brazenly mock us with their existence. There was only one course of action…an anonymous, strongly worded email.

When I received a reply to my anonymous message, I learned there are stronger words than the ones I'd been willing to write. Words like my full name, my home address, and the name of my high school newspaper. I was hit harder than a He Hate Me tackle.

They went for blood. They contacted the newspaper award committees to sabotage not only me, but my hard working colleagues as well. When I told them they sucked, I did so with honor. But honor is a concept as alien to them as Social Security Tax.

So they strong-armed an apology out of me. They humbled me through threats and humiliation.

I've never forgiven them for this.

Amish, I know you're monitoring my profile, so know this:

You may have scared a child, but it's a man who walks towards you now. Each step I take is a grain of sand falling through the hourglass. Your time runs short and your hypocrisy goes unchallenged no longer. February 3rd wasn't just the beginning of the end for the XFL; it was the day that sealed your fate. What does the X in XFL stand for? It stands for "X marks the spot." And the spot is New Holland, PA.

I'm coming, as soon as I'm through with Intercourse.

Other than a few self-aggrandizing flourishes, that's exactly what had happened in real life. Yes, I was that kid. The high school senior easily (if a bit facetiously) enraged by the federal tax policy. Yes, it led me to write an angry email to several Amish webmasters, ending with the phrase "You suck." Yes, one sent back a vaguely menacing response full of my personal details that suggested, among other things, a deep familiarity with IP address technology.

And yes, I backed down immediately.

I knew that my Facebook friends would remember the incident and that it would remind them of how strange life can be. It also struck me as a good opportunity to continue a story that had just sort of stopped. Here was my chance to write the missing next chapter—and I could say whatever I wanted. After all, in light of the apparent Web savviness of the Amish, what do any of us really "know" about them? They're somewhere off to the side of our cultural radar. They are the Facebook friends of our cultural landscape.

Now that I had revived this old feud, I could write almost anything about it…I just had to write quickly. The moment I posted my proclamation, I'd subjected myself to the unrelenting deadlines of creating fiction in real time. While Facebook grants plenty of opportunities for second-guessing after posting, there's no room for revision. There's only a never-ending sense of urgency—every passing moment is a part of your story. Everything is happening "now." And while each of my posts had the potential to create a loose thread that could unravel the whole story, a lack of posts would raise suspicion, too.

Earlier, I described Fakebook as a giant red button marked "Do Not Push." Now the button was flashing. Was it an ignition? Or a self-destruct? Either way, I carried it around in my pocket at all times—even at the grocery store.

In the chips and dip aisle of my neighborhood grocery store, my eyes lingered on a nearby candy display. I took out my phone, logged on to Facebook, and sorted through my photos until I found the images I'd prepared. I smiled nervously at the ridiculous thing I was about to make true.

All I had to do was press a button, and it would have happened.

But I hesitated and put the phone back in my pocket. I bought a pack of M&M's and walked out of the store. The clock continued to tick.

The first few weeks of Fakebook hadn't gone as planned. I was completely stunned by its immediate impact, and I'd desperately come up with ways to avoid taking the next step. Like it or not—and I didn't like it—my profile was my reputation, and I had put it on the line for something I'd started but really didn't understand. Was I just doing something funny and entertaining, or was I exploiting my friends and their repressed longings? I didn't know. I still don't know. I just knew I needed to land this thing on my own terms.

I stopped at an intersection. I ate a handful of M&M's without really tasting them. I glanced across the street. People were walking out of the costume shop with their store-bought make-believe, and I took my phone out again. The clock was ticking. I had to do this now, or it was all over.

"To hell with it."

It was almost Mischief Night, and I wanted to toilet-paper something.

So I did.

Dave Cicirelli

Like · Comment · Share

Julia Park wtf?...

less than a minute ago via mobile · Like

Dave Cicirelli

Oh my god am I in trouble...

Like · Comment · Share

Jay Patterson Do we have to subscribe to your blog for details?

32 minutes ago via mobile · Like

Matt Riggio what the hell did you do? Is that TP?

28 minutes ago · Like

Pete Garra ???

24 minutes ago via mobile · Like

Matt Campbell Don't even tell me the Amish have security cameras.

24 minutes ago via mobile · Like

Pete Garra all i can picture is dave chained and being forced to churn butter or make candles. It's horrible. Maybe a scene for saw 7?

23 minutes ago via mobile · Like

Dave Cicirelli

Ok…So apparently it's a "hate crime" to vandalize someone's property because they're Amish. Also, my profile and phone are obviously filled with "evidence." This is not good.

Like · Comment

Matt Campbell I was going to voice my concern about it being called a 'hate crime' but didn't want to jinx it… You used TP…not like you burned down a barn…

2 hours ago via mobile · Like

Ted Kaiser don't be scurred

about an hour ago via mobile · Like

Dave Cicirelli Dude. Regardless of how we feel about the definition of hate crimes, it makes this much more serious. And out here, being 26 isn't young, where they'll go easy on you.

I have no idea how this will play out.

about an hour ago via mobile · Like

Pete Garra wait, were you actually arrested?

about an hour ago via mobile · Like

Matt Riggio Dave, I have a friend who is a lawyer down in the Pittsburgh area. Call me on my home line if you need me or would like his number.

about an hour ago via mobile · Like

Joe Lennon damn i love following your adventures. best of luck with the amish war machine.

55 minutes ago via mobile · Like

Steve Cuchinello TP is a hate crime?!?! What is this country coming to? The Amish are almost unstoppable. I told you to TP the horse—you have to immobilize them.

8 minutes ago via mobile · Like

Dave Cicirelli Yeah, Steve. Good thinking. Having PETA on my ass feels like a great next step.

4 minutes ago via mobile · Like

Steve Cuchinello Get PETA on their asses!! They can use cars but choose not to. They ignore modern machinery and instead continue to exploit horses, cows, pigs, etc. Hypocrites.

less than a minute ago via mobile · Like

Dave Cicirelli …Machiavellian…

just now via mobile · Like

Dave Cicirelli

I think we may work something out, outside of court.

Like · Comment

Matt Campbell Wow. Thank god man. I was thinking the worst when I didn't see any posts for a while.

about an hour ago via mobile · Like

Tara B. I'd say you lucked out, but I still don't know if it will involve suspenders. Lesson learned this time?

about an hour ago via mobile · Like

Ted Kaiser ur disappointing me. Your big trip for revenge is ending with you wussing out over some toilet paper crime.

38 minutes ago via mobile · Like

Dave Cicirelli Who the hell do you think you are, Ted? What USC branded mesh shorts are you wearing that give you the cajones to sit back in your comfortable chair and call me a nancy?

37 minutes ago via mobile · Like

Ted Kaiser I believed that you were going to go to Amish country and set this thing straight. Instead you fold over a misdemeanor. The hope I had has been extinguished.

35 minutes ago via mobile · Like

Dave Cicirelli

I have to pay the Amish back as a personal debt. I'll be working and living here in exchange for dropping all charges. I feel like I was sentenced to be their butler.

Like · Comment

Gregory Kumm All I can think of is you coming out of the barn with two buckets full of milk. I woke up early and took the liberty of milking your cow. We don't have a cow, we have a bull.

26 minutes ago via mobile · Like

Joe Moscone Do they raise barns this time of year? I hope they make you wear a dress. Or, if not, grow one of those stupid chinstrap beards. Or maybe they'll make you pull that carriage you vandalized, and that poor horse can get a few days off.

18 minutes ago via mobile · Like

Jay Patterson Did you get your gear back? I'm already glad I subscribed to your misadventure. Good luck with your future travels man!

14 minutes ago via mobile · Like

Elizabeth Lee Are you serious? For how long? All you did was a little toilet paper…don't let them bully you.

9 minutes ago via mobile · Like

Steve Cuchinello Dave, if it makes you feel any better, I would rather be milking cows in Amish country than watching AJ Burnett pitch right now.

less than a minute ago via mobile · Like

Mission accomplished.

"Don't take my picture."

I was sitting in a booth at one of the many East Village faux dive bars, with my hand extended out to block the camera's line of sight. I was at a birthday party for one of my coworkers at Handler, and it had only been a few hours since I branded myself a hate-criminal farmhand.

"Damn paparazzi," I said.

"Are you serious?" the confused birthday girl asked.

"Yeah, I am—I can't be tagged in photos at some bar. People think I'm living on a farm."

"You're so weird."

"No, he's brilliant!" Joe stepped in. "And so is Fakebook."

"Thank you, Joe."

"It's also kinda fascinating." Christine joined the fray. "He's discovering what people are willing to believe—how much of what they see online they're ready to accept."

Joe rolled his eyes. "Whatever."

They debated for a bit, and I let them have at it—I was on both sides of the argument. The conversation eventually moved on, but my thoughts lingered.

I'd been well accustomed to the thrill of a successful prank, but this one was different—the sense of danger was weirdly divorced from the moment. There was no grand catharsis, no single instant for me to realize that I'd "gotten" them. I was never in the room to watch my audience's reaction. I had almost no sense of whether I was fooling everyone or even fooling anyone.

Meanwhile, the usual suspects were posting on my wall, but they only made up a fraction of my hundreds of Facebook friends—so what did that mean? How far down had the hoax taken root? How many people were falling for it? I just didn't know.

A large part of me was on that farm with Fake Dave, keeping tabs on the timeline, making sure his story unfolded at the right pace. Another part of me was back in Red Bank, wondering how my hometown was reacting to Fakebook. There was only a little bit left of me in the moment.

After a few minutes, my phone vibrated, rousing me from my thoughts. It was a text from an old friend, Jason.

"I don't do Facebook…but that doesn't mean I'm not following you. Hang in there. People love you."

Jay and I had been close friends back in grade school, but I hadn't seen him since his wedding a year earlier. I didn't know how to respond, so once again, I just ignored it.

I ended up leaving the birthday party early and started walking home along Avenue B, checking my profile at every street corner. Jay's text made it clear that my wall was a poor indicator of exactly who was paying attention. Were people just hesitant to get involved? Were they embarrassed to admit to being audience members? Whatever the reason, this was bigger than it looked. People were talking about it. If not over the Internet, then over beers.

I felt completely cut off and needed to check in. So I gave Ted a call, but he didn't pick up.

A beat later I got a text. "Not safe 2 talk. Call you later."

It's funny how Ted quickly became my closest confidant. Truth be told, I probably wouldn't have looped him into the hoax if he hadn't been part of the conversation that inspired it. He was one of my oldest friends, but our interests didn't entirely overlap. Based on fifteen years of going to Mets games but never to the Met, I'd wrongly assumed that creative endeavors like Fakebook were out of Ted's wheelhouse.

Besides, he was a notoriously dull Facebook poster. As I write this sentence, his actual status is:

Ted Kaiser
Freehold Mall for some shopping, stopping by the Monmouth-Nova game, Birthday Party for a bit, then out in RB for some Reggae Night.
Like · Comment

Guh. What makes him think my wall is his to-do list? His was exactly the type of profile I was trying to parody, and yet he'd turned out to be a tremendous asset—mostly due to his status as the "mayor" of Red Bank.

I can't say that I understood why everyone seemed to know Ted Kaiser, or why everyone turned to him for information when a rumor got out, but we did. He was never a sports star or a class clown or anything that typically makes someone the center of their social circle…He was just a natural master of networking.

Actually, I take that back. It sounds too calculating. He was just a guy—someone who everyone seemed to like well enough to be one of his two thousand Facebook friends. And as a result, he was the hub of all Red Bank news. So whenever someone stumbled onto my profile, Ted's corroboration of the story was often more than enough to get them to buy in, and best of all, he was able to relay the reactions of my hometown crowd to me. He was tending to my roots.

A lot of the kids I grew up with drifted back to Red Bank after having the college experience, and I might have been one of them…but the thing is, I didn't have the typical college experience. In fact, I bounced around three colleges in just four years, joking that I was "academically promiscuous."

I started at Syracuse and dropped out after a single semester. I don't regret leaving—I had my reasons—but I think part of me was looking to go back to the way things were. I was never the guy who couldn't wait to leave my no-name town in the dust—I like where I grew up and the people I grew up with. I don't carry a lot of scars from my teenage years. I had a good high school experience. I just needed to learn—the hard way—that the high school experience ends.

For a year and a half, in between my time at Syracuse and Rutgers, I went to Brookdale, the community college located…well, a few minutes from Red Bank. Turns out there's not a whole lot to do in a shore town in the dead of winter, especially when you're under twenty-one and all your friends are enrolled out of state.

And while a typical college experience is full of easy ways to make friends, meeting people at a community college is far more challenging. In fact, the experience hardly resembles anything that anyone's ever imagined college to be. There's very little in the way of elbow patches on tweed jackets. No pipe-smoking professors sitting at the top of the circle discussing Proust with their argyle-wearing students. There weren't even classic panty-raiding shenanigans going on under the nose of the fun-hating dean in the snobs-versus-slobs tradition.

At my college, it was all slobs, from top to bottom. Even the professors looked like they were just as likely to sweep up papers as they were to grade them. We were townies. We came to class, then we left. That was that. And when we came and left, it was either very slowly, back and forth from the Shadow Lake retirement community, or very quickly and very loudly, in a modified black, yellow, or purple Honda Civic. Gearheads and blue-hairs ruled the campus. The parking lot looked like the set for the next Vin Diesel movie, with a few Ford Crown Victorias thrown in for good measure.

The blue-hairs were just trying to have productive post-career lives, and I supported that. They'd earned it. But the gearheads were breaking my heart, working crappy full-time jobs while taking only two or three units every semester, putting all their money into spoilers and neon lights for their Civics. Five years passed, and these guys could have earned enough credits and money to join me at Rutgers, but instead they got bucket seats.

I'm not trying to damn the student body. It wasn't exclusively coasting gearheads and stir-crazy senior citizens. It was a cross section of everyone who couldn't or wouldn't go to a four-year school. It was people taking a second shot at education or saving money or staying close to home because of family obligations. In all fairness, it really was a place that provided opportunity.

None of that, however, reduced the drawbacks of such an eclectic student body. You had no way of knowing if the cute nineteen-year-old you were sitting next to in poly sci was actually a married mother of three about to celebrate her thirty-fifth birthday.

Inevitably, my social life suffered, and downtime began to center around jogs on the winter boardwalk and watching repeats of *Boy Meets World* (which I found oddly poignant). It was an isolated time.

But when summer finally arrived, it felt like a return to form. My friends were back. We were lifeguards and cashiers again, spending our nights hanging out and driving to parties before ending up at some diner. Just like always.

One night, as the summer died down, we found ourselves on an empty beach.

Every August seemed to have a night like this. We'd skip the diner and go to one of our beaches—the local spots that existed under the radar of the Staten Island and North Jersey BENNYs who migrate south. These beaches weren't particularly hidden or especially pristine. The weather-worn sand fences and odd stacks of litter surrounding the "Swim at Your Own Risk" signs gave the beach a certain lived-in quality. It was lived in by us.

I loved those nights. After a long summer of work and play, we Jersey Shore kids would get together and catch our breath one last time before the season ended and we had to return to real life. It always felt the same as every other year—except this time, it wasn't.

We weren't chatting about preparing for another year of high school or facing the great unknowns of college life. They weren't unknowns anymore. My friends were talking about returning to people I'd never met and places I'd never been. We were finally talking about experiences we hadn't experienced together.

We were the class of 2001, but this was 2002. People hadn't entirely moved on yet, but they'd begun to move apart. Most of us had already learned that the world was bigger than the semicircle we'd formed in the sand.

I didn't have enough perspective yet; otherwise I might have been able to find some significance in the setting—a connection to the sound of the changing tide, or maybe a sense of purpose in the Manhattan skyline just over the horizon. Maybe. I don't know.

What I do know is that a week later I was sitting on the same beach, alone.

Ted finally called back.

"Oh man, Cicirelli. You're a mad genius!" he said. "People were arguing about Fakebook all night. Steve was *loving* it—he buried you every chance he got."

"So people are talking about it?"

"Absolutely. I mean, everyone's known about it for a while, but now they're finally bringing it up. People wouldn't stop bugging me about you."

"But not a lot of people are posting."

"No? I'm not sure..."

"Well, it can be awkward. Like when my dad started leaving comments, people backed off—they weren't sure if it was any of their business."

"Your dad is great! The bit about law school? Classic."

Ralph Cicirelli If you had gone to law school like I wanted, you could have ended up with the farm rather than just working on it.
two minutes ago via mobile · Like

Joe Lennon This is the best facebook page/blog in existence.
one minute ago via mobile · Like

Joe Lennon Also, I dislike this post.
less than a minute ago via mobile · Like

"Yeah, he's crushing it," I said. "Hey, I threw out some crazy stuff. I need to know, what are people thinking?"

"Well, there's a lot of debate."

Ted's natural inclination toward diplomacy had served us well so far. Whenever someone asked him about Fakebook, he'd feign uncertainty about the things he'd heard, never painting either of us into a corner. He let people get comfortable with their own reactions and delicately swayed them to accept the uncertainty rather than dig for answers.

"A couple of days ago, there was a 'good for Dave' consensus," Ted said. "Now people are asking, 'What the hell's going on with Dave?' People are on all sides of it. You're a hero or you're going insane, depends on who you ask."

"That's perfect."

I wanted this thing to be hard to swallow, wacky enough so that people would begin to question the wisdom of my fake actions. I wanted debate, and I was thrilled that the conversation was about my motivations and not the iffy quality of my Photoshop work. "Does anyone suspect it's fake? I mean, I cited laws that don't even exist."

"Not really...people have said things like 'I almost don't believe this is happening,' and they'll doubt it for just a moment—I can tell—then just decide they're going to believe it anyway."

"I can't get over how nerve-racking it is. This was supposed to be stupid fun, not so intense!"

"I know...I think you're the only one who could pull it off. Everyone keeps saying, 'If there's anyone this would actually happen to, it's Dave.'"

"Wait? What? What do you mean? You realize I'm writing this guy as an idiot, right?"

"Dave, I'm not sure how to put it, but you've always done your own thing. I mean, the Amish story was based on actual events, you know."

"Yeah, I know...but people think I'm crazy?"

"No, they don't. Well, they kind of do. But they like what you're doing. They say you're like the guy from *Into the Wild*."

"That guy? The story ends with him dying alone in his van! Am I the only jerk who took that as the moral of the story?"

Ted laughed, but he could sense my discomfort. "Dave, it's not a bad thing. But yeah, people brought up a few stories. Matt Carew claimed he saw you in the audience of the Maury Povich show a few months ago, for example."

"He saw that?"

"So you were actually on the show?"

"Yeah, me and Eckhoff went. We were betting on the baby daddy results. It was maybe the most fun I ever had."

"This is what they're talking about!"

"It was so much fun! Why wouldn't I want to—"

"But it's not normal, Dave. He didn't see you at the Knicks game; he saw you on the Maury show. And you do that sort of stuff all the time—Elliott said he thought you were still living with those French women in Chinatown."

"I guess it's been a while since I talked to him."

"Dave, listen. Senior year, did you or did you not get thrown out of art class for the whole semester?"

"Ha! Yeah, that definitely happened. And I won the school's art award that night, too." I perked up out of pride for the decade-old victory. I hated that teacher. "She was pissed."

"You were the art guy, and you told the art teacher to fuck off. People don't remember the details. They just think—this is a guy who could do this shit. And Dave, you love those stories. They're the first ones you tell. You said you wanted people to think you'd gone crazy. It's working."

"Well, yeah," I said to Ted. "I was ready for people to think that I was going crazy. But I wasn't prepared to find out people thought I'd been crazy all along."

"Hey," Ted continued, "you think it's easy for the rest of us? People think Steve and I are complete asses because of what we've been posting about you."

"I'm sorry, Ted. I didn't think it through..."

"It's all right. We wouldn't do it if it wasn't funny. Actually, Steve was reveling in the attention. The reality is, people didn't think you were crazy, they just didn't think much about you. It's why they aren't shocked that you're acting crazy, and why they aren't shocked that Steve and I are dicks."

"Yeah, it's a *Black Swan* thing."

"The ballerina movie?"

"No, that's something different. *Black Swan* is a book—one of the ideas it asserts is that a million things are happening all at once, and it's only after the fact that we pick and choose the details that are important. We find evidence for an event once it's already occurred and convince ourselves it was obvious all along."

"Yeah, exactly. You tell people you're crazy, so they remember the crazy things about you. And so what? Since when do you care what people think?"

"Yeah, you're right. Screw it. I'll let them have the idiot they think I am."

"Right."

"They're doing exactly what I wanted them to, anyway—they're connecting the dots for me. They think I'm nuts, *great*. That just gives me freedom."

"Go for it, Dave!"

"And I'm not nuts, I'm an artist! This thing I'm doing is too big for them. It's Warholian…or, no, I'm like Banksy, and this is twenty-first-century street art. Instead of brick and plaster, I'm vandalizing their Facebook walls…tagging them with lies to reveal a greater truth!"

"Oh jeez…"

"I'm trailblazing. No one ever said it was easy being stuck ahead of your time, waiting for the world to catch up. Someday they'll get here, but by then, I'll be somewhere else!"

"Dave—"

I felt fantastic. Ted was right. I'd counted only two advantages in pulling this off: that the idea of Fakebook was brand new and that Facebook friendships were ambiguous by nature. But I finally understood there was a third advantage, one that I wasn't immediately comfortable with. The power of my own reputation. I had a résumé of oddities that stuck in people's heads, and now it was clear that the difference between the guy who would walk out on his life and the guy who would pretend to walk out on his life was too subtle for the casual observer.

It was a bitter pill to swallow, that the mockery I was making of myself proved to be more popular than the real me, but it was also liberating. If they simply believed me to be somehow heroically unhinged, then I thought I should own that conclusion…and challenge it with increasingly selfish behavior.

There truly were two of me. The real me was off the grid, living a life that was exclusively my own. The guy in the public's eye—the guy on Facebook—was someone else. Just in time for Halloween, I'd created a Frankenstein, stitched together from my own history and my audience's perceptions.

Nice to meet you, Fake Dave. Let's begin with a game of FarmVille.

4 friend request

As I quickly discovered, even fake FarmVille is boring.

Dave Cicirelli

Like · Comment · Share

Dave Cicirelli

I've been having a lot of fun lying to the Amish. They have a vague sense of what technology exists out there, but no real grasp of it (kind of like my mom). I told them that Twitter was an internet sex act, and that's why it's popular with celebrities. Easily the highlight of last night's dinner.

Like · Comment · Share

If it had actually been true, my life as an Amish political prisoner would have been just one stop in a long history of absurd living situations.

When I was a last-minute transfer student at Rutgers, for example, I was randomly placed in what was left of third-year campus housing. In other words, I got stuck with people who couldn't fill their own dorm. You know, the cool kids.

So I was the fourth man in a suite full of LARPers. If you don't know what a LARPer is, you've probably done something right with your life. LARPers are live-action role players. Unlike traditional role players, who hide behind the walls of someone's basement, LARPers fly their (literal) flags in public. They make homemade foam weapons and medieval costumes, go to a park, and play "sword fight." If one of the players gets hit in the leg by another player with a make-believe battle ax, he has to hop on one leg. It looks ridiculous if you're anywhere over the age of eleven, but exceptionally so if you are wearing a see-through beard and a homemade cape.

I learned something while sharing that dorm. I learned that dweebs are like zombies. In a one-on-one encounter you're faster than them, stronger than them, less awkward in social situations. But if they have numbers and you're in a confined space...shoot yourself before you're turned. I also learned that Hacky Sacks can be used to represent magic spells, but I digress.

The year after that, I lived with some friends in an off-campus house in New Brunswick. It wasn't the safest part of town, but if I had to get stabbed, I preferred the dignity of a real knife and not a fake sword.

I almost had my wish come true when my housemate threw a hobo party. To be clear, this wasn't a stick-and-bindle-themed party. This was a party where—without giving any heads-up to the housemates—one of the jazz dudes on the first floor invited the homeless of the community into our house to, like, listen to doo-wop or something.

And as altruistic a thought as that may have been, the reality of it was intense. Waking up to two dozen of New Brunswick's most mentally stable citizens, including a guy who mugged me, eating hamburgers and dancing to your housemate playing jazz flute... well, that's something you can't un-see.

And the year after that? The universe paid me back. Big time. It's best described by the first note I posted from the Amish farm.

OCTOBER 25: COURTING POSSIBILITIES

When I first lived in NY, it was in a Chinatown loft full of European strangers. It was a great chapter in my life that I owe entirely to diving into uncharted waters.

I'll never forget that first Friday night. The apartment hadn't filled up its eight (yes...eight) bedrooms yet, and it was just me and two of my new French roommates—looking for a place to eat on our first Friday night as New Yorkers.

I volunteered—after all, I knew a few places from my bridge and tunnel excursions. So I led us all to Peep, a Thai restaurant with a cool gimmick. The doors to its bathrooms are one-way mirrors. You can look out the bathroom stall, right into the restaurant, but no one can see in. It's strange, kind of interesting, and totally voyeuristic. Peep, to my New Jersey eyes, felt like a true Manhattan experience.

*What I didn't realize was that "Peep," to French ears, was slang for blowjob.**

Just imagine moving to France, and this strange Frenchman who sleeps under the same roof you do, he takes you to a "great little place" he knows, Fellatio's. Trying to explain that you're not a pervert is an uphill battle in a restaurant where the bathrooms let you watch people eat while you poop.

I had no idea what the next two years would hold. I didn't know anything about the other 40 or so people who would pass through that crazy apartment, or the parties we'd throw or the friends I would make. How could I?

All I knew was the feeling I had. A feeling that meant "you have a completely different life than you had on Monday."

It's a feeling I just felt again...while touching an udder. Here's to possibilities.

**Pipe is the proper spelling of the French slang, though it is pronounced peep.*

Ted Kaiser Just make sure that's an udder you're grabbing. There are bulls on that farm too.
just now · Like

I had hopes that the Amish chapter of Fakebook would look like these other chapters of my real life, where I'd bumble into an unexpected situation and perfectly unpredictable events would just present themselves to me. But, as I learned, the "waiting to see what happens" approach doesn't quite work when nothing's actually happening.

As it turned out, my masterstroke of turning Fakebook into a "real" version of FarmVille was a little too authentic. It was boring and pointless. Everyone hated it.

Dave Cicirelli

This duck won a blue ribbon. Respect.

Like · Comment · Share

Steve Cuchinello I've seen better.

less than a minute ago via mobile · Like

It felt so clever when I thought of it. In execution, it amounted to a lot of pictures of ducks. And people don't care about a duck winning a blue ribbon, even if they think it's a real duck.

Even readers who weren't my secret collaborators were vocally upset by it—a completely new development for Fakebook.

Matt Campbell ➡ Dave Cicirelli

I feel a bit disappointed by the reporting since the whole Amish debacle. There have been so many questions I have that I feel just have not been answered to make this whole event make more sense.

What are the terms of your servitude? Are you sleeping in the barn or in some Amish bed? How is the food? Besides fireplaces what kind of work are you doing? Do you grow your own tobacco and have a pipe with the men in the evening? Can they mix meat and cheese between bread? Do the Amish have pets; what kind?

Sorry to be so demanding, but I just feel that these little details can add volumes to our understanding and fascination. Thanks!

So after three weeks of pretending to actually do all the stuff FarmVille players only pretended to do, I realized I needed a new angle. But what?

Dave Cicirelli
I'm really beginning to hate it here. I mean, I guess it was naive to think they'd accept me into the community considering how I got here. But still…is it possible? Am I not as charming as I thought?

Like · Comment · Share

Erin Brennan Hanson impossible!
less than a minute ago via mobile · Like

Joe Moscone Very possible.
just now via mobile · Like

The days of engaging my audience just by taking naps at furniture stores or camping out on playgrounds were clearly over—they needed something more. But the possibility of a new destination had been taken off the table: I was stuck at the farm.

Once again I was confronted with the challenge of real-time storytelling. To maintain that delicate balance between the outlandish and the plausible, there needed to be gaps between the marquee events. But to maintain audience interest, I had to keep up the momentum. So how does one spend time between hate crimes?

I did what any creative hack would do. I brought in a sexy dame.

Everyone loves gossip. Even the suggestion of a fight between my father and me gave Fakebook's audience a petty thrill. People like seeing things they aren't supposed to see, especially if what they see is something they could have an opinion on.

And what could be a better engine for gossip than one of your Facebook friends dating an Amish girl? You'd be instantly invested in his story, waiting and wanting to see how it played out. You wouldn't be able to resist talking about it. And it would be so unexpected that you'd have a hard time coming up with a reason why it couldn't happen—especially if you'd already accepted Fakebook's story so far, as all of my followers seemed to have.

And best of all, the Amish have no digital footprint. She'd have no Facebook profile, no Facebook friends, no AIM account, no history at all. As far as the Internet was concerned, she'd be invisible.

It was so wonderfully clean. All I needed was a handful of photos from some random, willing girl no one could possibly know.

Yeah…that was a pretty creepy thought. So I called Jeff Shaw.

Jeff was a friend from my sole semester at Syracuse. It was surprising to me that we'd kept in touch, given the fact that we'd only spent four months in the same state—but we'd bonded. I felt like I could trust him to understand what I was doing.

And fortunately, because our close proximity had been so brief and so isolated, he knew hundreds of people who didn't know anyone that I knew. He was the perfect matchmaker to help me find a make-believe girl.

He e-introduced me to his cousin in Chicago, Kate.

Jeff Shaw ➡ Kate Moulton, Dave Cicirelli

Subject: SWM Seeking SWF…To Pretend to be Amish

Kate, meet Dave. Dave, meet Kate. The only problem I foresee—Kate you're Amish here, so do you have any photos of yourself where you're NOT drinking? *rim shot* Oh, he's such a ham.

Dave Cicirelli

Actually, I'm quite interested in the pics where you are drinking. *another rim shot*

First, thanks so much for agreeing to be a part of this, Kate. The storyline that's going to play out is that I run away with this Amish girl (who will be created using your photos). None of the pictures will be in poor taste, scout's honor, just your standard party pic fare. The captions will be used to fill in the blanks about the story that will—fair warning—not always show her in the best light, but nothing crazy! Ultimately, I just need a consistent likeness.

I'm going to login as Jeff to pull pics from your profile. Thanks so much, again. My profile is public, so please check it out and enjoy!

Kate Moulton

Hi Dave, Jeff,

Yes, I'm afraid I am seriously lacking in the being photographed around wooden furniture and butter churns department…but feel free to use whatever you can. This is hysterical.

Kate was perfect. And she agreed to pretend go out with me. I'd thought of everything…except my uncanny ability to blow it with even the surest of shots.

I think I need to make something clear...I'm actually a very good Photoshop artist. Honest!

Creating images in Photoshop is something I do for a living, and something I do well. I've studied illustration for years, and my experience with Photoshop's suite of tools has been one of the cornerstones of my career. But producing high-quality, convincing work requires time, preparation, and a healthy respect for the software's limitations, especially when combining several images into a single picture.

The most important consideration is the horizon line. Every image has one—it's the vantage point of the camera lens and the viewer's eye. It dictates the angles of every object in an image, determining if you're looking up, down, or straight at your subject. Combining photos where the horizon lines don't closely match will never produce a convincing image.

There are also basic lighting considerations. Every image has a light source that creates any and all highlights and shadows. If your background's lit from the left, and you put a subject who's lit from behind on that background, it's going to look fake. If you take a figure from low light and drop him into a sunny day, he'll look flat and out of place. If the photo was taken using a flash...forget it. All of the subject's details will be washed away.

If you're photoshopping parts of people onto other people, anatomy becomes a major concern. The body only moves in certain ways, and if you place a subject's head at one angle while the neck is moving in another, it'll stick out like a sore thumb (placed at a third, even weirder angle). And then there's the camera and the files it produces. Matters of focus, exposure, resolution, and flash photography vs. natural light. All of these need to match closely.

You can tweak and manipulate an image to compensate for

slight differences, but the magical Enhance button is pure spy-thriller fantasy. You can't manipulate data that isn't there. So taking a lousy thumbnail off Google Images and fitting it into a professionally shot background won't work. That's why the key to pulling off a successful Photoshop image is collecting as many pictures as you can. In hindsight, pretending to live in a community that is morally opposed to photography was a bad idea.

Dave Cicirelli

Everyone, meet Kate. We made out, and she baked me a pie.

Like · Comment · Share

The relationship was off to a rocky start—the image was awful. I'd committed every Photoshop sin at once—bad angles, mixing flash photography with outdoor lighting, attaching faces to heads that were tilted the wrong way—it was horrendous. So obviously, inescapably horrendous.

But at 2:00 a.m. when I'd made it, I somehow hadn't seen the problems. I wasn't looking at the image; I was looking beyond it—toward all the storylines it was about to open up.

So I hit the Upload button the next morning and went to work completely satisfied with my wit.

Dave Cicirelli

Everyone, meet Kate. We made out, and she baked me a pie.

Like · Comment · Share

Elliott Askew Wait a second…Why is it that you BOTH look like cardboard cut out people…WHAT HAVE THEY DONE TO YOU!? That is a fake person right?

10 minutes ago · Like

Joe Lennon Photoshop?

just now · Like

"Photoshop."

There was the word, right on my wall. It was the answer to a question I couldn't afford to be asked. Elliott, Joe Lennon, and anyone else watching were all just a little mental effort away from considering that none of my story was true. And the moment they considered that possibility would be the moment it all became obvious. I mean, what sounds more likely? Either I was an Amish indentured servant who'd abandoned his life so he could toilet-paper a horse and buggy, and whose pictures sometimes looked really fake…or I was just an asshole.

I spent the whole workday distracted by that feeling in the pit of my stomach. It made designing a website for a frozen-food sweepstakes seemingly impossible and increasingly trivial because all I could hear was the ticking of the time bomb I'd left on my wall.

I had no good options. Leaving the Amish Kate post online

would just give more people time to see it and doubt it. But pulling it would be suspicious, too, and only confirm their suspicion.

Tick, tick, tick.

I heard it in every click of my mouse. It was torture—realizing I was investing more time and care on this dumb website for a frozen macaroni client than I had on the most pivotal piece of artwork for the biggest personal project of my life.

Ultimately, exposure was inevitable. I knew Fakebook was unsustainable and that people were going to find out. But for any of it to be worthwhile, Fakebook's destruction had to be a spectacular crash that revealed something new—like an early jet smashing into the sound barrier. Instead of going out in a blaze of glory, this post was making Fakebook simply sputter toward the ground.

All I could think to do was use the old "shine a spotlight on it" trick. If there's a giant flaw in something you made…own it. I'd call attention to what an awful photo it was and hope and pray that people believed me—that they'd blame it on the shittiness of my third-generation iPhone camera.

Dave Cicirelli
Everyone, meet Kate. We made out, and she baked me a pie.

Like · Comment · Share

Elliott Askew Wait a second…Why is it that you BOTH look like cardboard cut out people…WHAT HAVE THEY DONE TO YOU!? That is a fake person right?
11 minutes ago via mobile · Like

Joe Lennon Photoshop?
less than a minute ago via mobile · Like

Dave Cicirelli Hahaha. Oh man, poor girl gets like one photograph a year and we look like cardboard cutouts. If I photoshopped that pic, I'd be embarrassed. This girls mad cool too. I'll have to take a better pic of her tomorrow (iPhones have no flash, and Amish have no lightbulbs.)
just now via mobile · Like

I looked at what I wrote. It was desperate. I looked at the picture. It was terrible. The bomb kept ticking, and every second was another opportunity for someone to stumble upon the photo and put it all together.

It killed me. All afternoon I weighed the risk of keeping the photo up and the risk of pulling it down. I changed my mind a hundred times before the workday ended.

After work, I found myself sitting on a bench outside the Flatiron Building. It was starting to get dark earlier and earlier, and the buildings were lit up. I faced north, looking at the Empire State Building over the trees in Madison Park. There was a chill in the air that my jacket wasn't keeping out. I just sat there in a cold daze.

I thought for a second that maybe the photo wasn't that bad. Maybe I was overreacting. I told myself it would be fine. Then I pulled up the photo and looked at it again. It was even worse than I'd remembered. So I pulled it.

Dave Cicirelli
Yikes. Jonathon didn't realize I put his daughter's picture on the internet. He's making me pull it—he thinks Facebook is some sort of pornography.

What a nightmare.
Like · Comment

Matt Campbell How did he find out? Do the Amish employ net-able people as spies?
less than a minute ago via mobile · Like

Dave Cicirelli I know…I keep half expecting to stumble onto the Bat Computer. Gossip man, like anywhere else. They're an insular people, and I'm this big X factor around here. Plus I've been flirting with Kate (the girl in the pic and Jonathon's daughter) like crazy. People talk man…people talk.
just now via mobile · Like

I sat there, staring at the screen until it went to sleep. It was a clunky, transparent fix.

I found myself back at square one. Amish Kate was off the table, over before it began. Fake Dave was still on the farm. I was back in the boring holding pattern I'd been trying to break out of, in even worse standing with my audience than before. Sensationalism was off the table for the foreseeable future.

A week after I'd pulled the photo of Amish Kate, I met with Elizabeth at the mega-deli on the corner of Madison Park. Her office was around the corner from mine, so on the rare occasion that we shared a slow day, we always made an effort to grab lunch.

I was still reeling and had spent the week rereading the boring FarmVille posts I'd put up to defuse my Photoshop photo bomb. At least they felt safe. There was no momentum to Fakebook anymore. My thoughts were scattered and my heart wasn't in it. I was scared to make another wrong move, and for the first time since I'd started, I wasn't getting any reaction—there were posts with no likes and no comments.

Fakebook lived on voyeurism, and disinterest was the worst end of this project. As Oscar Wilde once said, "If there is anything more annoying in the world than having people talk about you, it is certainly having no one talk about you."

Elizabeth grabbed a container of lettuce and handed it to the guy working the salad station, ordering the usual—beets, cranberry-raisins, walnuts, goat cheese, and balsamic.

It was too healthy for me and the funk I was in, so I grabbed a tray and wandered around. Sushi, pizza, Korean barbecue, tacos, wraps…all of it looked pretty good.

"Pretty good" is a low standard in a town where the "very good" version of anything is just a few blocks away, but variety is what made the Manhattan food courts an easy compromise. Besides, the cafeteria setting was appropriate for lunch with a school friend.

The art school bond is a special one. You spend thousands of hours together working on projects, exchanging ideas, helping each other figure them out. You live with each other's frustrations, triumphs, and failures, as you try, as Van Gogh put it, "to break through that iron wall between what I feel and what I express."

It was over one of these lunches that I'd first told Elizabeth about Fakebook, back when it was still just an idea. She'd loved it and promised to help, and of course she had. Her comments brought a balance to the testosterone-driven ballbusting from Ted and Steve—something I thought would be especially important after the introduction of Amish Kate. If only I'd gotten the chance.

"Dave…" she said, drawing my name out in her endearing, girl ish way. "That Photoshop was really bad."

"I know…" I looked down at the unwieldy piece of barbecue chicken I'd settled on.

"I mean, even the resolutions didn't match. You should always scale things down to the lowest quality image."

"Yeah, I don't know what I was thinking." I scooped up a forkful of runny sweet potatoes. They were pretty good. "The really scary thing is I loved it when I made it. I thought it was really funny. It was late—and I think I was just blinded by the joy I get out of doing ridiculous things. I know what you're saying, though. I could have been much more careful. Turns out I can blow it even with a girl I made up."

Elizabeth was looking back at me with her involuntary compassion.

"Well, maybe the margin of error is over. If you really want to keep doing this, you need to take it seriously. You need to set a shot list and give yourself a library of photos you can use with all sorts of different light settings. Be professional about it."

"This thing is really..." I tried to get out. "It's sort of a knot of a thing."

"What do you mean?"

"Well...it's hard to explain. There are all these threads, and each one I feel a different way about. Part of it is funny, part of it is twisted, part of it is mean or interesting or silly. Like...I feel guilty when people take it seriously. I feel excited and thrilled when people really believe it. I feel empowered when I create a new post and someone goes for it—when I've made something that makes their version of the world a little stranger. It's a crazy feeling.

"But then I feel powerless when I can't control their reactions. This version of myself I created as a joke is more important to people than the real me ever was. It's insane to become jealous of yourself. It's this strange feeling of rejection. At the same time, now that people are turning on him, I feel betrayed. It doesn't make any sense.

"And every time I sit down to write a new Fakebook post or make a new image," I continued, "I just feel crippled. I tug on any one of those threads, and the whole thing becomes more knotted."

"Maybe," Elizabeth said, "you just need to not think so much about it. If it's torturing you, I think you need to either stop doing it or stop worrying about the things that are making it difficult." She paused. "But I think you should keep doing it."

She sat there, collecting her thoughts. "It just feels…"

"Yeah…"

We shared an unspoken understanding. We'd spent hours and hours of studio time together. Fakebook, for all its frustrations and headaches, was unique. We both knew the value of a truly original idea. We both knew how rare those ideas were—and how delicate.

After work, I kicked off my shoes, plugged in my laptop, and sat on my unmade bed.

Dave Cicirelli
Here's another picture of a horse. Hope you like it.

Like · Comment · Share

Joe Moscone I'm bored by Amish country, perhaps even more than you are. Go somewhere with hot women and share those photos. Horses…carriages…children…enough already.
2 days ago via mobile · Like

Matt Riggio I must say, this is truly a far cry from the adventure that I've been expecting. Don't TP anymore, dude.
yesterday via mobile · Like

Joe Lennon How much longer before you move on?
yesterday via mobile · Like

Ted Kaiser seriously Dave this is just sad. You are their slave! You, Dave Cicirelli, a once proud, principled young man are now a lackey for some bozo Amish people. You're picking up horseshit.

5 hours ago via mobile · Like

Matt Campbell Ted, dude, Dave made an agreement as a gentleman. It requires that you be a man of your word or you are not a man at all. A commitment is a contract.

about an hour ago via mobile · Like

Another true-to-form post. I continued to limp away slowly from anything suspicious. Everything I did on my wall now reeked of caution. I felt like Fakebook was this beautiful but thorny flower I'd discovered but didn't understand. I'd spent the last month trying to protect it by locking it away, but I was just killing it, and I would have kept on killing it if I hadn't clicked onto Matt Riggio's profile.

Matt Riggio

Trivia night at Houlihans!

Like · Comment

Trivia night at Houlihans?

That guy has the audacity to call *my* posts boring?

I couldn't believe it. He didn't even know I was making this up, but he was giving me feedback. It was crazy.

Fake Dave was clearly on the cusp of—or in the middle of—a complete mental breakdown. Didn't these people have the decency to let him unravel in his own way? Or maybe they just couldn't see it. They were too busy projecting—dumping the weight of their fantasies on Fake Dave's shoulders.

And in that knot, out of all the different threads, the chord that was struck was an angry one. At that moment, there was no difference between Fake Dave and Real Dave. After all, they thought he was me. I felt like Maximus in the Colosseum, bellowing out, "*Are you not entertained?*" Because while they may not have known they were an audience, they sure as hell were acting like one.

I was new to the feeling—unprepared for it. At that moment, I resented their rejection.

And realizing how preposterous a feeling that was...made me want to keep Fakebook alive. Yes, it was a messy, horrible knot. But every single thread surprised me. The fact that some of the surprises were terrible and some of the surprises were thrilling only strengthened my belief that this giant, flawed, morally suspect thing had a point—as elusive as that point seemed. I was scared that I'd never discover what it was.

Desperation and pride kicked in. I wasn't going to act like Fakebook was a failure. I was going to push this forward, sputtering engine and all. If I crashed Fakebook into the ground, at least it would be with my hand on the throttle, not the brakes.

For a moment, I'd found my steel. Ted wanted rebellion; Matt wanted nobility. They both wanted a role model. So I gave my audience what they wanted.

NOVEMBER 8: BACK ON TRACK

It's not easy for me to admit this. Ted's right.

Although we've been friends a long time, we haven't always seen eye to eye. His mama's boy attitude always clashed with my DIY punk rock lifestyle. Back in high school, I'd drag race and Dead Man's Bluff and he'd organize a bake sale for the 4-H club. I was always sticking it to the Man, and he'd always water the Man's plants when the Man was out of town.

That's why it's so shocking to have our roles reversed.

Ted, I'm not sure what set of USC pajamas you were wearing when you wrote your last comment...but your words have the unmistakable sting of an unpleasant truth. And there's only one thing to do when you feel that sting.

Take action.

I hit the road seeking freedom and found a prison. Seriously, the only difference is that a prisoner has access to a television and a working toilet.

This is not a fate worthy of my legend.

I'M DAVID RALPH CICIRELLI. MY ONLY NATURAL WEAKNESS IS AT THE FREE THROW LINE. I gladly take it on the chin from the powerful, and wear my battle scars as a badge of honor. I'll uproot my life if my life feels wrong, because I believe in righteous confrontation!

A rut is not something you can leave behind, it's something you need to fill in. Otherwise you'll find yourself at the bottom again.

Matt Campbell defended me from Ted's criticism. As much as I appreciate his unwavering support, I have to disagree with his assessment. There is nothing gentlemanly about tricking a man into shoveling horse shit.

We didn't strike an agreement as gentlemen. I was dictated to.

If the Dave of just five years ago met the Dave of today, I'd kick my own ass. It would be an act of charity. The old Dave…the Dave I'm attempting to rediscover, wouldn't stand for this.

I know to some, Ted's assault seems out of place. Who is he to cast such judgment on me? The real question is, "who am I?" Ted's emotional response came from a place of pain…because I am his hero.

Ted, you've reminded me that you and others live vicariously through me, admiring the many ways in which I do what you're all incapable of. Thank you for reminding me of this responsibility.

I've let you down. I reminded you that sometimes heroes have feet of clay. But you've reminded me that I have a backbone of iron. Rest assured, I will fail you no longer. Your admiration is a responsibility I will no longer take lightly.

Tomorrow is my last day in Amish country (gotta pack my shit, dawg).

Steve Cuchinello "A nation that prefers disgrace to danger will find itself with a master, and deserve one." Alexander Hamilton as quoted by David Ralph Cicirelli.

Glad you have found your way.
yesterday · Like

Joe Lennon Congrats! Which way are you headed next?
yesterday via mobile · Like

Dave Cicirelli Not sure. Going to hitch a ride and see.

BTW, everything worked out for Hamilton, right?
yesterday via mobile · Like

Matt Campbell You're right. I forgot all about my anger about the threat of hate crime laws. I became complacent. How are you planning your escape?
yesterday via mobile · Like

Ted Kaiser I am glad you found your way Dave. So glad in fact, that I will let pass the subtle digs and your attempts at idolatry. You've been through enough lately. You should come back to NJ though.
yesterday · Like

Dave Cicirelli Ted, there's no shame in admitting I'm your hero.
yesterday via mobile · Like

NOVEMBER 10: LIFE IS STRANGE...

"It's often said that life is strange. But compared to what?"
—Steve Forbert

Here's the piece of the story I've been hesitant to talk about.

Ok…yesterday, it went DOWN.

If you read my last note, I basically verbalized it. "You strong-armed me, I'm not going to be intimidated by you, I'm Ted's hero…" blah blah blah.

Jonathon made it into this big ugly thing about the world outside of the Amish community, etc. He accused me of not being a man of my word…it got ugly. It basically ended when I dared him to stop me.

Storming out of a place filled with conscientious objectors isn't really that challenging.

It was unpleasant, but it's behind me.

…except it's not.

***

When I set up camp last night, Kate showed up.

Katie Fisher, the Amish girl I'd been flirting with…followed me out of Amish country. Jonathon's daughter chased after me like a lovesick teenager.

I mean, all right. She was my only friend out there. We made out one time, which was pretty cool. But…

…I was in Amish Country man!!!! It's like a hook-up in Cancun, except the exact opposite!

I didn't plan on leading her on, but I DEFINITELY didn't plan on taking her with me. This was all about independence.

Plus, I really don't know what kind of consequences my fleeing will bring about, I just know that having her with me will make matters more complicated.

But most important, I'm not sure what her expectations are. Does she think I'm going to marry her? Support her? I live in a tent.

The bottom line is I now have this woman with me who grew up in this strange place and is now relying on me to give her everything she imagined the rest of the world to offer.

I'm freaking out.

***

So now what?

We took a local bus to Harrisburg. From here, I figure we can take a bus to just about anywhere. We're in a cheap hotel. I couldn't exactly let her sleep in a tent. We went shopping at the Harrisburg Mall, I bought her some regular clothes. We'll probably hang out here a day or two then move on.

My cash supply is getting low.

She could have at least robbed her father before she fled.

Matt Riggio wow, Dave. This is heavy stuff.
about an hour ago via mobile · Like

Joe Lennon I'll think of something with more substance tomorrow because WOW.
about an hour ago via mobile · Like

Joe Lennon Also sometimes I feel like I'm being duped by these stories because they are downright unbelievable.
about an hour ago via mobile · Like

Matt Campbell So I guess you are over your boredom with Pennsylvania Dutch country? You definitely got the last word…so far! There are so many songs and stories about the 'farmer's daughter,' but not many have their plot in Lancaster.
22 minutes ago · Like

Ted Kaiser Did you hit that while at the hotel? All joking aside, I'd say watch your back. Jonathon is gonna come after you and you know how these Amish roll.
22 minutes ago via mobile · Like

Dave Cicirelli Classy as usual, Kaiser. We are fugitives, man. Both our lives were in flux, and passion runs high. It was high emotion, yet still tender and oh so right. Any more details, you need a credit card and a password.

Now if you are done imagining me making love to my lady, I'll move on.
19 minutes ago via mobile · Like

Elliott Askew Seriously dude…I wouldn't believe you…But…You CANNOT make this stuff up…shit like this doesn't even happen in fiction…
18 minutes ago via mobile · Like

Steve Cuchinello Dave, if she is of legal age: good for you. It was her decision anyway, you didn't ask her to come with you. But if she isn't my only suggestion is: RUN!! Run as far and as fast as you can (prolly a city block or two) and after that keep running. If that girl is under 18 her parents can and WILL do anything to get her back and this isn't a fun little journey anymore where Dave loses his mind and discovers his inner being, its straight up Dave going to jail. For the first time I am actually concerned for you.
14 minutes ago · Like

Carol Weng I lived in Harrisburg for about a year after graduating college. If you're still in H-burg, hit up Neato Burrito downtown. Or walk down the pedestrian bridge to City Island. There's also a civil war museum that I never went to, but might be neat if you're into that.

And about the girl…if you're not serious about her (i.e. have any future plans of marrying her), bring her back to her father. I'm sure he'd forgive you for everything if he had his daughter back.
11 minutes ago via mobile · Like

Mariko Nakatani Wow, this is getting wild. I wanna hear more! How is she adjusting to the "real" world? This must be a pretty crazy experience for her.
9 minutes ago via mobile · Like

Ralph Cicirelli Dave,

What are you thinking? I know you feel you were threatened and wronged by some Amish years ago, but taking this girl away from her family is not going to right that wrong. Let it go!

It's bad enough you created angst within your own family, do you need to destroy another family? Leave her to the insular life she knows and move on! In fact, abandon this half a** pursuit and come home…

Dad

8 minutes ago via mobile · Like

Dave Cicirelli Frankly, Ralph, there's only angst in our family because of your dismissive attitude. This is obviously important to me. You choose to insult me rather than support me, and make what's already difficult into something often unbearable.

How dare you blame me for "destroying another family." I may have spoiled whatever YOUR expectations are for MY life, but to treat Kate's own journey as collateral damage for your black sheep son is beyond unfair.

P.S. You don't need to sign your Facebook comments. It's not a letter.

7 minutes ago via mobile · Like

Kelly Murray dang! This is getting good…<pops some popcorn>…looking forward to the next part of your journey!

just now via mobile · Like

5 what's on your mind?

Half days are the longest.

They aren't very productive, either. I mostly sat at my office desk, staring at the little digital clock on the corner of my screen.

Who could work? It was the Wednesday before Thanksgiving!

It's my favorite weekend of the year. Unlike most holidays, where you're looking for a Christmas miracle or someone to kiss at midnight, there's very little room for disappointment. The only promise Thanksgiving makes is sharing a meal with your family. How perfect is that? It's just so uncomplicated. At least most years.

This was to be my secret return from exile—the first time I'd be in Red Bank since I started this mess. Even on a normal visit I could count on running into an old classmate or a neighbor, but this was homecoming weekend. The town would be packed with Facebook friends.

Despite how much I was looking forward to turkey dinner, I dreaded the train ride getting there. Penn Station would be an absolute bottleneck of Red Bank–born New Yorkers. The holiday would filter out the hundred or so people in the city I couldn't be seen by and put them all on the same handful of trains.

I looked over at my desk and sifted through a pile of promotional swag. I grabbed an oversized hoodie branded by a fitness product and a clunky pair of shades that say "Stay cool" on the sides. This would be my disguise for the eighty-minute ride home.

My office phone rang. It was an unknown number.

"Hello, this is FedEx," a voice said on the other end. "We have an oversized package to be delivered to you."

"What? I'm not expecting anything oversized," I said. "Where is it coming from?"

"Lancaster, PA."

Amish country? I was instantly excited and suspicious. "*Who is this?*" I yelled into the receiver.

The only response I got was a dial tone.

It clearly wasn't FedEx, so I assumed it must be Joe or Ted or someone having a little fun with me. But with the memory of my Photoshop debacle still fresh in my mind, the phone call unnerved me. I tried to put it out of my mind and went back to the important work of watching the clock move. After all, I had a train to catch, places I couldn't go, and people I couldn't see.

On the train, I grabbed a window seat and put my hood up with my forehead to the window, blocking me from most angles. The disguise must have made me look like a real scumbag—but an anonymous scumbag. My reward was a mercifully uneventful train ride home.

Waiting at the station for Ralph to pick me up, however, was excruciating. The time dragged, as I felt raw, exposed, and left behind by my own splintered identity.

In New York, I was able to suppress this feeling. After all, to my coworkers and my closest friends, I was still me, and Fakebook was just a thing I was doing. In Red Bank, however, Fakebook wasn't a thing I was doing—it was who I was. Being physically in the town, surrounded by the people who now thought I was someone else, was viscerally disorienting. My entire being was a liability.

"Where the hell is Ralph?" I thought.

My call to his cell phone went straight to voice mail. He must have been, as usual, saving the rechargeable battery.

"Ralph," I barked into the voice mail. "It's Dave. Keep your phone on. As punishment, I'm going to let this message run until it times out so you have to sit through it."

As I filled his voice mail with dead air, I warily watched people walk by. I was compelled to look at everyone who passed me to confirm they were strangers. It felt like only a matter of time before one of them recognized me and knew I wasn't supposed to be there.

It figured that my attempt to blend resulted in forcing lots of eye contact with everyone around me. After all, my "disguise" of a loose-fitting, gray hooded sweatshirt and blocky sunglasses made me look like a police sketch of the Unabomber. Combine that with lurking in the shadows sizing everyone up, and it painted the portrait of a drug dealer trying to get caught.

After a full ninety seconds, I reached the "message size limit" on my dad's phone and hung up. I walked over to a support beam and leaned on it with my back to the bars that lined Broad Street. In a couple of hours, the street would be packed—tonight was one of their big nights.

I'm sure it's the same in many towns. The night before Thanksgiving, the bars fill up with the returning prodigal sons and daughters. People jump on the opportunity to go out with the friends they normally never see and enjoy random encounters with their pasts. Despite our connectivity, there is still something wonderful and irreplaceable about sharing the same space.

I felt really wistful for this shared experience I couldn't have and a little ashamed for disregarding these peripheral relationships to create an online prank turned social experiment. They were so much more meaningful than I'd imagined when I tossed them aside. Tonight's annual bar crawl was just another communal touchstone that I'd carelessly thrown away.

What if I just show up? I wondered. What would happen if I brazenly walked into the Dublin House and just acted like I didn't know what anybody was talking about—acted like they were the crazy ones?

I couldn't do that, of course…but what if I went the other way and totally embraced the story? I could be Fake Dave for a night. All it would take was a single post: "Hey guys, Kate and I decided to spend Thanksgiving with our families. See everyone soon!" If I really wanted to sell it, I could even post an injury on Facebook and then show up to town in a cast, getting people to sign it.

I entertained this thought for a while… It could be kind of fun. I'd be greeted with a hero's welcome, and I could finally enjoy some of Fake Dave's popularity.

But with Fakebook, I was beginning to realize, the stage was more interesting than the performance. It wasn't about pretending to be someone else; it was about having someone else pretending to be me. The two lives needed to be quarantined from each other to really measure how much one impacted the other. To blur the lines between my online persona and my real life would turn Fakebook into just another hoax instead of whatever this was turning into.

Sadly, Fake Dave would have to spend the Thanksgiving weekend on his own. Or rather, I would be the one spending the weekend on my own—he had company. My gamble of introducing Amish Kate had actually worked. Fakebook had people's attention again.

Dave Cicirelli

We slept in. I was kinda hoping having an Amish girlfriend would be like dating Buddy the Elf, where I'd wake up and she cleaned all the clothes in the sink and churned the non-dairy creamer into a cheesecake. Guess not, haha.

Like · Comment

Stephen Ortez Dave, your story totally saved my work day. I am glad my cousin turned me onto this. I said it before, and I'll say it again, Godspeed.

less than a minute ago via mobile · Like

The previous few weeks had been Fake Dave and Amish Kate's "honeymoon" in Harrisburg. I thought it wise and believable to give them a little downtime after their explosive departure from Lancaster. And even though the slow time on the farm had dragged on a bit too long, I still thought it important to weave in these periods of quiet. Events needed to settle before I stirred them up again. Otherwise it was exhausting—both for me and for the audience.

And now I had found a status quo that was far more engaging than the original FarmVille parody. Having Fake Dave usher this girl into his particular idea of modern life was a gigantic gray area and had great opportunities for a little cultural satire.

Dave Cicirelli

I think a 'blooming onion' was a bad idea.

Like · Comment · Share

Ted Kaiser woah Dave what are you doing to this girl? That's a short dress for a fair Amish lady. Did you buy her really slutty clothes and tell her this is what normal American girls wear? If so, good job.

2 hours ago via mobile · Like

Brendan McDermott Dude, I am well accustomed to American food, and a bloomin' onion is just too much for me.

2 hours ago via mobile · Like

Dave Cicirelli Hey man, I had a craving. What would you eat after a month in Amish country? Some how a salad didn't seem satisfying.

about an hour ago via mobile · Like

Mike Center Bloomin' onions are wonderful and it's a shame those cowards at Chili's caved and removed the awesome blossom from their menu. I knew what I was getting into when I ordered that. We all did.

about an hour ago via mobile · Like

Dave Cicirelli

What a night.

Like · Comment · Share

Matt Campbell Mixed drinks!?

35 minutes ago via mobile · Like

Elliott Askew You must be opening up her world like the Dalai Lama did in Tibet. Just watch out for the Chinese, man.

18 minutes ago via mobile · Like

Dave Cicirelli What a highbrow reference, Elliott. Please relate it to The Simpsons so I understand.

12 minutes ago via mobile · Like

Erin Brennan Hanson i have a motherly instinct to cover her up. Who is dressing that poor girl?

5 minutes ago via mobile · Like

Dave Cicirelli Listen, Tali-Brennan. I let her buy whatever she wanted. I'm not the monster you think I am.

just now via mobile · Like

I couldn't help but laugh at people's judgmental reaction to Amish Kate. All across the country, twentysomethings nursing hangovers were judging me for introducing this girl to their own lifestyles. I took Kate Moulton's photos—the same photos most twenty-five-year-old girls have on their Facebook walls—and showed that lifestyle back to them. "Look at what you did to that poor girl in the mirror," they complained.

Screw it, I thought. Haters gonna hate, and Fake Dave and Amish Kate were having fun. Plus, there was a lingering instability between them that would keep it compelling. Fake Dave's whole journey was about being unattached, being free. Now Amish Kate was a responsibility, albeit a hot blond one. Her presence undercut his attempts to be a "citizen of the road." Having Fake Dave not necessarily on board with this—but not immediately sending her back, either—created a world of texture.

She also created a new context for my audience to assess Fake Dave's behavior. Before Kate, it was easy to be supportive of this adventure since even at its most immature, there was no real victim (other than that toilet-papered horse). But now? An innocent woman had been ripped from her family and community, all because she was seduced by some drifter's modest worldliness.

What was Fake Dave's responsibility to her? How much personal responsibility did Kate have for herself? Was this journey still worth doing? Was it romantic or reckless? Insane? It was impossible not to have a point of view.

NOVEMBER 19: UPDATE FROM THE ROAD

I've spent a lot of my nights awake, staring at Kate.

Honestly, at this stage of the game, I have no idea how it's going to pan out. Long-term relationships were never my strength, but I always did my best to treat women well. Even though I feel bullied into this situation.

And this situation WAS forced upon me.

As much as I like have the best "how did you meet?" story of all time, I can't help but hold a little resentment towards her.

I mean, if you separate yourself from the story for a moment, its crazy…right? Because she's Amish, everyone gives her a pass on unusual behavior, and we all just consider her an innocent. That's really not fair to me.

If she was just some girl, and not some Amish girl, following me would be considered CRAZY. Not kooky, but crazy. She may be crazy. I barely know her. But I do like her. The first few days were something…

Elizabeth Lee I understand you're going through some stuff…and that I obviously do not understand this journey you're on…but stop saying this was forced on you. You always have a choice. You obviously want to be where you are, or you would be home. Anyways, stay safe…and NY misses you.

yesterday via mobile · Like

Joe Moscone No doubt your current situation is unique. But who am I to say what you should do with this girl; I likely could not pick an Amish out of a lineup of Orthodox Jews, let alone begin to understand her culture/lifestyle and what she's bringing to the table that you're so infatuated with. Keep putting one foot in front of the other, but don't lose sight of the fact that you embarked on this journey for yourself—not her or anyone else.

yesterday via mobile · Like

Graciela Meza I have to agree with Elizabeth that none of this was forced on you. I believe people do things they want to do and let things happen that they want to happen. I guarantee that if an unattractive smelly Amish girl wanted to follow you, you would have found an effective way of telling her no.

Sorry Dave. No matter what happens, you have my ear, let me know if there's anything you need.

yesterday via mobile · Like

Matt Campbell I love this adventure.
yesterday via mobile · Like

Dave Cicirelli Graciella...exactly how shallow do you think I am? Seriously. You seem to have an excellent read of exactly how shallow I am.
19 hours ago via mobile · Like

Joe Lennon Who said she was unattractive?
19 hours ago via mobile · Like

Dave Cicirelli BTW, Joe. I think you misunderstood Graciella. She's saying that IF she was ugly and smelly, I would have found away to turn her away. Don't worry about it, art school friends are often nearly illiterate. She is correct, however, about my stance on ugly and smelly people.
17 hours ago via mobile · Like

Graciela Meza Speaking of nearly illiterate, my name is spelled with one L.
17 hours ago via mobile · Like

Elliott Askew Besides really enjoying following your adventure your experiences have shone light on just how different men are from women...I think that the great majority of women posting serious comments have expressed negative opinions on almost everything you have been doing...

Or maybe it's just that the loud minority leaves a greater impression on me. It's been very interesting though... Not to say that all the guys have been supportive...But it just seems like we get what you are trying to do to a greater degree.

I support everything you are doing Dave...And I believe that all of the obstacles you have faced and will face in the future are really essential aspects of the experience. Keep it up man. We have your back.
16 hours ago via mobile · Like

Elliott Askew PS…I don't plan on posting anything serious for a while…I just felt like throwing down the gauntlet and getting this sex war started…

16 hours ago via mobile · Like

Dave Cicirelli Bros before Hos.

16 hours ago via mobile · Like

Dave Cicirelli

Gettin some love at dinner. Going to head to some sports bar to meet friends of hers. She makes friends quick. By comparison, once again I'm confronted with the possibility that I may not be as charming as I thought…but who could be?

Like · Comment · Share

Elizabeth Lee you look really happy! :) maybe this isn't such a crazy thing you're doing.

2 hours ago via mobile · Like

Dave Cicirelli Yeah, she's all right. I'm starting to feel a little bogged down though. I didn't uproot myself to settle down.

2 hours ago via mobile · Like

Elizabeth Lee Seriously? You're being a jerk! I take it back…this whole thing is crazy then.

about an hour ago via mobile · Like

Elizabeth Lee I cannot even believe you'd say that. I'm really pissed off.

about an hour ago via mobile · Like

Dave Cicirelli Hey! Don't make me the bad guy here. I didn't invite her along, she invited herself. I'm supposed to be living in a tent, and stretching my cash supplies a hell of a lot longer than I can support it now. I'm going to have to get a job soon! Listen, she's a sweet girl, and I feel responsible for her…but this was thrust upon me. I'm taking responsibility, but I never made a commitment, so cut me some slack!

36 minutes ago via mobile · Like

Terrance J Riley You are like a "punctured bicycle on a hillside glistening," lol. Your girlfriend is beautiful; Congrats on that.

24 minutes ago via mobile · Like

Elizabeth Lee She is beautiful! Appreciate what life has brought your way! And yea…maybe it is time to get a job! Get back to real world! I am cutting you no slack, grow up. You took yourself there, you intruded on her life! You've allowed her to stay with you. You have chosen this.

18 minutes ago via mobile · Like

Dave Cicirelli And Terence, I think even Morrissey hasn't covered this situation yet, haha. Maury has. But not Morrissey.

17 minutes ago via mobile · Like

Joe Moscone Wait is she hitchhiking with you or is she pregnant? Because it's my understanding that we're talking about the former, in which case you owe her nothing at all.

You did NOT intrude on her life; don't listen to that crap your "friend" is spewing. You were "sentenced" to stay there in her community, it wasn't a choice. And even with your obviously limited charm, to her—living that lifestyle and with her upbringing—you're like Don fuckin' Juan! (And she doesn't even know who he is!!) That's on her, not you.

Go about your travels…live your life…and make the most of this awesome experience however you wish.

Plus, regardless of her beauty, the baggage this girl will bear for years and years to come isn't anything you want to deal with. Shit, if/when her people catch up with her, if you're there, you're going right back to shoveling horse shit! Not worth it.

5 minutes ago via mobile · Like

Dave Cicirelli Joe's right! I can't be held responsible for HER feelings. I mean, listen. Elizabeth, you blew this up and attacked me. I was fine seeing where this curve in the road takes me, but your judgment and Joe's points are making me take a hard look at this. I left NY for reasons. I wanted to re-center myself as a person and as an artist.

SHE intruded on my plans. Forget whatever fairytale visions you have Elizabeth, a cute "how you met" story is no reason to avoid taking a hard look at this. She followed me, and that, frankly, is a little crazy.

She had the poor judgment to follow the drifter who vandalized her farmhouse. I'm not sure why I'm obligated to cover her mistakes.

Man, this got me angry when before I wasn't. I have some thinking to do.

3 minutes ago via mobile · Like

Joe Moscone Atta boy! Write her off as collateral damage and move along on your journey.

just now via mobile · Like

This was a comfortable place to keep things, but not for long. If it were a different time of year, I might have maintained this status quo for a while and have the controversial "it couple" continue to live off Fake Dave's unspecified cash reserves for longer. But tonight was the night before Thanksgiving, and it was a great opportunity to expand my audience.

I was convinced that many people simply hadn't noticed Fakebook on their news feed yet. The same qualities that might make a YouTube video a hit don't make a Facebook profile go viral. In fact, a cornerstone of Fakebook's appeal is that it's *not* meant to be theater—or at least not meant to be perceived that way. It's supposed to be real events happening to a real person—and the audience isn't supposed to think of themselves as one.

It's engrossing to watch a guy get in over his head with an unexpected girlfriend and to follow his constant pattern of sabotaging any chance at stability, but a crucial part of that appeal is that it's none of your damn business. To post a comment is to admit you are looking.

I'd noticed that as people's interest in Fake Dave and his adventures deepened, their discretion also grew. Fakebook, in many ways, was a ripe staging ground for old-fashioned gossip—and tonight, when everyone got together to catch up on each other's lives, I safely guessed there would be a lot of gossiping.

Dave Cicirelli
Some of our friends from town are throwing Kate a going-away party. Yes, they actually called it "Kate's" going-away party. Women are just not taking my side on this one.

Like · Comment · Share

Joe Moscone You're not foxy enough to have parties thrown in your honor. (And, no, your own birthday bashes don't count.)
5 minutes ago via mobile · Like

Dave Cicirelli Joe...You clearly are not aware of my genetically perfect teeth.
less than a minute ago via mobile · Like

I got them back on the road, hiking west along highways as my audience traveled east, back to the shore.

"Jeez," Ralph said as he finally pulled in to the train-station parking lot. He gave my Unabomber disguise a look. "You look like hell. I thought you were a bum."

"Thanks, Pops."

"Come on, your mother's waiting."

"Whose fault is that? I was out here for like half an hour."

"I was at the liquor store."

"That's some good parenting, Ralph."

There's another reason I didn't bring Fake Dave home with me—one unrelated to the integrity of the Fakebook social experiment, but entirely related to the Fakebook hoax. At the end of the day, despite all of the rationalizing, I knew I was lying. I was lying every day, over and over again. But it was abstract lying, so most days I could pretend it didn't count.

To walk around Red Bank, however, and come face to face with people who had shown me nothing but support—that was too aggressive, too personal. I didn't have the stomach for it. I'd leave that task to Ted and Steve.

Before I saw my mother, I saw her handiwork as I entered the house: a hand-drawn sign on the living room chair that said "NO CLOTHES ZONE" with a little drawing of a shirt crossed out in a no-smoking-style circle. In the long-standing "dirty clothes go in the hamper" stalemate in the Cicirelli marriage, that chair was the floral-printed Gaza Strip.

"Your mother treats me like one of her kindergartners," Ralph said in a tone closer to pride than shame.

"My kindergartners listen!" Mom chimed in from the kitchen, where she was stirring a pot of sauce.

I walked over and gave my mom a hug and a kiss on the cheek. "Is he giving you trouble, Mom? Normally I don't pick favorites, but on Thanksgiving, I love you more than Dad."

My mom scooped out a couple of meatballs, and making good on her Fakebook promise, she served them to her son who had come home.

"What a momma's boy," Ralph said as he grabbed a handful of blueberries from the refrigerator. The closing door offered a glimpse of the Thanksgiving feast to come.

"That's breakfast food!" she yelled out.

"He's only acting out for the attention," I said in as patronizing tone as I could muster.

"You guys like to gang up on me," Ralph said, as he turned away to protect his prize.

It's true, we do gang up on him. After all, a poorly behaved kindergarten student isn't the worst description of my dad. He's usually in trouble for stealing treats between meals or making a mess when he comes in from the yard. It's also true that he likes the attention. He was smiling ear to ear as he cried victim.

Besides, it's not like he shows restraint when someone else has the target on their back. In fact, by bellowing out the made-up term of "breakfast food," my mom placed it squarely on herself. Early bedtimes and rigid routine are a couple of her hallmark areas for teasing.

"It's almost seven," I said to Mom. "I thought you'd be in your pajamas by now."

"She wishes," Ralph said with a mouthful of breakfast food.

"Yeah, he's right," Mom said with a laugh. "As soon as I'm done with the dishes."

Within a half hour she was dressed for bed, and we all sat down to watch TV. Their DVR held nothing but backlogged episodes of *Say Yes to the Dress* and *House Hunters*, the perfect cocktail to bore the hell out of me. After two hours of watching strangers buy things, my solar-powered Mom went to bed, and Ralph had already dozed off. I looked at the clock, barely past 9:00 p.m. Now what?

I woke up to the sound of a vibrating phone on a wooden end table. "Whaaaa...what time is it?"

"Dude. It's only like 10:30," Ted answered.

"Oh...You in Red Bank?"

"Yeah. I'm with Steve, and it sucks," Ted answered.

"Wait, why are you calling? You guys haven't given anything away, have you?"

"No, we're keeping your secret," Ted said with a little more bite than I expected. "It's easy because people are ignoring us. They seem angry at us."

"Angry at you? What for?"

"Probably for the way Steve and I have been treating you online. For all the things we write."

I thought about how so many people, including those who resented Ted and Steve, were reluctant to even post on the Fakebook wall. I thought of the many Facebook-era conversations I'd had that disingenuously started with "What have you been up to?" I thought about how distracting all this secret public knowledge could be.

Then I remembered the specific things Ted and Steve had been posting.

"Well," I said in a sly tone, "you were saying some pretty harsh things about that sweet Amish girl."

He hung up.

I texted an apology. I had been completely out of line. Fakebook was my Frankenstein's monster; now Ted and Steve were out there facing the scorn of the townsfolk to defend it on my behalf. I went back to sleep feeling awful. In the morning, there'd be work to do.

I woke up around six and went downstairs to an empty kitchen and opened the refrigerator. I looked at all the prepped food for the afternoon feast and snuck a pinch of uncooked stuffing.

It was peaceful, the quiet before the storm of overlapping cooking times and family arrivals. Soon enough, my mother was up and running around the kitchen. Any offer to help was rejected—she wasn't letting me anywhere near her masterpiece. It was just a matter of sitting around and waiting for Thanksgiving to start.

So I sat around in front of the TV. America's favorite new genre of unscripted television—obnoxious people with quirky professions—began to take hold of me. I sat there for hours, watching encore presentations of fat guys building theme motorcycles. It was mind numbing, and I felt myself both wanting to see how it turned out and wanting to jump out a window. It made me nostalgic for the days when cable TV was all about minor celebrities remembering stuff from past decades. I finally turned it off, itching to do something productive.

Naturally, I turned to Fakebook. In light of last night's revelations, my original plan of acknowledging Thanksgiving with an exterior shot of a Boston Market didn't seem sufficient. So with that same mix of boredom and anxiety that had triggered Fakebook in the first place, I was inspired to create a new picture.

I looked at the clock and saw it was almost 11:00 a.m. I'd have to work fast, so I began a frantic search for images. This work was going to be rushed and barely passable, but it felt important. Besides, with the option of attending my high school's homecoming football game squarely off the table, photoshopping was the best way to pass the time before Mom finally let us unwrap the antipasto.

I scoured the Internet and took poorly lit photos with my parents' Canon PowerShot, locking myself in the basement to meet this pressing deadline. I could hear my brother Jeff and his wife, Elisha, arrive from the airport around noon. I heard the footsteps of Mark and his fiancée, Lisa, enter the house an hour later. By 2:00 p.m., all my aunts, uncles, and cousins had arrived, and the house got very loud.

I'll say hello as soon as I can, I thought, *but I have to get this image made. I'm under deadline.*

An hour later, I had Fake Dave post from a homeless shelter:

Dave Cicirelli

What kind of Cicirelli would I be if I wasn't first in line?

Like · Comment · Share

I closed my laptop, feeling a little uncomfortable about what I had just done. It wasn't just the very, very poor Photoshop quality this time. It was the content. Right after I posted it, I realized it was an utterly obnoxious thing to show. Even though this never happened, it still felt exploitive. In the moment, I found it impossible not to think of Fake Dave as me. We shared the reputation I'd just soiled and that suddenly bothered me.

But it was done. All I could do now was cross my fingers. Ted and Steve were getting a hard time for calling me out as the bad guy, so I owed it to them to prove them right. Above me, I could hear the loud din of the full family.

Sometimes I try to look at us through the eyes of my sisters-in-law—what we must have looked like to them as they first shared a holiday with us. It's a good family. We love each other; we all have lived upstanding lives free of police records, substance abuse, and most other black marks; we look good on paper. But get us all together, and we are chaotic and loud.

At first glance, other than the lack of spray tans and hair spray, we don't offer much to dispel the stereotype of a big New Jersey Italian family. At any given time, everyone is engaged in at least three loud conversations—two of them arguments. Politics, personal lives, nothing is sacred. Anything anyone says is mocked, interrupted, or undermined.

But from the basement, all the overlapping arguments compressed into the single sound of steady laughter. It was a good reminder of why Thanksgiving is my favorite holiday. It's not about what you can get; it's about appreciating what you have. It promises nothing more than sharing a meal with your family. It's uncomplicated, even this year. It was my home, my town, my family—all as they are.

There's honesty to it.

If only the whole Thanksgiving holiday could have ended with pumpkin pie, a scoop of vanilla ice cream, and a football game. It would have been a nice ending after a frustrating start. But the thing about Thanksgiving is that it's on a Thursday.

By the time Saturday night rolled around, the holiday weekend was seriously getting to me.

If my brothers hadn't been in town, I would have bounced Friday morning. I'd be back in the city that was big enough for me to be anonymous. I'd be able to grab a drink in a place where the bartender wouldn't know I was supposed to be outside of Harrisburg.

Ironically, if I wasn't supposed to be in Harrisburg, I wouldn't have been so eager to go back to the city. I would be going out with my brothers in the town that was abuzz with how exciting my life was, instead of tagging along on my parents' DVR routine before turning in early. I was beginning to forget what 10:00 p.m. looked like.

And Saturday night…I couldn't even count on TV with my parents. It was pizza night.

Luigi's Pizza is the one thing that we, as a family, all agree on. While there's good pizza in New York, there is no Luigi's. Luigi's doesn't have a brick oven. It doesn't burn coal or wood or use fresh buffalo milk mozzarella. Instead, it offers a true pizzeria pizza, just perfected.

As I tortured myself with the Food Network—watching an attractive lady I'd never meet cook food I'd never eat—Mark, Jeff, Lisa, Elisha, Mom, and Dad were sitting at a table with multiple square pies coming out of the oven.

I imagined the thin but substantial crust—how it never yields under its own weight like a lesser slice. The bottom is crispy without being burnt and has inherited the textile quality of the large-grain flour the raw dough once rested on. The crust is soft on top, absorbing the flavor of the shredded mozzarella—just a hint on the salty side and with a touch of oil, but no grease—and, of course, that spectacular sauce. It's a vivid red with a touch of sweetness, and the occasional tomato chunk accents the otherwise smooth composition. And when you eat the crust—and in my family, you'd better—it's like a palate-cleansing sorbet, ensuring that "first bite" sensation remains from slice to slice.

It's the best. It bonds us. But for all our love of Luigi's Pizza, no one in my family has ever savored a bite. To savor one bite is to endanger the next. Everyone at that table—including my mother and sisters-in-law (my brothers made sure their wives were Cicirellis in appetite before they make them Cicirellis in name[3])—wants every single slice. Of course you want the corner slice and the biggest slice and the one with the air bubble. Each is different and special in its own way, and each selection is a Sophie's choice: You know that choosing one slice means there's another you will never have.

So to secure the first pick of the second round (and third round and fourth…), we eat quickly. Really quickly. We're like an elite black-ops team. We swoop in with speed, efficiency, and minimal conversation and then leave, with no evidence that our target ever existed. We're a school of piranhas, and after a few minutes of frenzy, all that's left are an empty tray and the unused metal server.

And before you know it, we're in the car on the way home, expressing astonishment at how slow that one family with all the leftovers was. We're a family. Luigi's is our second home.

But I was stuck on house arrest, trusting my family to eat their fill and then bring me home a personal pizza (but, you know, sized for a family) in one piece. Mark promised me they'd bring me home pizza, one piece. I didn't even feel secure in that.

"Hey, Dave!" Ralph said as he walked through the front door, with the rest of the family closely following. "You wouldn't believe this one family," he continued as he carries a large delivery box. "They had pizza on the table when we got there, and they were still working on it when we left!"

Before I even got up from the couch, the pizza was on the island in the kitchen—surrounded on all sides by people still wearing coats. I jumped into the fray to grab a slice, but I would have had an easier time freeing a gazelle carcass from a pride of lions.

---

[3]I have to make this clear—despite being good eaters, my sisters-in-law are both very thin. If I give the wrong impression in a published book, I will be in trouble for years and years.

"You too, Mom?" I said as she grabbed a coveted corner piece.

"Well…I thought I wasn't hungry anymore. But now that I'm eating…"

I knew better than to continue to talk, but I darted Mark a look that said, "I thought this was my pizza." He didn't even notice.

I got just enough to get a taste, enough to crave it and feel wildly unsatisfied. This, I imagine, is what half a fix feels like.

I hated Fake Dave. Estranging me from my friends—so be it. Ruining Steve and Ted's reputation…well, there was bound to be some collateral damage. But this? Just a day before, I'd felt bad for Fake Dave—for making him act so immaturely at that homeless shelter. After missing pizza night, however, I was more than happy to have him reap what he sowed.

So for the first time all weekend I stayed up until midnight, and through a garlic-powdered haze, I scoured the online portfolios of movie makeup artists to find black eyes and bruises, and took perverse pleasure in photoshopping the consequences of Fake Dave's Thanksgiving tour of poverty.

Dave Cicirelli

For the first time in my life, my famous Cicirelli charm let me down. I got a little jacked up Thursday night, but I'm fine now and finally got my stuff back. Flashing electronics around at a soup kitchen was a bad idea. We're probably going to be walking all night. I've had it with this part of the country.

Like · Comment · Share

Joe Lennon Are you going to tell us what happened exactly? Glad you're ok.

3 hours ago via mobile · Like

Elliott Askew Umm...Can we talk about what is going on with your face?

3 hours ago via mobile · Like

Dave Cicirelli I waited until that son of a bitch got blackout drunk on hooch he bought with my money to get my shit back.

3 hours ago via mobile · Like

Elliott Askew It looks like he had a pretty good right hook...Thank god you got your stuff back...You're looking more like Indiana Jones everyday (post fight with the Nazi on the tank).

I will reiterate that you were looking for an adventure. I hope you are not getting discouraged by all the negativity.

2 hours ago via mobile · Like

Dave Cicirelli Elliott. You are right. I seek adventure, and I'm definitely finding it. Even Indiana Jones got his ass kicked every once in a while.

2 hours ago via mobile · Like

Ralph Cicirelli Dave, what happened? I won't even think of telling your mother. She will lose it if I do.

This Thanksgiving was very sad. Your mother set two extra places at the table in hopes that you and your lady friend would show up. My heart was heavy when I saw her tear up.

Dave, you know how I feel about this misadventure, but you know that we love you. The greatest gift we could hope for this Christmas is that you come home and make two aging parents very happy.

about an hour ago via mobile · Like

Dave Cicirelli Ralph...I know a thing or two about what it feels like to be punched in the gut. This message hit me hard and hurt a lot. I don't know what kind of son makes his mother cry, and it hurts me a lot to think

I've become one...but I will not be manipulated by the guilt you've instilled in me.

Referring to yourself as "aging parents" is heavy handed, and your agenda overt. Referring to my new life as a "misadventure" is so incredibly dismissive of something that is clearly very important to me...it defies words.

Perhaps your Christmas wish should be that your son finds what he's looking for, wherever that may be.
about an hour ago via mobile · Like

Joe Lennon Dave, let your shit fly free. You are living an adventure men only dream of.
about an hour ago via mobile · Like

Ted Kaiser Kate's looking good. I think she's a catch.
about an hour ago via mobile · Like

Dave Cicirelli Ted, you horny son of a bitch, stop looking at my girlfriend. Everyone likes her more than me.
about an hour ago via mobile · Like

Ted Kaiser I noticed your face and I feel bad, but Kate's was worth mentioning. Damn...
53 minutes ago via mobile · Like

Dave Cicirelli Ted. Yeah, she's pretty hot. We are the premier "it couple" of the derelict community.
47 minutes ago via mobile · Like

Michèle Malejki Cicirelli, you're looking pretty rough here! Hope it's healing okay...Def support the adventure but go easy on the food kitchens—Rock on.
22 minutes ago via mobile · Like

Steve Cuchinello You mean the ACTUAL poor people were pissed off at a guy showing up on THANKSGIVING for free handouts with hundreds of dollars worth of electronics and his hot Amish girlfriend acting like he is as poor as them??

Let's call this a "learning experience."
18 minutes ago via mobile · Like

Dave Cicirelli Seriously Steve, kiss my ass. At least I'm having experiences. One day when you get your ass kicked, and with your personality that seems inevitable, I'll treat you with just as much compassion. What an ass clown.

13 minutes ago via mobile · Like

Steve Cuchinello Dave, I call it as I see it. Maybe I'm more of a friend by giving you a reality check from time to time, rather then kissing your ass.

3 minutes ago · Like

Dave Cicirelli Steve, your strategic use of ALL CAPS to emphasize your sarcasm is not being supportive. It was a veiled expression of how much more clever you think you are. Since you've got it all figured out, I'll be sure to consult you about proper food bank etiquette before my next meal.

less than a minute ago via mobile · Like

Steve Cuchinello OK Dave, you're right. That's what I was going for, to show you how smart I think I am and how foolish you are. Somehow you've become an arrogant hobo.

just now · Like

There. I did it. I hurt Fake Dave. I gave my collaborators a legitimate defense for their criticism of me. I finally had a halfway decent Photoshop job. It felt pretty good.

But man, I sure could go for some more Luigi's.

That Sunday evening I got off the Delancey Street F train, still wearing my branded Unabomber hoodie and NJ Transit disguise, and approached my apartment.

What a strange weekend. I'd pegged it as an important weekend to reach out to people—and had succeeded. While I sat at home, voyeuristic gossip of my adventure spread as whispers over beers—far more freely than it could via proclamations on the Facebook permanent record.

Brian Romatelli ➡ Dave Cicirelli

Dave,

I heard about what you've been doing on Wednesday night. I went home and spent 2 and a half hours reading through all your posts. Dave, you have my total support! No matter what everyone may or may not be writing about this life-changing adventure I think they all know in their heart of hearts that they wish they had the courage to do the same thing. Maybe not now in their lives or maybe it was in the past or forthcoming, but at some point in ALL our lives we need drastic change and I think your story is the perfect example of someone in touch with the pulse of reality and willing to take the risk to become what they are destined to be.

Thank you for inspiring me; I will not soon forget the absolutely wonderful morning I had today reading about your journey. You really made my day my old friend.

Go international and soon!

Unbelievable. This guy thought I took requests.

Still, I'd gotten new fans and I'd given them a show—albeit at the cost of my real relationships with them. Besides, I'd take a house-arrest homecoming to a homeless Thanksgiving any day. That made me realize how deep into Fakebook I was. I was seeing this through, and it felt almost liberating.

When I arrived at my building, a FedEx box was leaning against the door of my apartment. This was unusual; I had everything shipped to my office. But remembering the strange call I'd gotten from Fed Ex a few days ago, I pushed back the hood on my Unabomber sweatshirt and cautiously picked up my suspicious, unsolicited package. It was maybe a six-inch by six-inch base and about a foot high, and it had some weight to it. Once inside my apartment, I grabbed an X-Acto knife and cut through the tape along the box's seams. I reached in and pulled out a small…pot of flowers.

From whom? I'd never gotten flowers before. I was confused and somewhat flattered. There was a small card:

"Dear Dave, Happy Thanksgiving. I'm thankful that I found you. Love, Katie Fisher."

Katie Fisher? Who is Katie Fish…Wait. *That's my fake Amish girlfriend!*

Someone knows.

6 tagged

"Hey, Steve," I said into my phone while glancing over at the mysterious pot of yellow tulips now sitting on the small round table I had bought in the restaurant supply district.

"Hey, Dave," Steve answered. "What's up?"

"So…um. Did you buy me flowers?"

There was a pause. "No…" Steve answered, drawing out the sound of each letter. "Do you want me to?"

"Nah, I'm cool." I quickly hung up.

I took a deep breath. I thought one of my collaborators might be having fun with me and had to check them each off the list. Steve was my first guess, and I hoped my call to my second, Joe Moscone, would be less awkward.

It wasn't.

Then Ted, my father, even sweet Elizabeth. But it was a series of humiliating dead ends.

I swiveled my chair toward my laptop and took a long look at my Facebook friends. I reread every post and every comment, looking for a change in attitude or some subtle clue to who the mystery sender could be. Everyone was a suspect.

I was impressed by this operation. This secret foil of mine had managed to subvert my subversion—turning Fakebook into a personal playground the way I aspired to do with Facebook.

I sat at my desk, staring at the card in my hands. "Dear Dave," the card read. "Happy Thanksgiving. I'm thankful that I found you. Love, Katie Fisher."

It was a generic type of message that didn't offer a clue as to who wrote it. I concluded it wasn't someone who knew me well—otherwise there'd be a trace of personality in it or a reference to an inside joke. There'd probably be less effort to conceal their identity.

This was simply a declaration: "I know your secret."

But it had to be someone I knew at least a little. After all, how could they have gotten my address otherwise? I tried to put myself in this guy's shoes, tried to imagine what it would be like if I'd just discovered that the sensational Facebook page of an old, forgotten friend was totally fake. It would be tempting to immediately expose it and let everyone to know how clever I was for figuring it out. That was the easy, obvious thing to do.

But that's not what happened. Whoever this was took a step back and decided to go about this in a much more calculated way. This person wanted to protect the hoax because it gave them power. They wanted it to continue, just on their terms.

The comic-book lover in me was completely enthralled by the thought of having a real-life supervillain. I imagined a Machiavellian figure silhouetted by light from the large screens monitoring my Facebook page.

"Good…good…" the faceless voice said calmly as he petted some sort of jungle cat.

Part of me didn't want to know who my secret foil was. Then again, part of me did. I felt challenged by a worthy foe. He'd already shown patience, cunning, and a willingness to spend $19.99 on the "Yellow Sunrise Surprise Bouquet."

I took another look at my flowers. I had to admit that they freshened up the place.

I picked up the phone and called the Send-Flowers.com customer service number on the back of the card.

"How can we help you today?" the operator replied.

I leaned back in my chair and put my bare feet up on my desk, facing my kitchenette. "A few days ago your company delivered flowers to my home on Delancey Street. Order number F dash seventeen, thirty four, B."

"Was there a problem with the order?" the bubbly customer-service rep asked.

"Oh no, not at all. They are positively beautiful! It's just…it's that I don't know who they are from," I said in my best Woody Allen voice, "and it's making me very nervous."

"I see," the operator said.

"It may be some kind of joke…but I've had trouble in the past with unwelcomed suitors, and I'm uncomfortable with this gesture. Very uncomfortable.

"I have to know," I continued, "who sent them? Where did they come from?"

"Unfortunately, sir," the operator replied, "the purchase contract legally forbids us from disclosing that information without a police warrant. Would you like instructions on how to pursue legal action to obtain one?"

I was stunned. Send-Flowers.com had a policy in place to assist with restraining orders? It made sense, I guess, but it still felt a little extreme.

"Oh, I don't know…it may be a big practical joke," I said. "I don't want to take it that far, not yet anyway. Is there anything at all you can tell me?"

"I'm sorry, sir," she said graciously. "Good luck!"

I hung up the phone. It was a dead end—all I'd discovered was my own unwillingness to delve into the dark side of Internet floristry. I'd simply have to patiently wait for clues to come to me instead.

After my awkward phone call with the Internet florist, I let the active mystery recede to the back of my mind. Yet, the residual excitement that remained had rekindled my lagging enthusiasm for the Fakebook enterprise.

For the next few weeks, I truly enjoyed Fakebook. One of the reasons I had started the project is that I like to jump into something completely unknown and experience the surprise and delight of seeing what happens. That attitude had gotten me into MTV headquarters and landed me in an eight-bedroom apartment in Chinatown where I was the only American. And now it had delivered me mystery flowers.

This new dimension—something out there that I couldn't explain—renewed my excitement. It was fun, frivolous, and wonderfully absurd. This spirit began to infuse the story, so I eagerly pushed it forward.

Using the night of Thanksgiving violence as justification, Fake Dave and Amish Kate were back on the road and heading west. But this time, looking to build a little momentum, I had them abandon their on-foot plans and try their hand at another hobo staple, the freight hop.

DECEMBER 9: SLIPPIN' ON BANANA PEELS

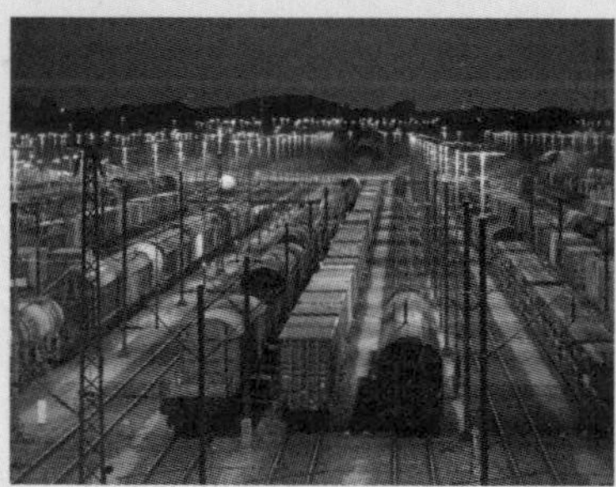

Ever since I saw a man slip on a banana peel, it's been my life's work to witness clichés.

I've seen a pie in the face. I've listened to a man preaching from atop an actual soapbox. I've even witnessed a violin player appear at the peak of self-pity!

When that magic happens, a cliché is a beautiful and rare flower that blossoms unexpectedly and only for a moment… but its sweet fragrance lingers in your mind forever.

Yet so many elude me still. I caught dozens of fish, but never a boot. I've seen sheets of glass delivered, and I've seen high-speed chases, yet never at the same time. And what does a guy have to do to see a tumbleweed during an awkward pause?

It's obvious. Move to the desert.

I've had it with the Northeast. Monday we're breaking into Enola Freight Yard hopping a train to Atlanta, then west to Arizona.

Something about the desert just feels right. Plus, it's the birthplace of Barry Goldwater, my Republican idol. I'm embarking on a new chapter, one that hopefully will be hotter than the last. But a dry heat, of course.

Now if you'll excuse me, I need to work out some logistics. I plan on making love to my lady at the exact moment our train enters a tunnel.

Dave Cicirelli

I'm not the biggest fan of graffiti, but credit where credit is due…that's a sweet tag.

Like · Comment · Share

Dave Cicirelli
This ride is amazing since I gathered the stones to open the door a bit. I'm feeling so patriotic right now. The scenery is so amazing.

Like · Comment · Share

It was thrilling. I felt like I was on that trip with them.

Christine wanted a smoke, and I needed some air.

We stepped out onto the street and into the crowd of smokers in front of The Charleston—a small music venue in Williamsburg, Brooklyn. Our coworker Pete was doing a set there, and a few of us came out to support his rock-and-roll persona.

I'd found that support at work for my alternate persona was a little less universal. No one objected to it outright; the Handler crowd just continued to have a mixed reaction to Fakebook. Consequently, small talk felt like a gauntlet of bafflement and skepticism.

"So why are you doing that thing on Facebook?" my colleague Michelle had asked as she took a sip of beer from her plastic cup.

"People actually believe this stuff?" Matt had asked when we were walking down the stairs.

"I don't get it," Danielle had said point blank.

By the time Christine wanted to step outside, I was eager to join her.

"What'd you think of the show?" I asked Christine, as I buried my cold hands inside my pockets.

"It was really good!" Christine said as she lit a cigarette, "but the real show is on the street." She nodded toward a midriff-baring guy riding a fixed-gear tall bike.

In an era of anti-bullying legislation, I'd like to cite Bedford Avenue as a cautionary tale for the world we're courting—a world where people's need for attention goes unchecked without any fear of judgment. How else could you explain a grown man in a child's T-shirt riding a ten-foot bicycle without brakes?

"Those guys are ridiculous," a fellow smoker said to us. He was wearing bifocals.

"Yeah," I said. "I've never actually seen anyone get on or off those things. It's one of those New York mysteries, like how you never see a baby pigeon."

"Gross, I know," Christine said. "It's like they hatch fully formed—wait, do they even have nests?"

"No one knows..." the bifocaled twentysomething said, doing mystery hands. He seemed harmless enough but also emblematic of my discomfort with the neighborhood. In the past twenty years, Williamsburg has transitioned from one of the worst neighborhoods in Brooklyn to, well, one of the worst neighborhoods in Brooklyn. Violent criminals were somehow being displaced by ninety-pound hipsters who brought with them a showy form of creative culture.[4] Bifocals were no exception.

How to describe a hipster: These are adults who don't look attractive and aren't interesting, so instead they've settled on looking interesting. Williamsburg is now overrun with men in ironically waxed mustaches and women wearing misplaced belts over vintage dresses.

---

[4]Seriously, criminal element, how did you let that happen? Step up your game.

And it's not that the neighborhood is a ridiculous place—I kind of like the weirdness of it—but that it's an insincere weird. I mean, I went to art school, so I've met a lot of genuinely offbeat people. I've also met a lot of people who think of themselves as offbeat, and they all moved to Williamsburg.

In some ways, living in Williamsburg is a purchased credential or a check mark in a column. There's a paint-by-numbers quality to many of its residents: their passion doesn't lie in the art so much as in being seen as an artistic person. It's creativity worn on your flannel sleeve.

"So what did you think of the show?" I asked Bifocals.

"It was pretty good, I guess. I mean, the whole shoe-gazing surf-rock thing is pretty tight if you are looking to play it safe. I like things a little more challenging."

Guh. What is with this competitive drive of hipsters to be bored by something first? What's the endgame? To take pride in experiencing the least joy?

"You know," he continued, "lo-fi noise pop, like Sega Book of Genesis." He took a long drag on his American Spirit. "Their early stuff."

The way he spoke—aggressively dropping in musical genres and subgenres—started to grate on me. He was like the kid who tries to impress the teacher with the longest words in the thesaurus. Except this wasn't homework. It was music. It was supposed to be fun. This guy embodied what bothers me about the whole scene. It isn't about creating. It's about collecting. The hipsters seem content to be remembered for remembering.

"I'll have to look them up," Christine interjected.

"Please," I said—deciding then to out-obscure him. "They are just doing what the Ninja Bin Ladens have been doing for years. They are practically a cover band."

"Yeah..." he defensively responded. "That's sort of true, but they infused a rockabilly rhythm that set them apart."

"What are you talking about? That's exactly how they were most influenced!"

"I'll relisten—but Sega Book of Genesis took it someplace unique. Anyway, I have to run to a basement show. I'm seeing The Recently Trained Lovers. They're like a cross between the Ninja Bin Ladens and Dr. Sparky and the Drunk-by-Noons. You should check them out."

"Definitely will," Christine replied.

And with that, Bifocals wandered off into the Williamsburg night, joining the ranks of the skinny-jean catwalk of Bedford Avenue.

"Bifocals..." I said. "That's a new one. How long until the 'ironic toupee' becomes a thing?"

"Ha!" Christine burst out, before she took the final drag from her cigarette.

I looked over, smiling slyly. "Want to know a secret?"

"What?"

"Ninja Bin Ladens is just some band name I made up."

"So you just lied to that guy?"

"Yeah, totally."

She stared at me, clearly not sharing my sense of pride and amusement at my successful ruse.

"I mean, it's not really lying," I added quickly. "I just don't take these one-off conversations too seriously. It's more fun when you mix it up a bit. He's an extra, you know?"

"An extra?"

"Yeah, the extra theory. That's a guy I'll never see again—he has a small walk-on role in my life. Everyone you walk by on the street, all non-speaking roles, just filling out the background."

"That's kind of terrible."

"Nah, it's not! Because to them, I'm an extra, too. We're all stars and we're all extras. It's just liberating to think that way..." I didn't finish the thought because Christine was looking at me completely unconvinced.

"I can't believe you are still doing that thing on Facebook," she said.

"I thought you dug it," I replied, feeling almost betrayed by one of my earliest supporters.

"Yeah, but that was, like, months ago. It's been going on too long. It feels like lying now."

"I'm doing it for six months. Doing it for a little while isn't really interesting."

"Six months? All the way until April?"

"Yeah, I'm wrapping this up on April Fools' Day."

"Clever," she said flatly.

"Well," I said a little deflated, "a little, yeah."

"It's gone on long enough."

"I don't get this at all. You were the one that convinced me to draw this out! If it weren't for you, this would just be a big goof. You even got your mother involved!"

"I know," she said defensively, "but I've changed my mind. It's lying to a lot of people, all the time! Don't you ever feel guilty?"

"Sometimes, sure," I said.

"Because you know it's wrong. David, you need to go to confession."

She'd just dropped my full name and told me to go to confession? She might as well have said that she thought she'd raised me better than this. I started to blush in shame.

I squatted down on the sidewalk, not quite sitting, with my back against the wall. "Listen…I do feel guilty about it. Really guilty when I stop and think about it, especially when people seem moved by the story.

"I really do try," I continued, "to make Fake Dave not heroic. I always have him doing stupid and selfish things—the way he treats his girl, the way he yells at his audience, the way he flakes out on things. It's all to make the joke on me, you know? But the real joke is that people respect him way more than they've ever respected me."

Christine's look softened as I yielded. "Of course they do, Dave," she interjected. "It doesn't matter what you make him do or how dumb he acts. You know how many people fantasize about people leaving their jobs?"

"Yeah…" I said. "I do. More than most. In Red Bank, I've been told, my name has become synonymous with peacing out—you know, 'I'm ready to pull a Cicirelli.'

"It doesn't matter," I continued, "that I had him get jumped the night before or vandalize a religious community. They give me a pass because they are still so impressed with the balls it took to disrupt my life."

"But you didn't."

"That's not true at all!" I snapped back. "Why do you think I go to *every* work party now? It's the only social life I can have. My life's been pretty goddamn disrupted."

"Don't take this out on me!" Christine responded loudly. She stopped as we both realized we were making a mild scene. "It obviously bothers you," she continued in a calmer, almost compassionate voice, "because you know it's wrong. Just stop all the lying, and go to confes…"

"*Dave!*" we heard from across the street. A blond girl was running toward us, looking stunned and dumbfounded. "Is that you?"

Wait…I know her! It's Lauren…we were on the high school newspaper together. She was a grade under me…Oh no. *No!*

"Are you back? Are you back from your journey?"

Stunned, I was overwhelmed by an unstoppable urge to run away. As I bolted, I turned my head and saw Christine doubled over from laughter.

At first, I should have been terrified as I ran away through a blur of the theme bars and theme people. I would have expected myself to be distraught after nearly being caught like that—with Lauren thinking she saw me. I wasn't sure what would happen next: if she was going to expose me, or if her uncertainty would keep her quiet. But suddenly, I felt an overpowering sense of exhilaration as one word dominated my thoughts.

"Journey."

Being spotted by Lauren wasn't a failure; it was an accomplishment. I'd gotten a twenty-five-year-old woman to say the word "journey"—outside of a karaoke bar. What a strange and wonderful thing my lies had made real.

I ran ten blocks south before I finally stopped, resting on the guardrail of the bike lane entering the Williamsburg Bridge. I crouched down to catch my breath and felt the sweat on my brow start to cool in the cold winter air.

Emotionally wired from the encounter, I decided to decompress with a walk over the bridge to my Manhattan apartment just on the other side. After ten minutes of walking through the repeating geometry of the red-truss structure causeways and a half-mile of graffiti, I walked out onto the observatory platform.

It was a cold December night, and even colder up there. Unobstructed views of the city, I'd quickly learned, come at the cost of unobstructed East River wind. I chose to endure it and leaned out on an overlook, splitting my gaze between the Brooklyn and Manhattan late-night skylines, catching the Empire State Building just as it turned off its outside spotlights lit for Chanukah.

The cold kept most pedestrians off the bridge, and it was unusually quiet—save the ambient noise of the traffic below and the occasional rumble of the passing J train. At a busier hour, I probably wouldn't have noticed my phone vibrating with an incoming text.

I assumed it was from Christine, asking me where I'd gone off to. It wasn't. Instead it was a number I didn't recognize but an area code I'm very familiar with: 732—central Jersey.

"You never said thank you for the flowers."

My eyes widened. I was completely struck by the surreal quality of the moment. I took off my glove and began to type. "Who is this?"

"Katie Fisher."

"Impossible. She's from Pennsylvania Dutch country. This is a New Jersey area code."

"Your ass is from Dutch country."

Huh…maybe my stalker was a professional wrestler.

"Well, my ass does reflect the levels of craftsmanship the Amish strive for. I'll ask again. Who is this? I will find out."

"John Fisher."

I stood there, completely aware of…being there. It's hard to describe the feeling exactly, this mixture of amusement and exposure—of being completely at someone's mercy. It felt like I was being watched, and I was in a heightened state. This person had total leverage over me. I had nothing…I was impressed. I was terrified. If this was a girl, I might be in love.

"I smell a conspiracy," I texted back and stared at my phone, waiting for the reply.

It came only seconds later. "You should know all about them. After all, your ingenuity is the reason I follow your game of misadventures in the realm of online social-networking pretend."

"That's quite an articulate accusation."

"Flattery will get you everywhere, young man. That famous Cicirelli charm, no?"

Before my cold fingers could finish typing a retort, another popped up from the mystery texter. "My friend, have no concerns about exposing my 'suspicions.' I am only interested in games. You do like games, don't you? I had the most fun discovering yours."

As the bitter cold wind kicked up, I now pictured my foil as a beautiful woman in a black dress, sipping a glass of wine in front of a warm fire as she toasted my demise.

"Are you Carmen Sandiego?"

"Ha! Catch me if you can...but you may not need to search the world to find me. I may be closer than you think."

A moment later I received one last text—a photo of a box. At my doorstep.

For the second time that night, I began to run. This time I wasn't fleeing, but in pursuit. I rushed down the bridge as fast I could on the pathway that slowly descends from overlooking the rooftops of the East Side projects to the street level and my apartment's front door.

I bolted off the bridge and across Delancey Street. I elbowed my way through the popped-collared crowd trying to get into the club next door and sped past the undercover cop car always parked at the mouth of the bridge.

Sure enough, there was a box, but no Carmen Sandiego. I grabbed it, burst through the door to my apartment, and tore it open like an animal, grabbing a corner of the tape with my teeth. I dumped the contents onto my coffee table, and from a puff of packing peanuts emerged a single book. What else could it be—a copy of *A Million Little Pieces*.

Sigh. If I'd wanted irony, I would have stayed in Williamsburg.

7 | relationship status

I ended the year as a ghost in my own life. The diversion I'd thought up in the fall had completely taken over by late December, and it was going to be a long, cruel winter. The exhilarating highlights of being spotted in Brooklyn and the cat-and-mouse game of my secret foil began to feel like they'd happened a long time ago.

I was back in the routine of Fakebook, and the real-time demand for content and the surprisingly heartfelt nature of my following had worn me down quickly.

I was ready to relax, ready to see people, ready to have fun—after all, it was almost New Year's Eve—but that wasn't meant to be. New Year's Eve parties draw out the extended circles of friends that I desperately needed to avoid. Having no life was the ironic cost of having two lives. Being a hermit was the cost of being popular.

So it seemed an opportune moment to visit my brother, Jeff, and his wife, Elisha, in Evanston, Illinois, far from the people back home who, ironically, thought I was even farther away. Fake Dave's December had found him putting his illustration skills to good use as an assistant at Tatooine—a very real tattoo parlor in Glendale, Arizona, whose owner agreed to participate in Fakebook[5]—with his runaway Amish girlfriend at his side.

---

[5]I reached out to the owner of Tatooine, Chris Bailey, on Facebook. He immediately got the point of Fakebook and accepted my friend request. He granted me permission to use his shop as a set piece and to use his photos as a base for Fake Dave and Amish Kate's life in Arizona.

Dave Cicirelli

Good morning…I just saw a rattlesnake. That shit's better than coffee.

Like · Comment · Share

Matt Riggio holy fuck

3 minutes ago via mobile · Like

Kim Paquet I love your posts, they decorate my news feed.

2 minutes ago via mobile · Like

Dave Cicirelli Thanks Kim. That means a lot to me.

less than a minute ago via mobile · Like

Dave Cicirelli

I've been working for 24 minutes, and I've already gotten the nickname "Shore House." MTV has much to answer for…

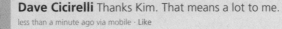

Like · Comment · Share

Elisha's brother and sister, along with their respective spouses and a six-month-old nephew, joined us for New Year's Eve. The night held the promise of watching TV with three married couples and a baby...and man, did it deliver.

It was a far cry from the previous year's festivities. Last December 31, I'd somehow found my way into the Times Square Alliance's private party, an elite event thrown by the organizers of the ball drop, complete with a cordoned-off, private section of the street for viewing the countdown. In other words, at 11:59, I was able to excuse myself from the crazy-fun open-bar dance party crawling with socialites and walk onto a pampered stretch of 42nd Street to be a part of the million-person crowd cheering and screaming their way to midnight.

Three hundred sixty-five days later, instead of watching the ball drop in Times Square with the mayor, I watched it from a couch in Illinois, the only single guy in the room not in a diaper. I literally spent the last moments of the year watching a live broadcast of the party I'd spent the first moments of the year attending.

But for Jeff and Elisha, New Year's Eve wasn't about meeting new people or kissing strangers. It was about spending time with friends and family.

In reality, I only knew two of the seven people in the room. Distance had created something of a veil around my sister-in-law's family, and my brother's adult persona had been hidden behind it. So while I was reasonably engaged in the conversation, part of me was a fly on the wall, observing my brother for the first time in an entirely new context.

They were all so comfortable with one another, using nicknames and sharing inside jokes. There was excitement, yes, but it centered around the baby. It was like going back to a time when my parents, aunts, and uncles were forming the relationships I'd grown up taking for granted. In some visceral way, I started to see a stable family life not as a jumping-off point, but as a destination. That particular New Year's Eve proved to be strangely satisfying, in a way that the outrageous ones can't.

Jeff and Elisha were new homeowners, and my visit was peppered with errands and car trouble, all sorts of "life" stuff. Jeff's problems were practical, not existential. He'd invested his time in real relationships, in the real world, and as a result, he was growing roots in a new place with new people. He had his act together in a way that was far from flashy but increasingly appealing to me. Jeff gave me a window into a completely different stage of life.

I, on the other hand, was twenty-six and only beginning to feel real adulthood creep up on me. I'd drifted through my first twenty-five years on potential but was learning that being capable isn't the same as being accomplished. In fact, I couldn't really think of anything I had to show for myself other than a few good stories. I'd spent my time, but I wasn't sure that I'd ever invested it.

My brother had a wife, a house, a growing family…I had an imaginary girlfriend. Turns out the only place I'd invested my time was in my fake life. And sadly, it showed.

I didn't know exactly how it had happened, but somewhere along the line, my alter ego had started faring better than the real me. Fake Dave had a steady girl and was making friends at the tattoo shop. He was enjoying eighty-degree weather and the admiration of everyone I'd ever befriended on Facebook. In contrast, I was single and obsessively isolating myself, bundling up for a freezing winter, and undermining the integrity of my relationships.

I was jealous of Fake Dave's stability. So I decided to take it from him.

Recent Activity

Dave went from being "It's Complicated" to "Single."

Dave Cicirelli
Watching the Sugar Bowl. Katie cheated on me last night. Happy New Year's.
Like · Comment

Kevin Conway Typical...
6 hours ago via mobile · Like

Todd Stern Poor guy...I like how this shit happens to the most honest, trustworthy, stand up dudes.
6 hours ago via mobile · Like

Ted Kaiser Never trust the Amish.
5 hours ago via mobile · Like

Stanley Shih Are you kidding? Like she pecked some guy on the cheek? Or real Tiger Woods-level cheating?
5 hours ago via mobile · Like

Erin Brennan Hanson It's the freedom you've been waiting for baby, take it.
4 hours ago via mobile · Like

Brendan McDermott Oh no Dave. Sorry dude.
4 hours ago via mobile · Like

Dave Cicirelli Nothing to be sorry about. She proved to be a floozy. It's not the cleanest break in the world...I don't quite have the heart to kick her out of my tent.
4 hours ago via mobile · Like

Brian Morrisson A wise man once said, "If her name begins with K, just stay away." Trust me.
2 hours ago via mobile · Like

Kristen Scalia Obviously Brian doesn't take his own advice. Either way I'm really sorry, Dave. If you need me to kick her ass, just let us know and I'll fly over there. Happy new year?
2 hours ago via mobile · Like

Dave Cicirelli Thanks Kristen, but perhaps Brian is the authority. He has the wisdom of experience, no? Besides, his advice rhymes.
2 hours ago via mobile · Like

Matt Campbell Weak dude. Is it a cultural thing? Are Amish secret swingers? It would explain everyone looking the same…easier to adjust to random partners.
about an hour ago via mobile · Like

Steve Cuchinello Despite the fact that I think your trip has gone too far, I just want to say what Kate did is terrible.
about an hour ago via mobile · Like

Anthony Del Monte yo what is up with u? are u still livin in the city?
43 minutes ago via mobile · Like

Joe Lennon Dude, we literally had a conversation about Dave and his travels in front of you over Thanksgiving.
28 minutes ago via mobile · Like

Anthony Del Monte bro i dont even remember seein either of you that night i was recked. come on, me sober?
less than a minute ago via mobile · Like

Dave Cicirelli Tone…I miss you most of all.
just now via mobile · Like

I knew that word of Katie's infidelity would elicit a strong reaction, but it surprised me how many of the voices were new to the stage. The implosion of Fake Dave's fake romance had finally drawn out some of the voyeurs. Responses also varied. Some were compassionate, some judgmental, some angry. And some were unintentionally hilarious. Still, it seemed everyone had something to say.

So I capitalized on this new enthusiasm. The breakup played out as an on-again, off-again phase, full of mixed feelings and the open question—what exactly did Fake Dave owe Kate? I played up the ambiguity of the situation and the indecisiveness of its main players to keep the comment section robust and, for me, emotionally compelling.

Interestingly, as the relationship deteriorated, factions appeared, falling along gender lines.

There was Team Elizabeth, the girls who voiced their sympathies for Kate and clung to the love story as some sort of fairy tale, a relationship destined to work out. And there was Team Moscone:

Dave Cicirelli
Moscone's right. Screw this. I have to show up to work today to make back the money she made me spend on her and the money that got stolen because of her. I'm being a chump!
Like · Comment

Joe Moscone She's a damn symbiote.
3 hours ago via mobile · Like

Gina Lopez If you were strong enough to quit your job and just take off in the first place you should have no trouble moving on without her. Take it as a lesson learned.
3 hours ago via mobile · Like

Dave Cicirelli Starting over again sounds…difficult. I'm pretty sure Kate was the only stability I had left, but you're right. It needs to be done. Thanks, Gina.
2 hours ago via mobile · Like

Elizabeth Lee Before I say what I want to say…you totally do not deserve to be treated like this, and you're a great guy who deserves a great girl. But just stop for a second and put yourself in her shoes. She's never experienced ANYTHING. She might need to go a lil crazy before she can be the girl you want to settle down with. Think of her as a college freshman who went to an all-girls high school. She's gonna make some mistakes.
2 hours ago via mobile · Like

Dave Cicirelli Wow, Elizabeth. I know you want what's best for me, but I think you want a happy ending for the "love story" a little bit more. If I get back together with Kate, I'll humiliate myself.
2 hours ago via mobile · Like

Elizabeth Lee Well…loving someone is putting yourself out there…you're vulnerable. But, at the end of the day, if you love Kate, then screw everyone else. They aren't out there (wherever you are at the moment) living life by your side. They're just here…on Facebook, making comments. As cheesy as it sounds, follow your heart.
about an hour ago via mobile · Like

Dave Cicirelli Is loving her enough?
about an hour ago via mobile · Like

Alula Medhen Well Dave, there's a couple ways to look at this. There are those who don't believe in life after love, but I say love's a battlefield, you gotta know when to hold em, when to fold em, and when to walk away.
45 minutes ago via mobile · Like

Graciela Meza Alula, wouldn't that mean love is like a poker game?
44 minutes ago via mobile · Like

Alula Medhen Hey Graciela, long time…what I meant by invoking the wisdom of Kenny Rogers was it's time for Dave to cut his losses before he bets the farm (figuratively speaking)…I think a better game to compare love to would be roulette, one minute you've got it all and the next you're routing through dumpsters looking for a hot meal…
38 minutes ago via mobile · Like

Dave Cicirelli In my case, I dug through the dumpster looking for my next hot meal while my relationship was at its strongest. The open question is, which Morrissey song best sums up my experiences?
9 minutes via mobile · Like

Alula Medhen I'll concede that one. I know better than to argue with you about anything even vaguely Morrissey. If the question is simply which song by any artist best sums up your experiences, I'd say even parts Offspring's "Self-Esteem" and the Buzzcocks' "Ever Fallen

in Love", baked in a nice "Where Is My Mind" by the Pixies, topped with Cake's "I Will Survive" and just a dash of Nancy Sinatra's "These Boots Were Made For Walkin." For pep.
less than a minute ago via mobile · Like

Stephen Ortez holy shit the above statement is awesome!
less than a minute ago via mobile · Like

Seeing all these comments, I couldn't help but feel weirdly embarrassed for Fake Dave and his (sort of) girlfriend. They were being judged—even told what to do—by people whose understanding of the situation amounted to little more than having seen a change in "Relationship Status."

Fake Dave was mixed up, confused, and possibly in love. His life was in flux and he was looking for something to hold on to. That had been Kate, but then she'd proven to be fool's gold... It was a lot to deal with. Sure, their relationship had started in a weird place, with Kate running away from Amish country and inviting herself on Fake Dave's journey after he vandalized her family's horse and buggy...but what unfolded was a shared experience. The bum fights and freight-hopping must have brought them together in a way only they could understand. Or maybe it hadn't. Maybe Kate's cheating was her reaction to an emotionally distant boyfriend who'd never moved his relationship status past "It's Complicated."

Either way, somehow, Tone Del Vecchio's "Nice!" seemed like an inadequate response.

As I looked over the spectacle and put myself in Fake Dave's shoes to gauge the best way to respond, I began to remember what it was like to have my heart broken, trying to make sense of conflicting feelings and wavering convictions. Above all, I remembered the need to talk to anyone who would listen. Without Kate as his confidante and with the bridge to his family burned down,

Facebook was the only outlet Fake Dave had. It was his only sense of community.

So he posted…a lot. He posted his feelings as they came, no matter how fleeting. But moments don't pass on Facebook, they just move down your news feed. When his audience saw the inevitable contradictions compressed into just a few inches of digital space, some saw a hypocrite.

I'd spent the past three months telling stories about Fake Dave's selfish behavior, desperately trying to court people's judgment of him. By accident, I'd finally succeeded—and it was the one time he didn't deserve it. I couldn't imagine the isolation he felt. All I could picture was him curling up in his tent and playing The Smiths' "I Know It's Over" on loop for hours on end. That's what I would have done, if I'd had his life and my playlist.

Interestingly, the din of opinion did benefit one relationship—Fake Dave and I had made it through our rough patch, and we were getting along better than ever. I became sympathetic to his misfortunes and found him more relatable with every passing moment. In the spirit of my own initially dismissive attitude toward quiet suburban life, he'd been quick to abandon the tangible for the abstract "something else."

For the first time he was seeing the value of what he'd given up, just as I was seeing the value of what I'd rejected. Now we were both paying out the hidden cost of our longing.

In a note entitled "Roots vs. Wings," he wrote:

JANUARY 5: ROOTS VS. WINGS

In my heart of hearts I wanted to be home for Christmas.

But have you ever walked through your old high school? It feels familiar and foreign at the same time. You may be back in your old desk, but you aren't back in class. You were once a part of the environment, but now you can only visit.

I can go back to New York, or even New Jersey, but home is both a time and a place. While the place may remain, the time has long since passed. So it wouldn't be home, and I wouldn't be the same person.

I've learned that you can have roots or you can have wings, but you can't have both.

Maybe one day I'll land somewhere and new roots will grow into a new home, but for now I'm adrift.

The theme of roots vs. wings began to move Fake Dave's story forward again. In the early days, he'd walked with an aimless ambition, the desire to court adventure; now he sought substance. He felt changed but also lost. And I figured the added turbulence of his love life and the stress of his burgeoning self-doubt would be more than enough justification for his increasingly erratic behavior and poor judgment.

Dave Cicirelli
I think I'm going to get a tattoo today.
Like · Comment

Danny Ross bad. ass.
yesterday via mobile · Like

Anthony Del Monte I don't know you anymore.
yesterday via mobile · Like

Joe Moscone A dream catcher on the small of your back?
yesterday via mobile · Like

Ted Kaiser Tramp stamp?
yesterday via mobile · Like

Jennifer Huang If a guy gets one, is it still called a tramp stamp?

22 hours ago via mobile · Like

Danny Ross It's called a trampo stampo in spanish, for boys. For girls: trampa stampa.

22 hours ago via mobile · Like

Dave Cicirelli I never thought about a tramp stamp. What a great way to let people know I'm down to party!

19 hours ago via mobile · Like

Matt Campbell Think it through dude, Make sure the design is what you want, now and in the future. Don't just pick the Indian song cuz you're in Arizona.

17 hours ago via mobile · Like

Justin Blaser How about a freight car, like the one that took you to AZ...

14 hours ago via mobile · Like

Dave Cicirelli Freight car's kinda cool. It has meaning without pretension. I kinda like that.

12 hours ago via mobile · Like

Matt Campbell Mr. Peanut. That's classy and fancy.

11 hours ago via mobile · Like

Trish Acciavatti TRAMP STAMP

11 hours ago via mobile · Like

Dave Cicirelli The problem with the Tramp Stamp is I'd have to start buying midriff-baring shirts. I think that may make me too sexy to handle. I want girls to think I'm approachable.

11 hours ago via mobile · Like

Trish Acciavatti Or, you just find instances where you'll have to bend over a lot.

You could also get some sort of tribal tattoo band around your arm. Those are always cool. ahahahahahahahah

Or you could embrace the Jersey Shore attitude and get an Italian Flag on your back...

All good options.

10 hours ago via mobile · Like

Dave Cicirelli What I have in mind is almost as goofy. I'm having second thoughts, but it makes me smile. My Dad's going to completely disown me.

10 hours ago via mobile · Like

Dave Cicirelli WAIT! SPONSORSHIP OPPORTUNITIES?!

3 hours ago via mobile · Like

Michèle Malejki In tribute to old Simpsons, be like Bart and attempt to get that "Mother" tattoo...then get interrupted halfway, so you only have "Moth". What a throwback...

less than a minute ago via mobile · Like

Dave Cicirelli That's what I like about you, Malejki, you're a season 1 kind of gal.

less than a minute ago via mobile · Like

Jonathan Tatkon-Coker get a unicorn with a dolphin jumping over its right side and a rainbow going over its left side, all as a tramp stamp.

less than a minute ago via mobile · Like

Joe Moscone You're going to be the hit of the cell block.

less than a minute ago via mobile · Like

Dave Cicirelli

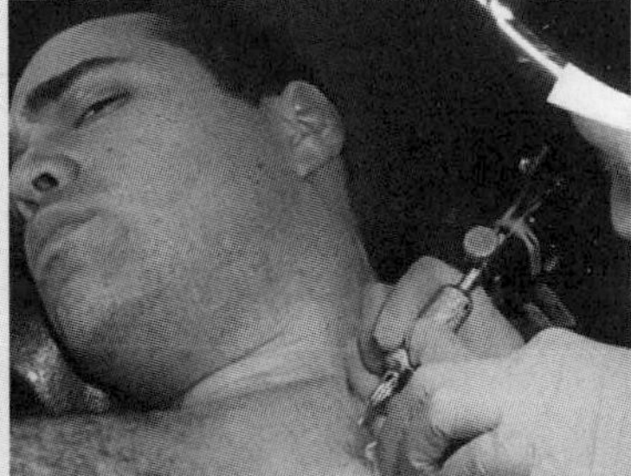

Like · Comment · Share

Joe Moscone Please tell me you got the Super Grover logo on your chest!
less than a minute ago via mobile · Like

Rolando Alvarado Yeah…That's about right.
less than a minute ago via mobile · Like

Katia Tron LOL
less than a minute ago via mobile · Like

Elizabeth Lee I'm with Katia on this! That pic is hilarious!
less than a minute ago via mobile · Like

Dave Cicirelli I'm glad I went with a funny tattoo, since all the girls are laughing at me anyway…
less than a minute ago via mobile · Like

Chris Mitarotondo so i'm pretty sure that this is a tattoo of michael jackson's glove
less than a minute ago via mobile · Like

Dave Cicirelli

Like · Comment · Share

Ara Arnn You are truly a gentleman of wealth and taste!
4 hours ago · Like

Jeff Shaw Dude, that is effing ridiculous. Is this your formal birthday suit? *rim shot* Thank you! Don't forget to tip your waitress!

P.S. You DO know tattoos are permanent, right?
4 hours ago via mobile · Like

Yolanda Paskovich Whoa!!! Dave, is that real?!
4 hours ago via mobile · Like

Dave Cicirelli An ascot didn't work as a tattoo. That was my first choice.
4 hours ago via mobile · Like

Michèle Malejki Phenomenal.
4 hours ago via mobile · Like

Dave Cicirelli The thing is, and I really gave it some thought, it's going to be adorable when I'm an old man.
4 hours ago via mobile · Like

Jenna Taylor Please tell me you're getting a pocket watch and chain tattooed down your leg.
3 hours ago via mobile · Like

Ted Kaiser i hope that's henna.
3 hours ago via mobile · Like

Dave Cicirelli Ted, let me explain what "peacocking" is. By creating visual interest, I'll easily attract a new mate.

Haven't you heard of the professional lover "Mystery?" He's a weirdo who used goggles and other Carrot Top props to score with women who have confidence issues.

But seriously, it's bitchin'.
3 hours ago via mobile · Like

Brendan McDermott I remember "Mystery." He apparently got mad chicks cuz he was "alpha" and had props. Girls like props.
3 hours ago via mobile · Like

Chris Mitarotondo no michael jackson glove, no love
2 hours ago via mobile · Like

Joe Moscone Thank you, Dave. For the rest of my life, I'll be telling the story of my friend who lost his

mind and up and quit his job to walk aimlessly across the country, leaving his family and friends behind only to allow himself to fall in love with an Amish parasite AND…get a ridiculous bow tie tattoo.
2 hours ago via mobile · Like

Steve Cuchinello I'll second Joe on that…my god.
2 hours ago via mobile · Like

Daniel Timek I imagine you sitting your kids down one day, and then a couple weeks later you finish up the story of how you got this tattoo.
about an hour ago via mobile · Like

Elizabeth Lee Well, I'll give you one thing…it'll be cute when you're an old man.
about an hour ago via mobile · Like

Joe Moscone Elizabeth, let's be serious—how many guys with chest/throat tattoos live to be "old men"? As if the cards weren't already stacked against Dave living a long life, this all but seals his fate…I fear in another couple of months, Dave's FB updates will be nothing more than "Hey, can someone Western Union me some cash. My veins are itchy and I REALLY need a fix."
about an hour ago via mobile · Like

Anthony Del Monte dave im sorry but after seeing that i think im going to delete u on FB…
less than a minute ago · Like

Dave Cicirelli Come on, Tone. Not every tattoo needs an Italian Flag on it.
just now via mobile · Like

The funny side story of awful-amazing neck art aside, the way Fake Dave's new perspective resonated with my audience didn't surprise me, but the way it resonated with me did. For the first time, Fakebook also became an outlet for my own anxiety, as the idea of roots vs. wings lingered in my mind.

My sense was that I had neither. Living in New York felt like trying to grow roots in a raging river, where people passed through but never stayed put. Needless to say, I had a lot to think about during my twice-delayed flight back to New York after New Year's Eve. I stared out the window at the blinking red light on the wing of the plane and thought back on my own romantic history.

The truth is, I'm no good at relationships. I think the reason is that I don't handle ambiguity very well. That uncertain stage before all the cards are on the table is crippling for the overly analytical like me. The vast majority of my relationships were either long, drawn-out false starts or short-lived, low-stakes flings. I mean, I broke up my fictional relationship out of jealousy—I could stand to be a little more self-assured.

And while I'm perfectly familiar with the hazards of nostalgia, that night I gave in and thought about the girls who got away and the girls I'd chased away. It's always been easy for me to canonize them, and maybe, for a moment, that's what I did. The truth is, I don't really know what I meant to them, and I don't have the courage to ask.

But it's not just our memories of the past that we need to manage—these days we have to cope with the present. Our profiles have us living in plain sight of one another; we don't even need to indulge in Facebook stalking to see how our old flames have moved on. For example, I never asked to see photos of my ex-girlfriend, Laurie, hanging out with a bunch of hot surfer dudes in Australia—as it was happening. But one day, there they were on top of my news feed, stirring up old feelings.

Witnessing the next phase of Laurie's love life unfolding at that very moment—from literally the opposite end of the Earth—created a surreal hyper-present. I'd moved on long ago, and she was completely within her rights to hang out with hot surfer dudes. But I didn't need to see it happening. Nor would she have been so cruel as to post them with the point of me finding out. I knew I was the furthest thing from her mind that night, just as she was the furthest from mine before the photos were passively presented on my news feed. But these snippets of unsolicited information still felt oddly pressing because I knew it was happening right now.

There comes a point when the past should be the past, when you need to get out of each other's orbit and escape that unintentional influence, those obstacles to new opportunities. But social media makes that almost impossible. How can we expect someone to be out of mind if they are never out of sight?

I didn't know what kind of impact this could have. I just wanted to not think about it anymore.

When I finally touched down, I walked outside the terminal through the bitter cold toward the JFK Air Train, which would connect me to the subway system for a long but inexpensive trip home.

Steps from the platform, I noticed a woman struggling to get her luggage cart over the curb.

"Do you need a hand?"

She turned around, and her blue-green eyes offset by her light-brown complexion caught me completely off guard. Standing nearly six feet tall, she was utterly stunning. "That's very sweet of you," she said. "Were you on the flight from Chicago? The delayed one?"

"Sure was. I've been on worse, though."

"Me, too. My name's Dhara."

"I'm Dave."

We began to chat, exchanging stories of delayed flight trauma. She seemed completely at ease, even though I'm sure I was tripping over my words. About halfway through one story, a train pulled up.

"Is this the right one?" she asked. "Actually, I'm sure it's the right train—I'm a natural at public transportation. When I was only seven years old, a set of train doors separated me and my little sister from our parents. I got us off at the next stop, switched to the other side of the tracks, and made it back to my folks, all before my sister had the chance to stop crying."

"That's pretty impressive."

"Oh, I know. My mom tells the story every Thanksgiving."

The train PA system announced the next stop. We were on the wrong train. "I promise not to cry for very long," I joked, looking slyly at her out of the corner of my eye.

"Well, this is all your fault," she replied, playfully hitting me on the shoulder.

"I think your mom's going to be really disappointed."

"You can't tell her anything! She'll be crushed to hear that my train skills are…deproving? Is that even a word?"

We ran across the platform and she leaned into her luggage the way a kid would before racing a shopping cart. You could see a manic brain behind her eyes, always darting from one thing to the next.

As we dashed onto the train through the closing doors, I turned and said to her, "We're halfway there."

She paused for a moment before cocking her head to a silent beat. "Whoa-oh," she sang under her breath, "we're living on a prayer!"

Had she just cited Bon Jovi? Could this be…a Jersey girl? I'd spent most of my life trying to dissuade people of New Jersey stereotypes, but it's true that it's absolutely impossible for someone from Jersey to hear the phrase "we're halfway there" without finishing the lyric.

"I have to ask…Are you from New Jersey?"

She laughed. "Well, sort of. I lived there for a couple years as a kid, and I went to college in New Jersey. But I was born in India, and I went to high school in North Carolina. I'm from all over, but

I'm enough of a Jersey girl to sing Bon Jovi. I'm guessing you're from Jersey, too?"

"Yep. I grew up on the Jersey Shore."

Her eyes went wide. "Really?"

"Yes, I'm an Italian American from the Jersey Shore. You're making me nostalgic for the days when that was only mildly embarrassing and *The Sopranos* was the defining show assassinating our character." I was starting to relax. "So you went to school in New Jersey...?"

She turned away and sheepishly replied, "Princeton." It was the first time she'd spoken without looking right at me. Ivy Leaguers can be strangely insecure about their accomplishments.

"I love Princeton. You can't walk ten feet in that town without tripping over a statue."

She seemed put at ease by my light response.

The truth is, I did love Princeton. In fact, as a Rutgers undergrad, I was Princeton obsessed. The two campuses are only sixteen miles down the road from one another, but light years apart in every other conceivable way. Princeton, both the town and university, is perfectly idyllic. It's almost like Main Street USA in Disney World—not a real town, but the true potential, the promise of what a town could be. Full of buffer spaces in between parallel parking spots and stores selling sweaters meant to be tied around shoulders (or as my roommate Paco put it, "sweater necklaces"). It's an oasis of calm compared to the urban sprawl of Rutgers's five campuses.

And contrary to what television has taught us, smart and nerdy-looking need not walk hand in hand. I was routinely floored by how attractive the Princeton women were. I even developed a couple of working theories—about the offspring of old rich men and their hot second wives. I wanted in. I shamelessly abandoned the Rutgers scene to go to Princeton bars with grand visions of being the dude a Princeton girl used to make her ex-boyfriend jealous. But all of these stunning scholars disappeared when the sun went down. It was completely maddening.

But I soon learned that I wasn't the first overreaching state-school type to develop a Princeton infatuation. Those overachievers locked us out by moving the entire social scene behind closed doors, inside members-only "eating clubs." With the Princeton women quarantined away, I'd all but given up on my dream of being used like the piece of publicly educated meat that I aspired to be.

And yet here I was, hitting it off with Dhara on a shuttle train. This was a landmark moment, not just for me, but for state school alums everywhere. If I'd known the Rutgers fight song, I'd have sung it.

"So what were you doing in Chicago?" she asked.

"Visiting my brother and his wife—and their house. It's like he's a grown-up or something."

"What does that make you?"

"Me? I'm clearly a child," I said.

She smiled and went on to tell me all about her family, and the initial wish fulfillment of talking to a Princeton girl quickly gave way to the simple pleasure of talking to, well, a charming and intelligent supermodel. This was someone I wanted to see again.

A few minutes later the Air Train dropped us off at the subway entrance and she said, "Thanks so much, Dave. It was really sweet of you to help me with my suitcase."

Her train was fast approaching, and as a commercial artist, I understand the importance of deadlines. I asked, "Do you have a card? I don't want you to think I had ulterior motives or anything, but…"

"Sure!" She handed me her number and stepped onto her Queens-bound A train before it sped off into the tunnel.

That night I was the happiest guy on the J line. Only in Bond movies had the inexplicable combination of nuclear physicist and lingerie model been revealed to me before that night.

Now, I had a date with a real-life Bond girl. The fifty-minute subway ride had felt like five. A light dusting of snow made the Lower East Side shimmer, and there was magic in the crisp air. I looked behind me and saw that I left no footprints. I was floating toward my building, right next to the base of the Williamsburg Bridge. My mind wandered as I shuffled through a week's worth of mail—until I found a letter from Kate's father.

That is, a letter from an imaginary Amish farmer. A letter from the imaginary father of my imaginary Amish girlfriend.

My nemesis had struck again.

Suddenly, it all came crashing down. The air wasn't crisp; it was just miserably cold out. I was simply confused—instead of the air smelling like wet garbage, it smelled like frozen garbage, which was a slight improvement. I lived under a bridge, like a troll.

I sent a quick text to Elizabeth, hoping she was still awake. "Hey. If you met someone on the subway, what are the chances you'd look him up on Facebook before having a drink with him?"

She wrote back immediately. "100%."

Great. Welcome to 2010. And Dhara was a Princeton girl; she'd definitely do her homework.

My entire profile was a red flag. My most recent post was an account of my bow tie tattoo being applied. The last several months would appear to be one act of poor judgment after another. Instead of seeing the real me, she'd see someone who antagonized the homeless and toilet-papered the pious.

A generation ago, Dhara would have been enticed to see me again for the same reason I wanted to see her—based on what little we knew about each other, we wanted to know more. That paradigm still holds true, but now, with the advent of search engines and Facebook, it's reckless for a young woman to meet a total stranger unless she looks up things about him. It's so easy to do, like flipping to the back of a baseball card for a player's stats.

We've always carried emotional baggage, but it's never been easier to shuffle through it. There's no "past" with Facebook, and there's no "distance." Nothing happened "then," and nothing ever happens "somewhere else." It all pools together, fossilizes, and creates a permanent but evolving here and now.

"Getting to know someone" is still the cornerstone of starting a new relationship, but Facebook has forever changed the process. How many conversations won't take place because we don't have to ask what someone's favorite book is anymore? How suspicious would you be if someone had the same answer as you? Does that coincidence lose its meaning online? I had no doubt that the new romantic landscape could lead to happy endings, but for an overly analytical fool with a fake profile, the landscape was a minefield.

Through Fakebook and because of it, I was simultaneously learning what it was like to start and end a relationship in the Facebook era. The morning of my flight, I'd woken up in the new home of a growing family. That night I climbed into an empty bed, fairly certain that my real relationship status was going to remain "single" for a very long time.

It's almost funny. "As I climb into an empty bed..." is actually a line from "I Know It's Over," the song I'd imagined Fake Dave consoling himself with. I fell asleep that night thinking of the girl on the train, while The Smiths sang, "I know it's over and it never really began. But in my heart it felt so real..."

Maybe I should have changed my status to "Married." After all, I'd sacrificed everything for the committed relationship I was in with my own Facebook profile.

8 share

"This is ballsy," Joe said, standing over my proposal on Handler's main conference table. "Your boss sign off on this?"

"Yeah. You know her," I said with a hint of pride in my voice. "She's gutsy."

We were looking at a proposal for our next promotional mailer—twenty-inch, high-gloss, fully printed shippable packaging. The idea was to get media members excited when our newest superhero toy line arrived on their desk and to ensure they opened the package. This was the fifth one we'd produced, and the mailers had been one of our most successful tactics.

"I'm just thinking back to last year," Joe said. "When the lawyers made us change our tagline a half dozen times."

"Oh right," I said. "We couldn't legally guarantee that our product 'makes you feel like a superhero,' right?"

"Yeah," Joe said, chuckling a bit. "It's ridiculous. But it's also why this makes me nervous. You want to create a completely original drawing of the main character. I don't think they'll let you get away with it."

He was right. This was a huge risk. The brand sent assets—beautiful high-resolution images created by the best illustrators in the business. Usually we'd use these images in our design. It was what we'd always done. But I couldn't do the same thing over and over. I'd gotten the creative itch and wanted to try something new. So I proposed going outside the assets and creating original artwork.

"And even if they approve the proposal," Joe said, "if you can't make the drawing look as good as the official images, we're screwed. And it's not just our client but all the licensing partners, too. This also would have to be approved by the publisher and the film studio." Joe looked up from the comp on the table and at me straight on. "Three groups of brand managers. Three legal departments. If I pitch this," he said sternly, "you have to pull it off."

I wasn't sure I could pull it off. I've always been a good illustrator, but it was a skill I'd sidelined. Now I was committing to do my best work ever, after years of rust. It was foolish of me to even suggest it—putting at risk weeks of work and the company's reputation. Yet, how could I not try?

I mean, I was a comic-book kid growing up. Deep down, I still am. I'd never forgive myself for passing on this opportunity.

"I can do it," I said.

"All right then," Joe said. "Let's pitch it."

I walked back to my desk, a little exhilarated and a little nervous. I knew I was making my life hard. A drawing like that—at the size it needed to be and the standard it had to meet—was going to take a couple hundred hours.

But man...I'd get to earn the next couple paychecks drawing a superhero. For once, it was more exciting than anything going on with my other life. Fake Dave was just sitting around feeling sorry for himself.

And people noticed.

Matt Campbell
I worry when I don't hear any updates for a few days.
Like · Comment

Dave Cicirelli Ha. Sorry pal. Even in my life there are boring days. I think I've earned a few.
1 hour ago via mobile · Like

I'd tried to be a little experimental with his downtime and had even tried to inject Fake Dave into a live event. From my couch in New York, I used Twitter to pull live photos from the night's Devils-Coyotes hockey game in Glendale, Arizona.

It was an interesting little experiment—a trial run for potentially sending Fake Dave to Vancouver for the upcoming Olympics. I liked infusing a live event with fiction—where Fake Dave's presence might make someone to tune in for the crowd instead of the competition. But having Fake Dave watch things was still not very engaging. Fortunately, it was just one night, and it did serve the need for some downtime.

This period of quiet also helped me serve another specific, if still hypothetical audience. I had a vested interest in not appearing insane if Dhara looked me up.

I looked at her card on my desk. It'd been a few days since our encounter. Now or never, I thought, as I gathered the courage to write her an email:

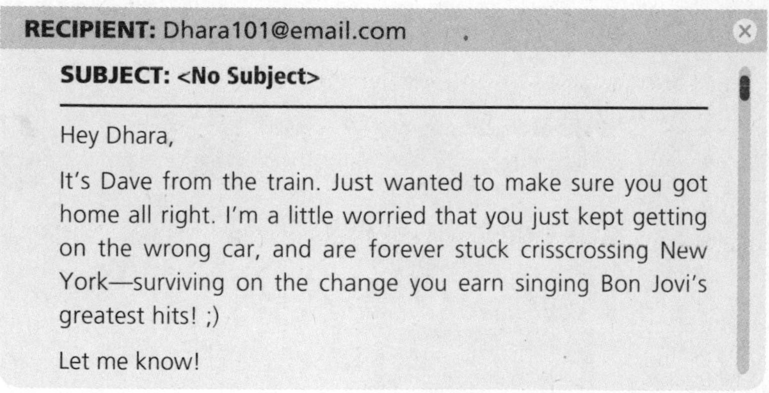
RECIPIENT: Dhara101@email.com

SUBJECT: <No Subject>

Hey Dhara,

It's Dave from the train. Just wanted to make sure you got home all right. I'm a little worried that you just kept getting on the wrong car, and are forever stuck crisscrossing New York—surviving on the change you earn singing Bon Jovi's greatest hits! ;)

Let me know!

I thought it was cute. I even went as far to use a winky-face emoticon, unusual for any self-respecting guy. For better or worse, that was probably my A-game.

I was still hoping against hope she wouldn't dig too deeply into the strange back story of my public profile. Though I did tempt fate by committing the cardinal sin of blue-state New York dating—Republican-themed humor.

Dave Cicirelli
I can't believe there is no good Barry Goldwater museum in Phoenix or Glendale. There's like a center where they have speeches sometimes, but that's it. Is it possible there is no market for the Barry GoldWater Park? Is my dream of an aquatic adventure land based around the founder of modern conservatism doomed to go unfulfilled? If I build it, will they come?
Like · Comment

Erin Brennan Hanson If that's the eventual end to your mission, you would have been better off staying home. And I say that because I know my husband would end up dragging me there for a day of Goldwater-themed "fun."
about an hour ago via mobile · Like

Dave Cicirelli You'd make a great Goldwater Girl, haha.
about an hour ago via mobile · Like

Michael Surabian My Mom was a Goldwater Girl. Apparently apples do fall far from the tree.
12 minutes ago via mobile · Like

Dave Cicirelli Your mother sounds both very wise and in need of a worthwhile legacy. Perhaps she'd be interested in investing in my vision?
less than a minute ago via mobile · Like

I could keep Fakebook in a holding pattern for a week or two—it made sense for the story. But ultimately I had to tell a story worthy of having a second life. Fakebook was my priority, and maybe that meant scaring away the girl from the train.

But to my surprise, all my concerns were for naught. An hour later, she wrote back.

"You find the place all right?" I asked with a smile. "There shouldn't have been any confusing transfers."

We met for drinks that Saturday at Vol de Nuit, a Belgian beer hall in the West Village. It was a cool place with a good beer selection and a unique red-lit enclosed courtyard. It had a casual but intimate vibe that felt right for a first date.

"Haha," Dhara said as she sat down. "I should tell you now, though. I have a friend's party that I have to go to later tonight."

"Yeah, that's fine," I said. "I have a late-night slice of pizza I have to eat in my apartment later." I got the message fairly clearly. This date was an audition.

"So be honest," I said, "you Facebook-stalked me, didn't you?"

"Well," Dhara said, "did you really just get a bow tie tattoo?"

I laughed and began to tell her about Fakebook.

"I'm not sure I understand," she said. "Why would you do this?"

"Well, don't you find the whole Facebook experience kind of strange?" I asked. "I mean, you suddenly gain access to the lives of people you barely remember."

"Well, I don't know," she said almost disinterestedly. "They are just people's profiles. I can't say it upsets me."

I was a little struck by her nonchalance toward social media. In my months of explaining Fakebook, not everyone understood why I would specifically do what I did, but everyone understood the underlying suspicion of social media's implications.

"I wouldn't say it upsets me…" I said.

I took a real look across the table and studied her for a moment. She was younger than me, twenty-two to my twenty-six. And while four years isn't much, the age gap felt significant all of a sudden. I became self-conscious and saw myself as an old man complaining about "how low kids wear their pants these days."

"It's just interesting..." I continued. "Something I think is worth playing around with."

The waitress brought us our beers.

"Tell me," I said. "What is it that you do? Are you a train conductor?"

She laughed a bit and then began to tell me about her job in finance. It sounded impressive and involved traveling to interesting places to do intriguing projects. She was clearly on a rarified track.

I'm not without exposure to this side of the world—I know Ivy League graduates. Hell, I even shared apartments with her European equivalents. But being with Ivy Leaguers still stirs up a weird insecurity in me. There's a perception that what I do is "fun." Design can be viewed as a hobby or something subjective, rather than the communication discipline it is.

When I describe the projects I'm excited by, especially to someone with a job like Dhara's, I sometimes feel like a kid with a pack of crayons, my work more suitable for show-and-tell than career day.

"I'm drawing superhero toys," I said.

"Really?" she said with a look of confusion. "Wait...are you, like, a toy collector?"

"What? No," I said in an attempt to downplay my enthusiasm and distance myself from our core consumer. "I create promotional artwork for the toy industry."

"But it is," I continued, while looking down into my beer, "kind of fun."

"Oh," she said. "That's neat."

There was a bit of a pause. Enough of one, anyway, to overhear a bit of the conversation from the table next to ours.

"So this girl," the guy next to us said to his girlfriend, "gives

Pauly D a shirt that says, 'I'...and like, an Italian flag, 'Jewish Girls!'" He was reciting a pivotal moment of *Jersey Shore*'s first season.

It's easy to forget how all-consuming *Jersey Shore* was when it first came out. No one had ever encountered a Snooki before, and we all were trying to process the four-and-a-half-foot package of spray tan and gusto.

I was uneasy with the world sneering at the negative ethnic and regional stereotype of my own people, but a sideward glance toward Dhara suggested she was into it. I swallowed my pride, and we joined their conversation as put-upon, real-life Eye-talians from Joisy.

In return, our two-minute interaction with the MTV-watching table injected a little sense of fun and absurdity into our night, and loosened us up. And things began to click again—like they had when we were mutually making the most of our delayed flight, when I was too tired to overthink anything and happy to jump into something without a plan or expectation.

And before I knew it, one drink turned into another. Soon we were bar-hopping around lower Manhattan with the same manic energy we'd had while train-hopping around the airport.

Eventually we ended up in the bar of the Bowery Hotel—a new place with an old feel. We sat in front of a large fireplace, on a dark brown leather couch.

"This place reminds me a lot of Princeton," she said.

"Yeah," I said. "It has a real eating-club vibe."

"You know about eating clubs?" she said, somewhat alarmed.

Uh oh. I'd said too much. "Um, just a little," I said. "From some friends of mine. Did you belong to one?"

She did. And she enthusiastically told me about all its formal events, full of pomp and rituals and traditions. We scrolled through photos on her BlackBerry, confirming every suspicion I ever had of college life sixteen miles down Route 9. Everyone in the photos looked like villains in an '80s movie—James Spader types complete with teal sweater necklaces and salmon pants.

I showed her some photos from my senior year at Rutgers. My album had a lot more passed-out friends with penises drawn on their faces. "You and I had very different college experiences," I said.

She laughed, but before I could elaborate, her phone chimed with a new text from her friends. She looked down at it.

"I don't think I can delay any longer," she said. "I wouldn't have double-booked if I was sure you weren't a creep."

"So I passed the audition?" I asked. "I can see you again?"

"Well..." she said with a smile, "depends what you have in mind."

"Oh," I said, faux offended. "There's a right and wrong answer?"

"I'm just trying to get the most information—I'm an analyst, after all."

"I can take you to a fancy Italian restaurant I know, and we'll order the second, no, the third cheapest bottle of wine they've got," I said. "You're worth it."

She laughed. "Interesting."

"Oh, I get it now. This is a negotiation," I said. "I can go as high as fifth cheapest—final offer."

She laughed again and gave me a little push on the shoulder. "How dare you, sir!"

There was a pause, and we stared at each other for just a moment. There was something intoxicating about this girl, especially when she returned my gaze with those piercing blue eyes. She was so beautiful and smart. She had true confidence, the kind that never flirted with arrogance. It simply felt good to be around her.

But there was something else, too. I can't overstate what it meant to me, within the context of my tangled lives, to have an uncomplicated night out with someone new. Because while I had two lives, I only lived one of them. And I lived that life in secret—locked away within a shrinking prison of caution. It wasn't until that night, when the burden was momentarily lifted, that I truly felt the weight of social media surveillance.

Because of Fakebook, I didn't have acquaintances or casual friendships anymore. They were all potential whistleblowers, each with the power to unravel my work. I lived with a constant fear of being spotted—or of having an unthinking coworker act out of habit and casually expose me with an errant post. Stadiums, concerts, holidays, or even the smallest of parties were no longer part of my life. My world had contracted to all but the closest of relationships in guarded environments.

That night, however, I didn't fear news accidentally rippling across the complicated network of everyone I'd ever known. The only mutual acquaintance between Dhara and me was each other—it could not go further than the two of us there, holding each other's gaze.

For the first time in months, my life didn't shrink. It grew, if by just one person for just one night.

"What are you thinking?" she asked.

"I'm a little embarrassed to say."

She looked at me suspiciously.

I gathered up the nerve to risk revealing my inner goof to this stunning, cosmopolitan woman. "I want to take you ice skating."

"Wait, you want to take me ice skating?" she said. "That's adorable."

"Yeah," I said. "I kind of have the dating sensibility of a fourteen-year-old girl."

She smiled. "Me, too."

"Congrats!" I heard as I walked into the graphics bullpen Monday morning. My boss was leaning against the open doorway to her office, with Joe standing just behind her.

"Huh?" I said. "I didn't tell you about my weekend yet."

"What?" she said with a laugh. "No! The client approved your superhero design."

A wave of simultaneous excitement and panic swept over me.

Joe looked at me. "So don't fuck it up."

I'm not a great cook, but I can follow instructions. I had the oven preheated to 350 degrees and my ingredients all laid out. I was halfway to a finished Broccoli Bake.

It was a recipe I'd pulled from the Amish cookbook that arrived in the mail today, part of a care package from my secret foil that included the "Deceitful Dave" mix, now playing through my CD radio/alarm clock speakers.

Based on the nature of these pranks, I began to suspect this person was actually a husband and wife. The whole thing just reeked of a "couples activity." I could almost see them walking through the aisles of Bed Bath & Beyond and stumbling onto the cookbook. "Oh my gosh, honey," the wife would say. "We just have to buy this for Dave!"

I smirked at the thought of how domestic I imagined my personal supervillain team to be—and how domestic I was, as I continued to chop broccoli while listening to adult contemporary.

My weird appreciation for this creative torture had grown. I admired them—and that initial sense of danger had ebbed a bit. It was clear, at this point, that they didn't want to destroy Fakebook. They enjoyed it too much.

Then a few lines from "In the Air Tonight" caught my ear.

I've seen your face before, my friend, but I don't know if you know who I am.

Well, I was there and I saw what you did. I saw it with my own two eyes.

Damn, I thought to myself, that's so on the nose. Whoever this person was, they'd pulled it off. They'd put together a mix tape that actually expressed how they felt.

Then, all at once, the sheer absurdity of this relationship snuck up on me, and I laughed out loud—right on cue for the killer drum break.

"That Phil Collins track," I texted to my secret foil. "Brilliant."

I put my bake in the oven and sat down on my couch, grabbing my laptop.

"Ha! Yeah, I'm proud of that one," he texted back. "It's nice to be noticed."

His reply made me feel even more in sync with this guy. We both loved attention.

The song switched to Elton John's "Rocket Man," and I began to prepare the posts for the next few beats of my Fakebook story.

Dave Cicirelli
Back on the road. Had an emotional week. I'm sitting down to write a note and wash up in the Starbucks bathroom like a homeless guy.

Also, if anyone at Starbucks wants to sponsor me I'd be happy to talk about how their Caramel Macchiatos give me that "get up and go!" I need to walk out on another life!

Like · Comment

Elliott Askew YES! back on the old dusty trail. I am very glad you are on the move again...Maybe you can steal a Native American girl next...That'll teach them to think they can screw us out of taxing their casino profits.

less than a minute ago via mobile · Like

Dave Cicirelli I see, you would like me to fill out my score card with the often neglected, often tax exempt, minority ladies...I'll see what I can do.

just now via mobile · Like

It was time to move things forward. I no longer needed to worry about keeping things calm for Dhara's sake. She was in on the joke, even if she didn't really get it.

Admittedly, the fact that she didn't get it initially tarnished things for me a bit. I recalled how she'd said, "They're just people's profiles. I can't say it upsets me." It upset me that it didn't upset her. Our four-year gap didn't seem like a lot, but when I thought of all the rapid change in those four years, the gap seemed like a gulf.

Facebook emerged as I was finishing college. She was still in high school. This is a huge difference. I found it jarring to be reconnected with people I'd lost touch with. If she graduated from high school with a profile, then she'd never lost touch with anyone…ever. So what was new to me was normal to her.

I mean, how would she respond if I sent her a mix tape? Had she ever even made one? I have no idea. Mix tapes…they were just a thing that wasn't going to be a thing anymore. They were barely a thing when I was growing up—downloading music on Napster arrived early in my high school career. By the time we were in college, mixes became playlists and tapes became links. Just describing how I used to listen to music—Columbia House Record Club, Napster, Kazaa, LimeWire, Pirate Bay—I was speaking a dead language. It's a weird concept to wrap your brain around: having grown up in a context that no longer exists. I felt an impulse to talk to someone who I thought would understand, who'd see things the way I do.

"Hey," I texted to my secret foil. "You're about my age, right?"

"I'll never tell!"

"No," I texted back. "I'm serious. I know you must be, or older. No one younger would ever think to send a mix tape."

There was a longer wait than was normal for the rhythm of our exchange. I got the sense that he was processing what I'd said or trying to figure out what my angle was.

"Is that true?" my phone chimed back.

"I think so," I texted. "Let me get real with you for a second. I just went out with this girl who is twenty-two. She didn't get Fakebook at all. Facebook is completely normal to her."

"That's kind of scary," he wrote back.

"Yeah," I wrote. "I know."

"You should stick with the Amish," he said. "This wouldn't be an issue."

Then a strange thing happened between me and my anonymous "pen pal." We went on to shed the cat-and-mouse pretense and had a genuine conversation.

Things were, of course, not even. He knew who I was and a lot about me. I knew nothing of him, other than an area code and his sense of humor. Yet, in a moment, none of that mattered. I needed someone to relate to, and I knew there'd be no better person—whoever he was.

We touched on definitive experiences, reviving them in our memory for just a moment. We talked about searching for out-of-print albums or back-issue comics before there was an eBay, an Amazon, a Netflix, or an iTunes—or being reluctant to go to a Blockbuster on a Friday night because of the crowds. We joked about how AIM was the planning center of our early social lives, and how going onto MySpace was like an archaeological dig. We referenced using pay phones to make a collect call, such as "Mom, pick me up," before affordable cell phones emerged and we were still tethered to set times and places.

I felt too young to be thinking like this, but clearly we had grown up in a world that no longer existed. Not only that, our entire upbringing was just a flicker—a brief transition period between the analog world of the generations before us and digital world of the generations after.

We matured along with the information revolution. When I

was ten years old, the cutting edge of information technology was typing text commands into a thirty-pound monitor plugged into a thirty-pound gray box plugged into a wall, and car phones were toys of the rich.

Sixteen years later, I casually tossed a five-ounce, buttonless glass sculpture onto my coffee table, where it looked perfectly natural resting with my wallet and house keys. Just then, it delivered a message—through a trillion dollars' worth of infrastructure, over land, sea, air, and space—with a friendly chime. I expected it to be another text from my secret foil and strange new confidant. Instead it was a Facebook notification. I had a new friend request. It was from Dhara. Her profile picture was her ice skating—a public image with a personal meaning between us.

Social media: The term may be new, but the concept isn't. From screen names to cell phones—hell, even mix tapes before that—media have always been social.

As I laced up my skates, I received a text message. "Good luck with Dhara," it said.

It was a message from my secret foil. He must have seen that I'd accepted a new friend request and pieced together that it came from the girl I had told him about. He was perceptive, that one.

"Thanks," I texted back. "I'm out with her now." I put my phone away for the rest of my night and stepped out onto the rink.

If you can't see the appeal of stepping out onto white ice set against the silhouette of Central Park under the stars and skyline, as Frankie Valli sings the main refrain of "I Can't Take My Eyes Off You" through a tinny PA system…well, you've just never been a fourteen-year-old girl.

I loved everything about the ice-skating date—helping a girl with her balance, holding hands, getting hot chocolate during a break as it began to flurry. It was so damn endearing—like living a Zales commercial. Based on the way Dhara pretended to wobble—allowing me to right her—I know she felt the same way.

We were loose. We joked. We attempted to outdo each other in some truly awful displays of figure-skating prowess. There wasn't a single lull or an awkward pause. We only stopped when ABBA's misunderstood "Take a Chance on Me" was interrupted by the ice cleaning announcement.

We grabbed our hot chocolates with marshmallows and ducked out of the main waiting area. We sat on the stairs of the stone patio overlooking the rink and found ourselves a quiet moment.

That night, like the night before, I felt free of Fakebook and was able to enjoy being in the moment. Unlike the night before, however, there were no plans hanging over Dhara. It was just me and this beautiful girl—with the whole night in front of us, and very little winter air between.

The next day, I get a text from my secret foil and strange new confidant. "I have to ask…How'd it go?"

An odd thought occurred to me: He literally did "have to ask," didn't he? How else could he know? There were no status updates and no photos posted on my Facebook wall. It was a night without a record—just a private memory belonging exclusively to Dhara and me.

It struck me that "having to ask" was soon going to join ranks of the mix tapes and "Be kind, rewind"—a relic of another time. How rare is it now that we have to ask? Facebook, in its simple grayed-out text, does the asking for us every time we log in:

"What's on your mind?"

It's such a simple question and so effective. With no other prompting or incentive, we answer volumes. We're a billion voices speaking at once, contributing to a thorough autobiography of our times and writing it in the moment. We're constantly reporting on ourselves and others—what we like, where we are, who we are with, how we feel. In short, we answer Facebook's question.

And Facebook catalogs every answer. Each post and every photo is stamped with a time, a place, and an ID. I mean…we "tag" each other in our photos, for Christ's sake. We make sure no detail goes unrecorded.

The scale of this gave me pause and frightened me a little. It still does.

Who could have guessed that all it takes to learn someone's secrets is to simply ask? I mean, George Orwell accurately imagined a world with more cameras than people, but he never imagined that we'd be our own photographers. If he wrote *1984* today, would he replace the ominous threat of "Big Brother Is Watching" with a friendly "What's on Your Mind?"

It's tempting to cast Facebook as Big Brother—and trust me, when you're trying to hide from the world, the comparison feels apt—but it's not quite right. What's compelling isn't simply that Facebook enabled us to be our own Big Brother; what's compelling is how we jumped at the chance. We were given a choice, and we rejected privacy.

And that day, after a really great night out with a smart and beautiful girl, I understood why. I realized Facebook has turned us into collectors of moments. And at times, actual experiences can just be a step toward the real goal of preserving the memory and placing it on display. Despite what I'd like to believe, my night out with Dhara didn't feel more special because it belonged to just the two of us. Instead, it felt diminished—locked away where it could never be validated on my wall. It wasn't a private memory, but a missed opportunity.

I looked up from my phone and swiveled my desk chair, taking a glimpse at my ice skates tossed in the corner of my living room. I was being melodramatic. A bittersweet smirk flashed across my face.

"It went well," I texted my secret foil. "If only it counted."

I fell asleep while writing this.

JANUARY 16: ON THE ROAD AGAIN...

I know I barely posted last week, and I'm sorry. I had a lot to sort through. Frankly, I needed the break. I've been back and forth with Kate and with my life, and I didn't want to say anything that I could be called out on later. Everything's on record. I didn't trust myself enough to post.

Anyway, last Sunday I won a LOT of money on the Jets, Ravens, and Cardinals games. Being from NJ, going to Rutgers, and living in Glendale paid off, ha. I'm a lot more reckless than I used to be.

But my whole life is a gamble right now, so what the hell. I've rolled the dice and made 2,000 bucks. TAX FREE! J-E-T-S!

So now I have 2 grand in my pocket. A woman who I don't know what to think of, and what to do with, and a bow tie tattoo that is in its bleeding phase.

The world is my oyster.

I'm so tired. haha.

I gave Kate a "severance package"...made the whole relationship feel cheap. But I just didn't have it in me to boot her with nothing. So I bought her off with $500 dollars for her troubles. That should get her on a train or whatever. Or maybe she'll go find that dude again. They can have a wild night out on me.

I'm going west. Then maybe north to Canada.

Do I need a passport to get in? The Olympics are in Canada, could be fun...Anywhere but here man. Anywhere but here.

Matt Campbell Is that a Willie Nelson reference? Two weeks in the Arizona sun took you from daft punk to country music? Kudos on the kick to Kate. Long time comin. What's your mode of transportation this time?

yesterday via mobile · Like

Steve Cuchinello Go North to Vancouver. If you can figure out how to screw up the Canadian hockey team's chances for winning gold in the Winter Olympics in a few weeks you could have a statue of your bust mounted in Washington, DC (bow tie included). What more could you want? Forget about Kate and go serve your country.

yesterday via mobile · Like

Dave Cicirelli I will go where the desert coyote tells me. I may go south and dive into the chaos of life or maybe I'll go to the north, and embrace the purity of frozen snow.

yesterday via mobile · Like

Dave Cicirelli

I'm seriously thinking of turning around and finding Kate. This walk is so lonely.

Like · Comment

Ted Kaiser Maybe you should call one of Jonathon's other daughters.

23 hours ago via mobile · Like

Mark Cicirelli hubba hubba

23 hours ago · Like

Dave Cicirelli I'm a little concerned that none of the girls are trying to stop me...aren't any of you just a little jealous? I mean I'm an unemployed drifter with an art degree. Haven't I proven myself as a provider?

4 hours ago via mobile · Like

Dave Cicirelli

To all the people who think I'm making a mistake:

I'm just looking for love, and couldn't find it at the Jersey Shore. Just like Snookers.

Like · Comment

Roger Kapsi LOL

4 hours ago via mobile · Like

Matt Riggio Dude, you're losing it.

4 hours ago via mobile · Like

Dave Cicirelli I'm finding it, buddy. I'm finding it.

4 hours ago via mobile · Like

Ted Kaiser Kate is probably coked out in a bar bathroom after a weekend-long drug and alcohol bender with two guys named Larry and Mason.

about an hour ago via mobile · Like

Dave Cicirelli Ted, you are the worst human being alive. Eat shit, Ted.

32 minutes ago via mobile · Like

Ted Kaiser You're right. That was harsh. But you need to move on. It's over. She was bad news.

26 minutes ago via mobile · Like

Dave Cicirelli You don't know what it's like man…She ripped the heart right out of my chest and churned it into butter. Please stop treating my life like some silly game.

Do you think my life would have turned our better if I got into the National Honors Society?

26 minutes ago via mobile · Like

Jessica Kouvel Munch i have been quietly following your journey. well, except for when i get together with Red Bank friends and we discuss your life and adventures. nice, right? But anyway, I just have to say, you are so freakin' clever. you're completely heartbroken, and you manage to make awesome pop culture references, this amazing play on words (churned your heart into butter), and then, to top it off, bring back these crazy memories of ridiculousness from high school (aka the huge hullabaloo from certain people getting in or not getting into national honor society). love it.

22 minutes ago · Like

Dave Cicirelli Humor is my coping mechanism :)…:)

less than a minute ago via mobile · Like

9 | wall

A quick Google search told me that Lobby Bar at the Royalton Hotel was the only spot between our offices with a fireplace. It was a perfect—albeit pricey—choice for a cold late-January weeknight. The warmth of the fire validated the expense, as did the way Dhara sat close to me as we sipped our over-named cocktails.

"This place is really nice," she said.

"Yeah, I come here all the time."

"You think you're pretty classy for a guy who still plays with action figures."

"Whoa...whoa...whoa," I said in faux outrage. "First of all, I do promotional marketing for the toy industry. It's an eleven-billion-dollar-a-year category, and next month's Toy Fair is its biggest annual event..."

"You better camp out," she continued to tease, "so you can be the first to get your little toys."

"Collectible figurines."

"So," she said with a pause, "there's a holiday coming up...Should we celebrate it?"

"Presidents' Day?"

"Yeah, goober. Let's have a candlelit Presidents' Day dinner..."

She repositioned herself a little closer. My chin now rested just above her head and my arms were able to hold her around the waist. I could faintly smell the scent of her shampoo. "Yeah. I mean, we've only seen each other a few times, but a Valentine's date could be kind of fun."

"Yeah, for sure," I said—swayed simply by her asking.

After another hour of cocktails and playful if somewhat cautious conversation, the night ended with one-dollar pizza slices and a long kiss good night.

I couldn't help but feel a sense of satisfaction. I was dating a beautiful, intelligent woman and made my living drawing superheroes. Things were finally going according to plan—*exactly* according to plan, just as I wrote when I was thirteen. I couldn't have made up a better life…so to speak.

And yet, part of me couldn't shake the feeling that none of this counted because it wasn't on my wall. It's funny how the fiction of Fakebook made my real life feel, somehow, less real.

Don't get me wrong. I was plenty happy to just be with Dhara, but I wouldn't have minded being seen with Dhara. I wish I was mature enough to not care at all about what other people thought, but I did care a little. I mean, for the first time in my life, every girl I had ever liked was paying attention to me—and I was with someone who would make every one of them jealous. Instead they saw my desert-heat-driven descent into madness:

Dave Cicirelli
I'm so damn lightheaded…I really feel nasty.
Like · Comment

Kristen Scalia Dave, just think, if you were home i would say "hey, come over, we can eat our troubles away with a couple pounds of cheese"…come back soon? :(
2 days ago via mobile · Like

Ted Kaiser you know, these symptoms below are pretty close to what you're sounding like. I'm not suggesting anything, I'm just saying…

Symptoms of gonorrhea usually appear 2–5 days after infection, however, in men, symptoms may take up to a month to appear.

Other Symptoms of Gonorrhea:

Fever, night sweats. Muscular aches, and extreme fatigue.

Nausea, feeling sick over certain smells, or foods. Lightheaded and dizzy. Feeling shaky inside and "not well." A strong inner sense of something being very wrong with your body. Listen carefully to your body, it is seldom wrong.

2 days ago via mobile · Like

Dave Cicirelli Gonorrhea? I thought Godzilla killed that bastard years ago and became the undisputed king of monsters! Don't fuck with that Ted.

2 days ago via mobile · Like

Steve Cuchinello ?????? You alright Dave? That made no freakin sense what-so-ever.

2 days ago via mobile · Like

Dave Cicirelli I'm laying on a rock. I'm a lizasd. Iraq. I rock. iRock. Hahahaha.

yesterday via mobile · Like

Pete Garra Dave I'm afraid you've lost your mind. You must remember to drink lots of water in the desert.

yesterday via mobile · Like

Dave Cicirelli People are after me because I know the secret of the ooze.

yesterday via mobile · Like

Joe Moscone ok, now i'm on board with the Gonorrhea theory

yesterday via mobile · Like

Dave Cicirelli

Wow...Found this pic in my phone. Maybe people are right, and I should turn back...That would have been an awful ending for Dave Cicirelli.

Oh, and by the way, I've been in the hospital since late last night. Apparently I was dehydrated, making me susceptible to some sort of flu. I was found naked and having fever hallucinations...I don't know where half my stuff is, including the laptop. What a mess.

Like · Comment · Share

Joe Moscone Ho.Ly.Shit! Dude, yeah it's time to come home. WTF do you look like today bc this is horrible. time to come home. all joking aside, enough already.
4 hours ago via mobile · Like

Ted Kaiser Maybe its time to end the silliness and come home? I told Eckhoff we shoulda driven out to Amish country when u were there. We let you get too far. It is our fault. We wanted to give u some space on the journey but what were we thinking? We shoulda drove out to PA, dragged your ass away from Jonathon and Kate, threw u in the car, and drove u back to Michael Drive to sort out ur life. Maybe we ought to consider finding u in Arizona or wherever the heck u are
4 hours ago · Like

Elizabeth Lee Omg feel better! U need to take better care of urself!
4 hours ago via mobile · Like

Dave Cicirelli If I turn back now, what was it all for?
4 hours ago via mobile · Like

Christine Clericuzio Don't listen to them—success falls only one step short of where failure overtakes you! Come home only if YOU want to, not because other people think you should! Strange pic to share, uhm thank you?
3 hours ago via mobile · Like

Danny Ross you might have had a rough night, but at least you are still, and always, dapper.
3 hours ago via mobile · Like

Joe Moscone This pic is still freaking me out. You look like a pug in distress.
2 hours ago via mobile · Like

Alula Medhen fuck that, keep heading west till you find a chippendales and use that money-maker to make some bank
2 hours ago via mobile · Like

Ted Kaiser on second thought, ill stay away from Arizona to keep from catching whatever it is u have. in fact, it might be best if u continue ur ridiculous journey rather than bringing ur infection/flu/disease or whatever it is, back to NJ.
about an hour ago via mobile · Like

Brian Eckhoff if you're going to try, go all the way. otherwise, don't even start.
about an hour ago via mobile · Like

Dave Cicirelli That's really moving, Phil. Thank you.

I'm a believer in that old philosophical question:

Can a man walk in the same river twice? Every passing moment, the river has changed…and so has the man.
about an hour ago via mobile · Like

Joe Moscone I agree with you, Dave. I think when you return to Jersey, you must march into the center of Midgetville and declare yourself their King.
3 minutes ago · Like

Dave Cicirelli I told you that dream in confidence, Joe.
less than a minute ago via mobile · Like

Chris Mitarotondo i'm disappointed in you. if you were a real man, you would have ran across the country like Forrest Gump did. i think you're just dogging it. i see right through you.
less than a minute ago · Like

Steve Cuchinello Wow. Maybe we can hire that private defense company Wasco is working for at Guantanamo Bay to take a chopper out to the desert

> and pick your diseased ass up. How close are you going to flirt with death before this isn't worth it anymore?
> just now · Like

Such is life. It was cruel but necessary to drive Fake Dave into such a dark place. This extended hospital stay would marginalize him—drive him off the grid so I could devote a little time to the real world.

The truth is, it was all starting to become more than I could handle. The stresses of my personal, private, and fictional lives were mounting. As fun as it sounds, the upcoming Toy Fair and the long leads for the summer blockbuster season made February the most professionally demanding month of my year. It barely left me any time or desire to power up Photoshop on the weekends and create the false evidence of a bohemian lifestyle.

Not to mention Dhara. Ignoring any weird pang of regret about my ill-timed privacy, I knew a real girl was more important than a fictional one. We were at a delicate juncture in our young relationship, and I really didn't want to blow it.

The bottom line was, I had a tough job, a real girl, and a fake life. Each of these was in competition with the others, and one of them was going to have to be neglected. I couldn't keep diffusing my focus—I needed to prioritize. This became especially necessary the day I got a letter from the State of New York.

"You have jury duty?"

My boss's voice traveled out of her doorless office and into the newly renovated graphics bullpen. The bullpen unified the previously dispersed department into a single open room. We weren't yet used to seeing each other all day long. Nor were we used to all of our unique relationships merging into a single dynamic. The adjustment left things a little…raw.

“Yeah,” I told her. “Grand jury.”

“Your timing sucks,” she said in a tone I interpreted as blame.

“It’s not my timing.”

“Yeah…I know,” she said flatly, with a trace of fatigue. “It’s just that the deadlines aren’t going to change, whether you’re in the office or not, you know?”

“Boss…if I get picked, I can still work all morning and put whatever I don’t get done on a portable hard drive and work at night. I’ll pull my weight. But either I go to court or I go to jail.”

“Well, just try not to get picked.”

“I’ll do what I can.”

As it turns out, there is no screening process for a grand jury, and I couldn’t do a thing.

A dollar bag of cashews and a Gatorade are no kind of lunch. Especially if they’re eaten at the same subway station where you bought them. Still, that was all I had time for during the fifteen-minute ride to the courthouse on Centre Street, and the combo would soon become routine. I arrived with just enough time to run a hard drive full of tomorrow’s deadlines through the courthouse security’s x-ray machine and find my way to the assigned room.

When I walked into the courtroom, I was struck by how little theater there was to it. With its drop-down ceilings and fluorescent lights, the space resembled a small lecture hall. I chose my seat in the front row, becoming Juror 9.

To the left of me was Juror 10, quietly studying from her textbook, though she looked slightly too old to be an undergrad. She was tall and slender, maybe five-foot-eight, with the type of slim figure that was meant for the fashionable clothes she was wearing.

With blue eyes and light brown hair against a porcelain complexion, she was very pretty and, to be honest, the reason I chose that seat.

Juror 8 sat down to our right. She had short graying hair and looked to be in her late fifties. She was wearing a red penny coat that was once expensive. Without her addressing me, I could feel her stare linger. It was making me uncomfortable, and I reflexively ignored it.

Relenting, she addressed the room as a whole: "Does anyone know how to get a monthly MetroCard?" Only one person answered her question, but everyone noticed how peculiar a question it was in a room made up of full-time New York City residents. There was something both sympathetic and off-putting about her—an impression confirmed by the acknowledging glance I exchanged with Juror 10.

The whole experience had a "first day of school" feel to it even before the bailiff, an old-school New York Italian, wheeled in a TV-VCR combo.

"Hi," the video began. "I'm *60 Minutes* anchor Ed Bradley, and you've been selected to serve on a grand jury!"

"What?" Juror 10 muttered under her breath in bewilderment.

"Hi, I'm Troy McClure…" I mimicked quietly. She and the people behind us laughed. Juror 8 didn't. Instead she attempted to write an email under the desktop, tapping away at the cracked screen of her first-generation iPhone. Her attempt at discretion was undermined by the default *tic* sound of each keystroke.

"What's a grand jury?" Mr. Bradley continued. "I'm glad you asked."

Pockets of quiet laughter cropped up around the room, along with (and partly because of) the din of *tic*, *tic*, *tic*, which was only interrupted by an audible "oh" and exaggerated recoil whenever Juror 8 mistyped.

"Grand jury is an important part of the judicial process. It's the grand jury's—your—responsibility to determine if a case has enough evidence to justify a trial, or if the case is to be dismissed."

The video then cut to testimonials.

"I found the experience really rewarding! It was a great way to get to know my community, while giving back to it!"

There was a handful of cynical groans. I was cynical too, but mostly about wasting tax money on landing top-tier talent like Ed Bradley.

"The burden of proof is much lower in a grand jury," Ed resumed. "It's the petit jury that needs a unanimous vote to prove guilt beyond a reasonable doubt. Because you aren't convicting, you just need eleven of a possible twenty-one votes to come to a conclusion."

I took a look at my twenty fellow jurors. A few of us—the jokers, the cynics, and the genuinely insane—had already revealed ourselves. As the month went on, so would the bleeding hearts, the authoritarians, the wealthy, and the disenfranchised. It was a true cross section and a reminder that New York is too big for any one person to see all at once. The city is a multifaceted gem with sides that are both rough and polished.

"And remember, you are not here to judge the laws. You are here to judge whether or not the laws have been broken. It's up to *you* to determine what probably happened."

And for the next month, we did. We'd take a four-hour stop in the middle of our day, pushing off the rest of life's demands, to see a procession of cops and robbers (and lawyers). One by one, they would come and tell their conflicting stories. Once again, I found myself in the peculiar circumstance of determining what was true.

It was half past noon and I anxiously watched my files transfer to the portable hard drive. I'd been on jury duty for just over a week, and getting my work done was harder than I'd thought. I worked straight through the weekend and was coming in each day two hours early—no easy task when most nights I was working at home until past midnight.

"I wish I had half days, too," Joe said as we crossed paths toward the exit.

"I'd love half days. But at this point, I'd settle for just full ones."

The conversation was all in jest, but I was annoyed. I don't know if I expected praise for working so hard around my civic obligations, but I wasn't getting it. I tried to get it out of my mind by squeezing in some Fakebook nonsense as I walked to the 6 train.

Dave Cicirelli
These nurses aren't as naughty as the ones I've seen in movies.
Like · Comment

The hospital story was working as planned, laying seeds for the next leg of the story without the need for heavy Photoshop work. And if I could sell it, the cult storyline I had planned—with "the Center's" strict rules about communication—could keep Fake Dave away from his camera phone, and all the time-intensive photoshopping that being on camera requires, for almost a month.

Dave Cicirelli
There are these frighteningly polite people that keep trying to talk to me because I have no visitors.

Like · Comment · Share

At this point, I was only teasing an upcoming cult storyline. I had my doubts that people would believe it…but it did make a certain sort of crazy sense. Fake Dave had a rough go of it the past four months. His decision to have a completely unstructured life had resulted in nothing but physical and emotional harm. The supreme order of a cult could, conceivably, hold certain appeal for a guy looking for meaning but worn down by the search.

I saw the appeal, anyway. I also had been living with uncertainty since Fakebook began. Juggling two lives and facing the constant risk of being exposed definitely can get to you. I'm sure it had no small part in making the institutional predictability of the Centre Street courthouse so strangely comforting.

After spending four months doing Fakebook and four years in the deadline-driven and crisis-prone world of marketing, I found that jury duty was the first commitment I'd had in a long time that was completely structured. I showed up at one; I left at five. I sat in the same seat, and I responded only to what was presented to me. There was nowhere else I legally could be, so I didn't worry about how else I could be spending my time.

Even though losing four hours a day as Juror 9 put a lot of additional pressure on my life, that time itself was an oasis. It was an island in the middle of hellishly busy weekdays that simply was.

I never took the responsibility lightly, but if I'm being completely honest, it often felt like entertainment. We saw three to six cases a day, making it an interesting cross-section of New York's criminal affairs. Undercover cops, surveillance, money laundering, and product drops—it was fascinating to get a real-world glimpse.

And the grand jury's lack of a screening process made things interesting. Every time Juror 8 called the prosecutor over, it was compelling to see them try to turn her weird MetroCard fixation into a relevant line of questioning. "The jury would like to know…whether you had a monthly pass or a pay-as-you-go MetroCard…in the purse…that was stolen…"

The deliberations were interesting, too. I'll never forget watching Juror 3 lose it when Juror 15 limply tried to explain how shooting two people was not attempted murder.

"What…in your mind…was he attempting to do?" Juror 3 reasonably asked.

"As he was shooting," Juror 15 began in his predictably wimpy voice, "he said, 'I'm going to F you N words up.' He didn't say, 'I am going to kill you.'"

At that, Juror 3 exploded. Thankfully, they were sitting at opposite ends of the room or we would have been witnesses instead of jurors.

And as callous as getting amusement out of the spectacle surrounding real people and real crimes may seem, it's important to remember that we sent no one to jail, just to trial. The weight of convictions didn't fall on us. With the lower stakes and an eleven-of-a-possible-twenty-one vote system to smooth out irrational points of view, we always made the obvious verdict. (Assault with bullets is, in fact, attempted murder.) It was almost kind of fun.

It was coming home that was hard. When five o'clock came around, I'd walk to my neighborhood (with new knowledge of my neighbors) and my second workday began. I'd leave behind other people's lives and dive back into mine, just as I left it—except with a fuller inbox and shorter deadlines. Every night I'd work at my desk in plain sight of my bed until I'd go to bed in plain sight of my desk. The next day, I'd do it all over again.

"Dave, are you listening?"

"What? Yeah, I'm sorry. I'm just a little distracted."

I was. I'd convinced myself that I had time to head out to Queens for Thai food with Dhara. I didn't. I had an incomplete proposal due to the client by morning. It was ambitious, trying to get a sign-off on that superhero project—to allow me to create a custom illustration for their biggest launch of the year. It was important to me, and I wasn't sure when I'd get to it.

"I was asking if you ever want kids one day."

"*What*? That's kind of an intense question for, what, a fifth date?"

"I'm not propositioning you, if that's what you're thinking."

"Ha."

"I'm not sure I could ever be with someone who would want kids if I didn't."

On some level, I picked up on her phrasing of "if I didn't," but I lacked the focus to pull it together. I paused for a moment and shifted in my seat. I gave what I thought was a diplomatic answer. It was something about how I'd be disappointed not to have kids, but I would compromise to live the life of…I don't know. My response probably didn't make sense. It was just an attempt to avoid saying anything definitive.

"I definitely want kids one day. I just wanted to see how you'd answer if I suggested I didn't," she said matter-of-factly.

"Hey, that's not fair. I trekked all the way out here so you could test me? I'm missing a new episode of *Lost* for this!"

"You know I used to date a body double for *Lost*, right?"

"Please tell me it was the fat guy."

"Haha. Maybe. I don't think I'm going to tell you who. It's another mystery of the island."

I took a bite out of the vegetarian dish she'd picked for us and ran a mental slide show of all the well-toned dudes on that beach. For the first time since our first date, I was finding her intimidating.

"Have you been following Fakebook at all?"

"Yes," she said.

"What do you think?"

"Well…it's kind of weird."

Dave Cicirelli
So I'm almost 100% positive that these strangely polite people that keep visiting me are a cult that is trying to recruit me! I feel like the belle of the ball. I may go with them after I'm released today. I think it'd be kind of amazing to see…Like when I used to argue with Scientologists at the subway station.
Like · Comment

Christine Clericuzio uh oh. please be careful
about an hour ago via mobile · Like

Dave Cicirelli I'm too mentally strong to be suckered.
about an hour ago via mobile · Like

Claire Burke mentally strong? Like the time you got out of jury duty? Oh…wait a minute…
about an hour ago via mobile · Like

Dave Cicirelli You know I can't legally discuss that…I'm in enough trouble these days!
about an hour ago via mobile · Like

Matt Campbell Just stay away from Kool-aid.
38 minutes ago via mobile · Like

Ted Kaiser Mentally strong? Like the time you quit your job and walked around aimlessly? Or the time you willingly served as a slave for an Amish family? Or when you traveled back to the desert to find some Amish hookup who ditched you? I don't know what to do with u anymore. Does Ralph know where you are?
34 minutes ago · Like

Dave Cicirelli
I'm sorry that I've been MIA on here for a few days. I'm fine and didn't mean to concern anyone. I'm staying at the "community center" for a bit, and they have some rules

about cell phones. Yes, that's as terrifying as it sounds. It's kind of absurd and crazy passive aggressive, haha. I'll write more soon.
Like · Comment

Matt Campbell It seems kind of ironic to me that you left Amish country early largely because of your disagreements with Jonathon. You talked constantly about how he was using 'pride' to suppress his family. You hated how they shun fancy things like electricity. Yet, here you are joining up with a cult at a community center that "has rules about cell phones?" Dude, wasn't this supposed to be an experience about freedom, no limits, doing what you want to do? Time for another re-evaluation perhaps.
22 minutes ago · Like

Ted Kaiser wtf are you talking about?
less than a minute ago via mobile · Like

It was Thursday, February 11, and I was exhausted. The trip for Thai food had pushed my work routine well into the early morning, and with very little sleep, I was happy to leave the office and head to court for my four-hour break. Saturday was both Toy Fair and Valentine's Day, and I had a lot to get done before both. I walked into the court, eager to focus on other people's problems for a few hours.

The first case we saw was the continued "Yellow Brick Road." We assigned all cases that spanned multiple days an arbitrary code name. To keep things fun, we had a *Wizard of Oz* theme that week and found "Yellow Bricks" kind of clever for a graffiti case.

It was a fairly cut-and-dried case. In fact, it only had been continued because there was simply too much evidence to cover in a single session. The deliberations went quickly, with the only hiccup being crazy Juror 8 choosing to singlehandedly legislate that street art is not a crime on the grounds of her membership to the Whitney. She was easily outvoted and we took a break.

I saw Juror 10 drinking a bottle of water in the break area. We seemed pretty like-minded in all the deliberations and had bonded a little over our shared reactions to Juror 8's weird antics.

"How often do you think they replace the burgers in there?" I asked, pointing to the White Castle vending machine.

"Oh god, I don't want to think about that. Those things are sketchy enough when you buy them from a restaurant," she said.

"I've never actually had one. I'm afraid of taking that step…buying hamburgers by the sack."

"Wise decision."

"So…have you heard?" she asked.

"Heard what?"

"Juror 8. She's an art critic."

"You don't say." We laughed.

"Yeah," I continued. "I like how she wants to put herself above the entire legislative process because she found an opportunity to remind us she has a newsletter."

"I'm sure it's the hit of her halfway house," she joked and we both laughed.

Juror 8 walked by and we quieted down quickly.

"Probably time to head back to the room," I said.

We were queued up for the next case, something about an alleged gang member who was found with a gun and then fled arrest. We'd seen this prosecutor before, a young guy who was a bit on the doughy side and came across as a little mean spirited. He called in the arresting officer, also young but with a muscular build. He seemed like the kind of guy who didn't see a lot of nuance in the world. After the initial and formal protocol questions, we got into the meat of the case.

"I was on a routine patrol when I saw the defendant, Amadi,

reach under a wheel well of a parked SUV. He removed a suspicious object and proceeded to place the object into the leg of his boot."

"Did you recognize the defendant?"

"I have not interacted with him prior, no, but I did know of him. He is known to be affiliated with NYZ, an Uptown gang."

"Upon seeing reasonable cause, what happened next?"

"As I approached the defendant, he fled."

The officer had a certain…I don't know if "attitude" is the right word, but impatience. It was the tone of a guy who clearly had other things he'd rather be doing. "My partner and I pursued him, and after a few blocks' chase, we subdued the suspect. Upon search, we recovered an illegal handgun."

The heavyset prosecutor submitted a photo of a handgun as evidence to the court, went through the usual legalese of confirming for the record that this was the gun in question, and read the official forensics report, where we learned the gun was loaded and its serial numbers filed off.

The police officer left the room. It seemed obvious that this was either a gun being sold or a gun about to be used, and this cop had probably stopped something nasty from happening in a nasty part of town.

The defendant's lawyer, a middle-aged woman with red hair, walked in. She began shuffling some papers around as we waited for the defendant to enter. I can't say what exactly our expectations were—or even if we had any—but no one was prepared to see the scared child who entered our courtroom.

He was sixteen, but he looked about twelve. He was skinny—maybe malnourished—and was wearing an old, oversized sweatshirt with a small tear at the collar.

"State your name for the court," the prosecutor said.

"I went to the youth center with seven dollars…"

"No, I said 'state your name.'"

This kid was overwhelmed. The prosecutor seemed…well…like an asshole.

"What?"

"I said 'state your name,' for the record."

"Amadi Johnson."

"Please recall for the court your recollections of the night of February 3."

"I went to the youth center with seven dollars. I had two dollars for my MetroCard and five dollars to go to the dance."

Juror 8's ears perked up at the mention of the MetroCard.

"Then what happened?"

"I was walking to the youth center, and I saw something on the ground, next to a Dumpster. I thought to myself, 'Whoa, I think that is a gun.'" His words were slow, deliberate. It took a lot of effort for him to get them out.

"What did you do then?"

"I put it in my boot to take it home. I had a phone number written down at home that I saw on the news. If I called this number, the police would take the gun and I would get a reward."

His lawyer squeezed his forearm and nodded in a comforting, encouraging way.

"What did you do when the police officer approached you?"

"I was scared, and I ran away."

"Why did you run away if you had nothing to hide?"

"I was scared and I ran away."

"What were you scared of?"

It's uncomfortable watching a kid get grilled. Your emotional response is to protect him. The whole dynamic was fucked. The kid was weak, uneducated, poor. He felt like the victim.

"Have you ever heard of NYZ?"

"No, I do not know who they are."

"You were not delivering a gun for NYZ?"

"I saw something on the ground, next to a Dumpster. I thought to myself, 'Whoa, I think that is a gun.'"

It was hard not to notice these lines he kept repeating—verbatim. It almost sounded rehearsed, but at the same time...If I were in his position, I would rehearse what I'd say too, even if it was the truth. And I was an adult—an adult from a good family with an education. This kid could barely afford the two-dollar MetroCard to get to the dance. If he was, in fact, in the wrong place at the wrong time, this is how I think he'd act. Everything he said was possible, and his words were convincing, particularly when his whole life made me feel guilty.

When the deliberations began, the experience was tense and draining in a way none of us had felt before. It was heavy. It was so less abstract than any of our other cases.

The thing is, there was no overt victim that day. We weren't certain that what happened that day was even a crime. If we voted one way, Amadi was just a kid in the middle of a big misunderstanding.

If we voted another, Amadi was a criminal...or our victim.

We were an arm of the same society that allowed him to fall through its cracks. It didn't feel like duty to send this kid to trial, and it damn sure didn't feel like we were doing good work.

There was a handful of adamant factions on either side, but by and large, no one knew what to do, what to think. There was a very soft middle of weak votes, and the handful of absentees ensured that we couldn't reach the necessary eleven votes for either conviction or dismissal. The case would have to be continued another day when more evidence could be gathered.

We assigned the case the code name "Tin Man" for no particular reason. We walked out of the courthouse and exchanged some quiet and awkward good-byes.

A weird mix of vulnerability, exhaustion, and emotion made me impulsively text Dhara.

"Hey, just wanted to say I'm looking forward to Saturday. It means a lot to me."

I knew the text was a mistake even before I sent it. We'd only been on a few dates. It was a dumb thing to say because it made Valentine's Day serious instead of frivolous—adding an expectation into our early courtship.

I distracted myself with a long meandering walk home through Chinatown. Eventually I made it to my street. It was barely seven, but it was pitch black and the wind was cutting. I wanted to just go to bed, but I couldn't. I had work to do, at least for a few hours. No more breaks, and I could be in bed by ten.

I grabbed my mail as I entered my building. There was a red envelope with a heart drawn on the back with the initials "KF." I smiled in recognition of my secret foil's handiwork and proudly read "Katie Fisher's" card to me. "All the roads I've taken have led me to you. Happy Valentine's Day." I tossed the card onto my coffee table and sat at the desk.

While my laptop was booting, I get the call I was expecting.

"Hey," Dhara said. "So…I got your text."

"Yeah…about that. I realized right after…"

"I just want to be clear, because sometimes I worry that I give the wrong signals. It's something I'm working on, but sometimes I make people think I like them more than…That's not right."

"I understand what you're getting at," I said. "You are worried we have uneven expectations."

"Yeah…the text you sent made me worry. Like, I haven't seen any reason to run away from you or anything. I just want to make sure we're on the same page."

"Totally," I said. "I just had a really emotional case…it wasn't…I don't know."

"All right," she said. "Good."

"We're still on for Saturday, right? The Valentine's Day date?

I promise you an event appropriate to your moderate affection toward me."

She politely laughed. "Yeah, that's the other thing. I was invited to go and visit some friends down in D.C. this weekend...Can we move it to Friday?"

"Yeah, that's fine," I said. "Works out better for me, actually. Saturday I have to work all day. You know, the Toy Fair. Got to get there early before all the good toys are taken."

"Okay, great," she said. "I have to leave early Saturday morning, so let's just keep it low key and have an early night."

"Sure."

Valentine's Day. I could feel the words unpack a series of complications I was not equipped to handle with this new dynamic. By establishing uneven expectations, I had trapped myself. Any effort I showed would be mounting evidence that I was a situation she'd eventually need to handle. A lack of effort, on the other hand, would just compound her waning interest.

What was I thinking? She was an Ivy League–educated stunner in a lucrative industry. I was a publicly educated graphic designer with inconsistent gym habits. Emotional day or not, it was just hubris for me to push this forward.

I looked over at my card from my other "girlfriend." Dipping into my other life seemed appealing at the moment, so I logged on to Facebook.

Jamie McAllister ➡ Dave Cicirelli

Subject: Thanks :)

Hey Dave,

So I've been one of your silent dedicated followers (Connie and I constantly share "Did you see what's going on with Free The Eggs Dave" exchanges). I have been going through a bit

> of an existential crisis myself lately with the commodities floor making me hate my life and I wasn't sure I was gutsy enough to quit.
>
> I am certainly not as gutsy as you, but reading about your adventures and the risks you're taking and stuff definitely made me feel like why the hell not. So many people have been giving me advice and telling me the smart sensible things to do and it was just nice to read about someone saying "F you" to the sensible people.
>
> Anyway I quit my job and I'm really happy about it. Like I said I'm not quite as adventurous as you so I won't be hitting the road (although I too have strongly been considering getting a tattoo, just not such a ridiculous one), but just wanted to say thanks for telling the Steves and Teds of the worlds to screw themselves. :)
>
> Good luck finding your lady.

I looked back at the card and picked up my phone. Grasping at hope, I texted the 732 number of my anonymous rival. "Are you Jamie McAllister?"

I placed the phone down on the table, next to the card. I leaned back on my couch with my eyes closed and waited.

The phone vibrated. "No."

I just stared at the text, feeling the last lingering hope that this was some sort of trick—a ruse from my secret foil—get dashed. All along, I'd held on to the rationalization that Fakebook wasn't hurting anyone. I was just telling a story. Playing a joke. That rationalization was shattered as my lie claimed its first victim.

Instead I just felt the burden of it all. This stupid commitment to a dumb idea I'd had four months ago…I could barely manage it when it only disrupted my life. Now I felt the full weight of Jamie's uncertain future. I placed my shaking palms on my forehead and pressed my fingertips into my scalp. I wanted to scream but couldn't…I was still far too lucid to not worry about how ridiculously dramatic that would be.

I just wanted to sleep, to take a break. I wanted eight hours to forget about this dumb fucking joke—to not worry about having a reasonable answer when people like Jamie eventually and inevitably asked why I would do this. I wanted one life again.

Oh god, my life…I wanted a break from that, too. I didn't want to think how I actually dreaded Friday night with Dhara. I wanted to not think about the sixteen-year-old kid and the gun concealed in his boot. I just wanted some fucking sleep. I'd been working every day and every night…with my only downtime while I was in transit between obligations. I just wanted to rest, to go to bed, and rest…to have nothing at stake for a few hours…to have no responsibilities for a few hours…to have no one watching.

I walked the handful of steps to my bathroom. I leaned forward onto the sink, and with both hands supporting me, I began to steady. Tomorrow was Friday. I could sleep on Friday, I thought. No, I had to work. And then I had jury duty. And then I had a date.

Saturday…no, not Saturday. It was the Toy Fair, and I had to work.

Sunday…maybe on Sunday I could rest. Maybe. Just make it until Sunday. Get it together until then. I had work to do. I had to keep it together. After all, Fake Dave didn't.

The next morning, I savored the walk to my half day of work. At jury duty, everyone was still shaken from the Tin Man case. Crazy Juror 8 told us she drove up to Morningside Heights—in what I assume was a wildly illegal act—to check out the scene of the crime. I like to imagine she used a big sleuthing magnifying glass.

Dave Cicirelli
There is not enough time to sleep.
Like · Comment

Dave Cicirelli
Expunging the toxic spirits to find the Center.
Like · Comment

I got home just in time to shower before meeting Dhara for our Valentine's Day date. I made her a "Lower East Side fixed-menu date" to play off the prolific restaurant deals. She had three venue choices for each course—dinner, dessert, and drinks. She noticed the grammatical errors before the effort, and the night had all the passion you'd expect from a woman who was going through the motions and a guy afraid of doing something wrong. I got an early night and a homemade card.

Dave Cicirelli
All the toxins in our mind create the weight that is the imbalance. The fulcrum of the Universe lies in the Center, and next year is quickly approaching.
Like · Comment

Saturday I worked at the Toy Fair, acting as security for toy collectors—the only crowd I could ever intimidate. It was the scene I had hoped for, full of the fun of toys celebrating themselves and the weirdness of a playpen filled only with adults. On my break, I shot out a few Fakebook posts on other people's walls—enjoying the heckler-like relationship the Facebook format allowed for.

Ralph Cicirelli
Dave, please give me a call. I need to speak with you about something that is very important. Also, I am worried about you. I have not heard from you in weeks and don't know where the hell you are. Please call!!!
Like · Comment

Dave Cicirelli Ralph, I cannot speak to you yet. You and mom gave me life which means you are the direct link to the ethereal toxins that have been poisoning me since pre-life. It is difficult to quarantine myself from the family, but how can I find the Path to the Center while remaining anchored to the Imbalance?

I forgive you.

Also, some people have brought up a good point about taxes. Can you handle that for me? I don't want to find myself in trouble with the IRS.

27 minutes ago via mobile · Like

Steve Cuchinello Yeah Ralph you were only good for giving life and filing taxes. Everything else has been poison. Good cult, Dave. Isn't there a comet you have to catch?

24 minutes ago via mobile · Like

Dave Cicirelli Steve, I know you only mock me because being dismissive of one discovering Truth is much easier than facing what it is that you fail to see.

I forgive you.

19 minutes ago via mobile · Like

Steve Cuchinello Dave, YOU have begun to bore me. I forgive you.

less than a minute ago via mobile · Like

Sunday, Dhara was back in town and I saw her at her request. Her text was short and devoid of whimsy. I arrived at the bar first. When she arrived, she offered me only her cheek. I asked her what she wanted to drink, while pulling out my wallet. She placed her card down on the bar.

I remember sliding a glass of Jameson in small circles around the booth's oak tabletop while I waited for my brother to arrive.

It's funny. In moments like those I'm more interested in holding the whiskey than I am in drinking it…the same way I've never felt an impulse to smoke but occasionally would like to gesture with a lit cigarette.

I guess I really am an artist—always concerned about the aesthetics. Like the way I couldn't help but think about how much this bar I'd stumbled into looked like a bar. There's nothing distinct about it; everything's made of wood, and there is some Irish name above the door. It feels like a bar "template," content to be unassuming and let the patrons fill it with character.

The places I usually go downtown, or in Brooklyn and Jersey City, tend to skew a bit younger and a bit more…novel. So many of those bars, like the people in them, seem to need some sort of statement—a twist to capture the interest of a purpose-hungry crowd. It's a bar meant to feel like a '70s basement or a speakeasy, or the bar that's all German imports… They all have to have something to validate their existence. As if being a place to gather wasn't enough.

I took a sip of the whiskey.

My brother, Mark, finally came in. Normally I didn't notice, but he had a specific way of entering. He stepped in quickly and sort of leaned forward as he looked around the room with an economy of movement. He was…focused.

I liked talking to my brother. He never patronized me with reassuring lies.

"Baby brother," he patronized. "What's the matter?"

"I got dumped."

"Is this the Princeton girl? You were barely going out with her."

"Yeah, I know. It was just another false start. It's frustrating. I can pull it together long enough to get my shot with a girl like that, but…"

"A girl like that? What does that mean?" Mark chimed in, taking offense at putting anyone on a pedestal.

I showed him a photo on my phone.

"Empirically speaking, that's the best you'll ever do."

"Unquestionably. There's something strange about dating a girl like that. She's so…unfamiliar with certain things. Uninhibited."

"Yeah?" Mark said with a slight, filthy interest.

"Haha, that's not what I meant."

"What do you mean, then?"

"Like, she lives in a world where people want her to like them…It's a stacked deck. Her sense of what's…normal…is somehow wider. I dug that, actually.

"But listen," I continued, "I'm under no delusions. I don't think she's one of the great loves of my life. I don't think this was 'meant to be' or any bullshit like that. What she is, however, is very bright. Very perceptive."

I paused, a bit of a lump rising in my throat. "I asked her to be honest, and she was. Her reasons were insightful…accurate." I paused again. "She handled everything respectfully…maturely…I can't say I'm even angry or hurt exactly. I just feel…"

I was embarrassed by how hard I was taking this.

"When Dhara was breaking up with me, her focus felt entirely on letting me down easy…like she didn't want to hurt me because I did nothing to deserve being hurt. I mean, that's what really stung. That…more than anything in particular that she said. It's that dismissive quality to it all."

"Right," Mark said. "Like the rejection was total."

I was startled by Mark's succinct description. He was right. That's exactly what I felt like. I was rejected not only as a boyfriend, but also as an equal.

Looking down, I slid my glass again in a small circular pattern. "Yeah…" I said. "I'm the 'nice guy' to her…and that's just not who I always viewed myself as…but I think that may be true."

"What does that even mean?" Mark asked.

"Hard to describe...like, I always aspired to be a 'good man,' but that's different, too. I think it's assertiveness. A nice guy is passive, accommodating. He's nice because it avoids conflict—he has no point of view. It's not admirable or anything you respect...it's just well-packaged weakness."

I paused for a moment, attempting to collect my thoughts. I tried to make it clear how I had fallen into the pattern of making half-stances, and how that had eaten away at who I was...allowed doubt to grow inside me. I needed to make clear how this all connected to the girl who didn't think enough of me and the career I compromised in and the audience whose respect I earned only by being someone else. How it was all part of this general frustration and anxiety of my stalled-out life.

"Like, I'm bright. I'm capable. I could have done what someone like you has done...have that kind of success."

"You're clearly too distraught to think clearly," Mark said.

"The point is, I had this creative itch. I decided I'd reject a safe road for the chance to be creative...but then I flinched. And now I live check to check in service of other people's ideas. It's...so...subordinate.

"But I always thought that was just what I had to do to make a living," I continued. "I don't expect people to pay me to do what I say, you know? But when I'm treated that way by a woman I thought a lot of..."

"I see," Mark said.

"So when that happens, it makes me think...maybe I am that 'nice guy.' What have I done that says otherwise? Maybe I am that guy who just does what I'm told. It's like I set out to be Superman, and I've arrived at Clark Kent."

"When most people look at Superman," Mark said, "all they see is Clark Kent." With an impatient tone, he continued, "What are you looking for exactly? Validation?"

"I don't know...maybe..."

"This girl didn't see it in you. So what? You weren't in love with her, so she's not important, an extra, a background character of your life who had a scene and now it's probably over. Professionally, if you think you're not able to go anywhere, then change your environment. Go somewhere else."

"Yeah, I just think I need..."

"Stop it. You always come up with another half-step instead of the big one you should just shut up and take."

"Yeah..." I said.

"It's a good thing to put a certain amount of pressure—to evaluate," he said in a softer tone. "But Dave, you're crippling yourself. Stop thinking about all these things you can't change or who you wish you were...Just focus on what you can do and let go of what you can't.

"Go home," he said. "Get some rest."

So I did.

The first things I saw when I got home were my two Valentine's Day cards from recent breakups in both my lives. I picked up Dhara's, which read: *I (Italian flag) Agnostic Girls.* It was a *Jersey Shore* reference—a show I only pretended to like. It struck me how funny it was—one card from a girl I'd made up and the other to a guy I pretended to be.

I put down Dhara's card. For just a moment, I felt unburdened. It was still Sunday. Now I could rest.

10 | link

I should have been stepping into bed. It was getting late, and the next morning a car was coming at the crack of dawn to take me to a 7:00 a.m. print run. But instead I was stepping into a running shower, fully clothed.

This must have looked completely ridiculous—but having already gone through shaving off a bow-tie sized square of chest hair, that didn't even register. Everything is relative, I suppose.

What an idiot! I'd forgotten the camera. I stepped out of the shower and ran to my living room, leaving a puddle with each step. When I grabbed my camera from the table, the errant strap grazed a dried-out blossom of my Thanksgiving flowers from my fake girlfriend, causing it to fall from the stem.

I could relate to the state of those tulips. After the past three weeks of being pulled apart by the competing demands of my professional, personal, civic, and fictional lives, I shouldn't have had the energy to stage a ridiculous, one-man photo shoot. Especially when its purpose was to further the cause of my recent troubles. But here I was, camera in hand, staging a Fakebook rainstorm.

The thing is, I did burn out. But there's something cleansing about the process. I felt lighter, somehow clearer, than I had in months. Years, even. I simply didn't have the energy to go through the paces of indecision. Jamie McAllister had quit her job because of my online hoax. Some stranger had complete leverage over me with his knowledge of it, and I'd spent the last few months pretending to have a girlfriend. My reputation was fucked. I'd come to accept that there simply was no graceful landing for this thing, so

I might as well enjoy the crash. So I let those fears go and felt a lot lighter for it.

And with the new "who gives a damn" attitude and the home stretch in sight, I decided to reinvest in my original absurdist vision. It was what I wanted to do. It was why I started Fakebook. I was done letting my fears dictate the life I scripted.

It felt good. Because when you stripped everything away, there was something about Fakebook I still enjoyed, and something about it that felt worthwhile. And I for damned sure wasn't going to let it whimper away after all I'd sacrificed. So every night I was at it, building a library of assets that I'd use in this crazy experiment's final chapter.

It wasn't just Fakebook I'd reinvested in. I was now about the business of changing things in my real life, too. The conversation with my brother hadn't exactly made everything clear, but it encouraged me to have momentum. I didn't know exactly what I wanted, but I knew I needed to stop thinking and start doing. As he put it, I needed to stop inventing half-steps. I wasn't even sure what I was looking for, other than options. So I spent much of my night scouring the job boards, finding out what those options could be.

And my personal life...I don't know how to describe it. It almost felt like I was getting over a hangover.

But all that didn't matter. I was moving forward. I was done being overwhelmed. I felt capable again. It might have looked ridiculous, me standing in a running shower fully clothed, camera in my outstretched hand—but it felt like I was taking control.

A box of Entenmann's powdered sugar doughnuts held my gaze, but I settled for pouring myself a tall black coffee instead. I needed the coffee more.

I might have been full of energy last night, but I was exhausted this morning. That's not to say I wasn't excited. My superhero promotional shipper—complete with my original illustration—was minutes away from going on press. All the late nights I'd spent on this were now in the past. The finished product was in my immediate future. I was filled with anticipation and now caffeine.

I sat down at the round faux wood table and took another sip of the strong coffee. The waiting area looked like anywhere else, with the standard grayish-blue carpeting below drop-down ceilings and fluorescent lights. The only difference was that the walls were decorated with a half-dozen large-format posters of cable dramas—the kind that get installed at bus stops and train stations. They must have been printed there, probably on the same press as my job.

Before I had a chance to open the paper, Fred, my print rep, came in and told me they were ready. I followed him off the carpet and onto the concrete floor of the warehouse. We walked down the hallway of finished flat sheets and fresh cover stock on our way to the press, where the technicians greeted us with hearty, ink-stained handshakes.

This wasn't a Kinko's where flyers got printed on a poorly maintained photocopier—it was a big operation with gigantic, million-dollar printing presses. In their glory, they had churned out hundreds of thousands of prints a day. I had a lot of reverence for these machines—the pinnacle of the four-hundred-year-old industry of spreading ideas. We were ready to begin.

CHOOM CHOOM CHOOM.

Forty-inch sheets bolted through the massive machine as each page was pressed by four unique metal plates with amazing speed and perfect registration—allowing four single-color images to mix on page and form an exact reproduction of my artwork. In a handful of seconds, the press recreated a few dozen times what took me a hundred hours.

Fred pulled off a sheet and, in a sweeping motion, placed a copy above the control panel. But it wasn't a copy of the work, was it? It was the work.

This was abundantly clear as I leaned over the sheet and realized just how *big* this thing was. I had this amazing feeling of actually discovering my own art.

"This is a cool one," Fred said.

"Yeah…I'm proud of it."

We went over it methodically, making a few marks with a Sharpie as we went. The side of my hand became slightly discolored from resting on the not-quite-dry press sheet.

"I think there's a little dust on one of the plates," I said. "And maybe we want to tone down the cyan on the left-hand side. It's probably my fault. I used blue in the shadows, but it's coming across as purple."

"You heard the man," Fred said to the technician, who adjusted a couple of sliders on what looked like a soundboard.

I was there to inspect the job and make any last-minute adjustments to make sure we got the highest-quality product for our client. I was there for business—but it was a pleasure. It was the moment when work comes to life—when screen becomes paper and pixels become ink. It was the moment when something imagined becomes real.

I went back to the waiting area with a rolled-up flat sheet of the approved art and again took a seat at the faux wooden table with my half-full cup of coffee, feeling like I no longer needed it. There was plenty of time to get comfortable. I had an hour before the first run concluded and the second side of the piece was ready for print, so I finally leaned back with the newspaper.

Ink from the paper mixed on my fingertips with the red ink already there. I found what I was looking for and began reading a recap of last night's Devils game.

As screens replace paper, the press check is becoming a dying ritual. Even in the five years I've been out of school, things have changed dramatically. More and more of my work is digital, and these big printed pieces have become rarer and rarer. For all the merits of designing for the Web, it's anticlimactic to have finished work living in the same environment you used to create it. There's no tangible sense of satisfaction in actually making an object, in having a project become unquestionably done.

But nostalgia can be a vice. You can only move forward. I put the newspaper down and picked up my smartphone—NHL.com should have video from last night's game.

The boys in the print shop hand cut and assembled a mock-up for me as the last step of the press check before the printed pieces went to another factory to be mechanically cut and assembled. It was an odd companion—a twenty-inch cube of high-gloss superhero. But I was really proud of it.

I rested my arm across it. I looked out the window as the black sedan drove onto the turnpike on-ramp en route to Manhattan via the Holland Tunnel—along the infamous stretch of highway that has all the sights and smells that live up to New Jersey's reputation.

When we drove by the Meadowlands, I couldn't help but rubberneck at the worst wreck the turnpike had ever seen—Xanadu. This proposed mega-mall was the latest attempt to turn Exit 16W into something other than a swamp—an endeavor that four major sports teams and a world-class racetrack couldn't pull off.

And the more you read, the more confounding this multibillion-dollar debacle became. A gigantic Ferris wheel overlooking the New Jersey Turnpike, an Egyptian-themed movie theater—complete with a rooftop lounge and helipad—and an indoor ski slope that almost seemed like a show of modesty.

But besides creating the world's most readable Wikipedia page, the project was an epic disaster. Construction was frozen, and corporate lawyers were hard at work trying to find escape clauses for the retailers. I felt bad for the people who were literally making it—the architects and designers. I've never been in a project of that scale, but I recognized the pitfalls of an open-air movie-theater lounge downwind from a Hess oil refinery.

Too many people had too much input. People—especially in a group—can become unable to view their work with unbiased eyes. The desire to do something spectacular overwhelms common sense, and mass delusion results in big, wrong decisions. And the handful of people who protest get drowned out by a committee that doesn't want to face the implications of the whole endeavor being a bad idea.

I looked again at my superhero shipper. I had a part in another billion-dollar project, didn't I? This project was part of a gigantic machine—a machine that churned out every piece of licensed product you can imagine, from breakfast cereals to school supplies to men's cologne. If you're paying attention, you'll notice that the image of this summer's superhero appearing in a Burger King Value Meal is the same image you see on a children's umbrella.

This is because before a licensor begins making that licensed T-shirt or pencil topper or laptop case, they are given guidelines as part of the licensing agreement. Any deviation from these guidelines gives the company the right to deny production. As a result, the country gets carpeted in millions of repeating superheroes. All in the same half-dozen heroic, generic poses—united in the mission to make sure the franchise has a singular image.

It's quality control. It's serious business. It's branding. And I deviated from that. Big time.

I didn't tweak an image or rotate a logo ninety degrees. I created a unique image of the title character. I literally redrew the face of the franchise. This is not something you can do. It's not allowed. I worked completely outside this gated garden on a project that will be the first glimpse of a major product line.

But it got approved.

I'd pushed my original image through the studio, the publisher, and the toy company—three distinct bureaucratic approval processes—and all it would have taken was one of them to chime in and send this the way of Xanadu.

But here it was, in my hands as I got out of the car and walked toward my apartment building. It was a ballsy move to commit to doing an original illustration, but judging by the reaction I was getting walking down the street, the gamble had paid off.

Every dude on Delancey was checking me out, ignoring their girlfriends as I walked by—all trying to gather the courage to say hello. So this is what a hot chick feels like, I thought to myself.

A giant box of toys…some things you just don't outgrow.

I put it up, on top of the dresser in my bedroom, and checked the time. I didn't have time to sit around, but I took one more glimpse. It was the accomplishment of my professional life.

Juror 10 was thumbing through her textbook, *Marketing and Social Media*, as we waited for the next case to begin. There were only a few days left in jury duty. Without Dhara in my head, I finally allowed myself to notice just how pretty a girl Juror 10 was.

Truth is, if I hadn't just dated Dhara, I probably would have found Juror 10 really intimidating. And the textbook—she'd gone back to school, which is a gutsy thing to do. You could sort of get that sense of independence from her. Maybe I'd ask her out. I mean, we did seem to have a similar sense of justice.

"Do you have to tweet your final paper?" I asked.

She smiled and brushed hair behind her ear. "Yeah, I have to keep it under 140 characters or else my grade is a Fail Whale."

"How's Fakebook going?" she asked. "Still convincing people you are in a cult?"

"Ha! Yeah, I'm wrapping that up," I said as I opened Facebook on my phone.

Dave Cicirelli
"Dave is no longer available."
Like · Comment

"Very ominous," she said with a smirk.

Our moment was interrupted when the bailiff announced the next case. "Tin Man."

It was a continued case, and everyone knew which one. We all steeled ourselves for a return visit from Amadi.

Instead we got a middle-aged Russian. He looked terrifying. His full black beard and unkempt hair made his piercing blue eyes seem to match his silver chain. He was built powerfully, an intimidating figure. Then he pulled out a badge.

"Please state your name for the court."

"Officer Patrick Malkin," he said in a thick accent.

"Please state your assignment."

"I'm undercover, part of a long-term investigation of illegal gun trafficking in upper Manhattan."

The usual line of questioning went on—the standard awkward legalese that gets all the formalities on the record. By the end of it, the "Russian gangster" had the same impatient attitude I'd recognized in Amadi's arresting officer.

"Are you familiar with Amadi Johnson?" the prosecutor asked, as he showed a picture of the defendant.

"Not by that name," he responded. "I know him as Nine Track."

"What is your relationship with Amadi Johnson, a.k.a. 'Nine Track'?"

"He delivers guns to me."

It hit the room hard. We sat there, absorbing this news. We'd thought, at worst, that Amadi made a bad decision that night. It never occurred to us that he might be a gun runner. Finding our worst suspicions not just confirmed, but exceeded, was devastating.

"Is this one such gun?"

The prosecutor pulled out a manila folder. In it were a photo and a forensics report on a handgun.

"Yes."

The prosecutor then read the report aloud. The gun was purchased without serial numbers and with bullets. The undercover officer had paid Nine Track seven hundred dollars.

Before we had a chance to fully process these details, the prosecutor produced another gun report from another sale. Another loaded gun. Another missing serial number. Another large sum of money.

It didn't make sense. Amadi was an underprivileged kid who barely had seven dollars to get to the neighborhood dance. He was scared shitless of the twenty-one adults sitting in front of him. Nine Track was a gangster who delivered guns to the Russian mobster who terrified the room.

A third gun report was produced. Then a fourth. And a fifth. And a sixth. We reached eleven before Officer Malkin was excused.

I thought about Amadi's testimony through a new lens, recalling how he'd repeated lines verbatim, like a rehearsed script. And the story—that he found a gun, tucked it in his boot, and was off to the authorities like a perfect little citizen—was ludicrous. It always was.

I thought back on Amadi and how he was presented to us. All the details: the wardrobe, having exactly seven dollars and not, say, ten. It all reinforced our discomfort and manipulated us into wanting his story to be true.

A handful of jurors clung to the discredited story. I hated it. I hated everything about it. But I couldn't stay silent.

I stood up and spoke against Nine Track. Because as comforting as it would have been and as much as it felt like the right thing to give him another chance—I realized that believing his story would have been a selfish act. Absolved from consequence, Amadi would return to his school and his neighborhood not as the scared kid we saw, but as Nine Track the emboldened gangster. The one we'd failed to stop. He'd be a PR win for the gang who exploited him.

And we'd be doing Amadi no favors, either—encouraging him further down a dangerous path. A path that led back to this courthouse, but the next time he'd be a little older and a hell of a lot less sympathetic, and under god knows what charges. Most of all, we sure wouldn't be doing anyone any favors if that trigger got pulled.

No, the only people who had anything to gain were us, the jury. We would have gained the delusion of living in a world where a scared sixteen-year-old kid was in the wrong place at the wrong time, and not in one where some fucking gang could seduce a desperate child to peddle their violence.

I want to live in a world where his story is true. But I don't. Instead I live in a world where I helped send Amadi Johnson, a scared kid who was dealt a shitty hand, one step closer to jail.

That night I grabbed my hockey stick and went to the handball court on Houston. In the summer, it's a madhouse, but you can count on it being deserted in the dead of winter. I was relieved to see that it was even plowed.

I wound up and took my first shot. It was as weak and inaccurate as ever, but the ball made a comforting "thud" against the wall just the same.

It was about as quiet a night as downtown can have, and the ambient sounds of city traffic were easily pierced by the various thuds and scraping sounds of mindless ball hockey. Combining with the deep breaths of cold winter air, it had an almost meditative effect on me.

I felt awful about what had happened in court. I couldn't get over how easily and deeply I had rationalized Amadi's story. I had forgotten how powerful a thing perception is. Truth can't be destroyed, but it can certainly be buried. And when it's buried, we have our hands on the shovel, don't we?

I wished Amadi's story to be true, and in doing so I was a willing participant in his lie—willing to connect the dots for him because I liked the picture that made. And for the first time, I truly understood how I was getting away with Fakebook.

The story I was telling tapped into the collective angst of my peers. Twenty-six is an overlooked age—not a kid anymore, but still not settled. The honeymoon phase of young adulthood is fading, and stretching out in front of us are the consequences of the course we set—a course that seemed like a good idea to the teenager who picked your major—for another sixty years.

When we were in our teens and early twenties, every ambition or goal was possible in the wide-open future—and our goals were wonderful ideals created by our imagination, not yet tarnished by becoming real.

For most of our lives, it didn't matter what our friends were doing with theirs. Whether they were going to a good school, playing in a band, or starting a landscaping business, no one had accomplished anything yet. It created the illusion that we were all the same. Everyone was at the beginning of their path toward a wide-open future.

But by our midtwenties, the future was beginning to narrow. We'd traveled different distances down divergent paths, and the gaps between us have turned into gulfs. And every time we log in to Facebook, the choices we didn't make, the lives we aren't living, are staring back at us through other people's profiles. Facebook can become a window to the world for each of us, just as the world begins to pass us by.

And we feel something. It's not jealousy, exactly. And it's not exactly nostalgia for our youth. It's a yearning—a sense of loss that comes with understanding that becoming who you are means saying good-bye to all the possibilities of who you could be.

And then there was Fakebook. Imagine that you're going through the motions of another Monday. After staring at a spreadsheet for the better part of the morning, you begin to lose motivation. In search of a thirty-second distraction, you click off Excel and log on to Facebook. Somewhere between the dozens of posts bragging about another great weekend, you stumble onto my page.

Here's a guy admitting publicly that, like you, he's in a rut. Like you, he doesn't have a plan. Like you, he doesn't know what he wants or how he's going to get it. But unlike you, he's not letting that stop him. So right when you are about to accept the inevitable narrowing of your potential—when you begin to acknowledge your only possible future because of the choices you've made—you see my story.

Dave, a guy you sort of know, walked away. He is walking away right now, while you're reading about it. He rejected the inevitability of the path he was on and has begun blazing a new one! In truth, it actually is only an escapist fantasy, but to your knowledge, it isn't fantasy at all. It could be you.

When I began Fakebook, I tried to remove people's emotional investment from the story. I thought it was messy and morally complicated. I didn't want people to care. Now, I realized that was never possible. My Facebook friends weren't simply unsuspecting victims of my hoax; they were its collaborators. Once they wanted to believe, Fakebook no longer needed to be convincing—it just needed to be rationalized. No one would believe Fakebook if they didn't believe in the *idea* of Fakebook just a little bit more.

The question was…was I starting to believe in Fakebook, too? Was pretending to quit my job and walk across the country just a pragmatic, quasi-believable premise to a practical joke? Was that all? Could I keep calling it a parody when, I realized now, so much of it felt completely sincere? Don't I also have a longing for a new adventure or the chance to start over?

I shot the orange street-hockey ball off the corner of the wall, and it deflected out of the court and into a grimy pile of plowed city snow. I scrambled up the pile with my feet cracking the dirty, iced-over surface and sinking in. As I plucked the ball out, I felt some of the city snow begin to melt into my socks. It was time to head home.

During the walk back, I sent out a post with a caption that felt as honest as anything I've ever written.

Dave Cicirelli
What a week.

Like · Comment · Share

Chris Buske where are you?
about an hour ago via mobile · Like

Dave Cicirelli Just south of the border. Long story. I'll fill everyone in a bit later. Playing on my iPhone is affecting my begging, ha.
about an hour ago via mobile · Like

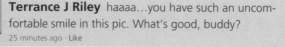

Terrance J Riley haaaa...you have such an uncomfortable smile in this pic. What's good, buddy?
25 minutes ago · Like

Enayet Rasul Can you smuggle some good tequila back to the good old USA?
3 minutes ago via mobile · Like

Dave Cicirelli I need to smuggle myself back first...
less than a minute ago via mobile · Like

Heh, I thought. It's almost funny: I longed to live in a world where Amadi Johnson wasn't a criminal. But my Facebook friends longed for a world where Dave Cicirelli was.

Tic, tic, tic, tic, tic.

Juror 8 typed away on her cracked iPhone.

"Can I help you turn off the sound?" I asked.

"Oh, I don't think that's a feature on this model."

Juror 10 and I exchanged a knowing look. At least I had tried.

The bailiff walked in. "No more cases for the day," he said, hands gesturing up in the air. "Thank you for your service. See you in seven to ten years!"

And with that, jury duty ended. A half dozen of us went out for drinks afterward in a crappy little bar just up the street. It was an easy environment to bond in—for the past month, we had all shared an experience. It felt appropriate to have a proper send-off.

But soon enough the crowd dwindled down, as people got back to their families or didn't want to trek home through the snow. Before long, it was just me and Juror 10.

We talked for a while about the things we saw at court—the characters in the jury or the funny behavior of some of the more harmless criminal cases. We joked about having a favorite stenographer, or that one lawyer who didn't know how to tuck in his shirt. Then we talked about our jobs, and how we both felt like it was time to try something new. How she was working full time and going to school at night, pursuing a new career in fashion journalism and marketing.

I told her how much that impressed me—that she had the guts to start something new. How I was finding myself especially impressed by that of late—by making a change in direction. Then I teased the aspiring fashion journalist for wearing giant snow boots.

She laughed and stuck out her foot, as if to model them. When she rested her leg, it was touching mine.

It was a snowy night, and I offered to hail a cab or walk her to the subway. She opted for the train. It was a long walk, considering the weather. But we trekked the two dozen blocks through puddles and slush, and she jokingly pointed out how dry her feet were inside those boots.

I suggested we cut through Washington Square Park because it'd be nice to see in the snow.

I'd had a lot of time during the month in court, during the time at the bar, during the walk through the park, to convince myself that she was too pretty to be interested in me. I'd had plenty of time to convince myself that the past month established a platonic relationship or that it was too soon to try something new after the Dhara disappointment. There were hundreds of reasons to protect myself from rejection.

But I didn't think about any of that. A little over a week ago, I'd completely exhausted myself with Fakebook, with work, with relationships. I'd crashed through the wall, and I was still in that echo. I didn't have the patience for overthinking, for indecision, for cowardice. I wasn't weighed down by worry. I'd lost interest in trying to navigate the haze of all the things I couldn't know.

Instead I focused on what I did know.

I knew that I was standing there in the center of the park with a beautiful girl in endearingly large boots. She brushed her light brown hair behind her ear. Her hair was dusted by freshly fallen snow. My feet were wet. Hers were dry. And the moment was lingering.

So I leaned in and kissed her.

Dave Cicirelli
Somehow I got down here without a passport, but apparently having one is pretty useful in getting back.

I'll fill everyone in on my daring escape that got me here in the first place, but first I need to cry for a few hours—mostly about these international roaming fees.

Like · Comment · Share

Elizabeth Lee Why don't you have your passport?
3 days ago via mobile · Like

Dave Cicirelli Shut up, mom.
3 days ago via mobile · Like

Dave Cicirelli Seriously, it's the same reason I left without a winter coat, the same reason I couldn't handle life in NY, and the same reason Kate cheated on me. I'm a screw up.
3 days ago via mobile · Like

Elizabeth Lee You're not a screw up. lol

There was no reason for the nasty comment, it was a

legit question. Can someone possibly mail it to you? You could rent a PO Box somewhere. Or, do you know anyone visiting Mexico any time soon? It's almost vacation season in Mexico.
3 days ago via mobile · Like

Dave Cicirelli Can some one even get it? I have no idea what was done with my apartment…I just left it. The landlord or new tenant probably used my passport to get a new identity…holy shit.
3 days ago via mobile · Like

Matt Campbell Find a US embassy. They may lock you up for being crazy after they hear how you got there…but you should do that before the Mexican police find you…
3 days ago via mobile · Like

Dave Cicirelli
I'm not sure how to make a poll on Facebook, so let's do a good old fashioned vote!

Now that I'm an illegal immigrant in Mexico, what ironic job should I try and get:

A) Day Laborer
B) Delivery Boy
C) Open a Mexican Restaurant
D) Border Agent

I'll also accept write-in votes.
Like · Comment

Danny Ross Water tester.
2 days ago via mobile · Like

Annette Pandolfo De Luca Open a restaurant. Then you can have your cousin the chef come and help!
2 days ago via mobile · Like

Mary Carroll Do they have a Home Depot parking lot? If so, everyday can be a new job.
2 days ago via mobile · Like

Stephen Papageorge Work for the cartels since they run Mexico…life expectancy may not be that long but at least you will have money to burn through.

2 days ago via mobile · Like

Ted Kaiser Find a coyote to get you back across the border. Although you probably have no money to give them at the moment so I guess try day laborer for a day. You did have a job doing driveways or something once didn't you? That can be useful now.

2 days ago · Like

Elizabeth Lee Option A.

2 days ago via mobile · Like

Elizabeth Lee Or u should work at a resort…You might make more cause you speak english.

2 days ago via mobile · Like

Matt Campbell Do they need landscapers in Mexico?

yesterday via mobile · Like

Dave Cicirelli

I'm at a bus stop. I found a church that set me up. I'm going on the move to a less heavily patrolled strip of border. I somehow crossed it once…

If I get into trouble, I can always rely on my signature tequila dance to get me out of a bind.

Like · Comment

Amanda Hirschhorn Just like Pee Wee Herman did during his Big Adventure!

yesterday via mobile · Like

Dave Cicirelli

"Keep, ancient lands, your storied pomp!" cries she
With silent lips. "Give me your tired, your poor,
Your huddled masses yearning to breathe free,
The wretched refuse of your teeming shore.
Send these, the homeless, tempest-tost to me,
I lift my lamp beside the golden door!"

Like · Comment · Share

Stephen Ortez good luck

about an hour ago via mobile · Like

Steve Cuchinello I would guess that it's a bad idea to try to climb that.

about an hour ago via mobile · Like

Matt Campbell You know there may be Minutemen on the other side of that fence? With rifles?

12 minutes ago via mobile · Like

Dave Cicirelli Yeah, the temple hooked me up with a group that does this a lot. I should be ok. The embassy is all the way in Mexico City, so I don't have much of a choice...

less than a minute ago via mobile · Like

For Fake Dave, things were moving again. It was a lot of fun putting him into a new adventure and having things move at a quicker pace. Nothing like a deadline to get things going.

But he wasn't the only one on the border of where he wanted to go. I was sitting on a leather couch across from a receptionist's desk, mentally rehearsing my portfolio presentation, about to have my first interview in over half a decade.

It's odd...I'd found all of my roommates in New York on Craigslist. I literally gave more than two dozen strangers from all over the world a key to my front door on the sheer faith that some unfiltered message board won't steer me wrong—but it felt weird looking on the website's job board, knowing they had a "hand job" board just one tab over.

But what did I know? Last time I looked for a job, Craigslist wasn't really a thing. Instead I had a New York graphic design directory and started cold-calling individuals, A to Z, looking for internships. I can't say I recommend that approach, either. It was long and grueling, and my calls were usually unwelcomed. So I bit the bullet and applied for this Craigslist posting.

Today, I maybe was a little nervous, but mostly I felt confident. I was hustling. The part of me that had cold-called a hundred art directors was reactivated, and it felt good. After all, judging by the reception area, this looked like a pretty legit operation. Who cared that I'd never heard of LiveWired Products? It was a bustling place, somewhere between cool and crowded. All sorts of people quickly walking around, talking about sales numbers and exchange rates and all sorts of things that you don't hear in the non-physical marketing practice. It felt like a place where real things happen.

"Mr. Cicirelli," the receptionist said. "Freddy is ready to see you."

I stood up and followed her to a large conference room overlooking Broadway, with Times Square just visible a few blocks to the north. Freddy was sitting at the large dark wood table. He stood up—he was a short guy, maybe five-foot-four, with his mostly gray hair slightly disheveled.

We shook hands.

"How are you? How are you? Please, take a seat."

You could tell right away that he was a bit of a character. Maybe a little bit of a hustler himself. I immediately liked him.

"So," he said. "Show me your work."

I pulled out my laptop and began to go through my portfolio.

"That's a very nice laptop," he said. "Is that yours, or does your company own it?"

"It's mine," I replied. "Yeah, a MacBook Pro, under a year old. I'm still paying it off," I said with a laugh.

"Very nice," he said in a serious tone.

He opened a bin and spread its contents out over the table. It was full of electronics and accessories. Computer mice, iPhone cases, brightly colored digital cameras geared for children.

"This is our current product line. Tell me what you think," he said.

I began looking through it, looking at both the packaging and the products themselves. It was pretty decent. It was not high end, but they seemed willing to try things.

"Be honest," he said to me. "I don't lie to people, and I don't like being lied to. You can say whatever you feel. If you think they are pieces of shit, say 'Freddy, these are pieces of shit.' If you think I'm a piece of shit, say 'Freddy, you're a piece of shit.'"

We both laughed. "I'm serious," he continued. "I've heard it all. 'Freddy, you're shit. I hate you. Go to hell.' I can handle it. I'm used to it."

"I think they're pretty good," I said. "I do. But there are things I would change…which I guess is why I'm here."

"Go on," he said.

"Well, these mice are really great. These metallic, pastel-colored accents really pop against the black body. It's a really nice product."

"It's our best seller," he said with pride.

"I believe it," I said. "But look at the packaging. You have them sitting on a shiny silver backboard. It overpowers the color—it kills the contrast."

I took a mouse out of its packaging, along with the silver backboard. I placed them both on the black table.

"See," I said, holding the mouse over the silver insert. "Your eyes are drawn to contrast, so against the silver, you mostly see the black."

I then removed the silver so the mouse was sitting against the dark wood conference table. "And now, your eyes mostly see the color—and it's these colors that make this product unique."

"Yeah, I do see," Freddy said.

I felt really good about what I saw. I could see us making decisions together, rather than throwing my work out to account staff proxies who then sent it to brand managers who then sent it to lawyers I'd never speak to. I could have a say here.

"I think we could use a guy like you," Freddy said. "We've been outsourcing all of our design work, but we're a growing company. We have products selling like popcorn. We want to build an art department. We're investing in it—spending lots of money."

My ears perked up a bit.

"We want LiveWired to have a singular vision, from the product to the packaging. All of it. How does that sound?"

"It sounds exciting."

"Now, I want to be totally honest with you. And you can always trust me. I never lie. But for the short term, you would be the art department. But we're building, and it would be building underneath you."

"That sounds like an opportunity," I said.

"Well, I don't want to keep you, but we'll be in touch."

"Thanks, Freddy. Great meeting you."

I hopped on the subway and returned to Handler from my "lunch break." An opportunity to build something, and it would be mine. That was tempting. When I walked back into the Handler PR graphics bullpen, I saw a reminder of how much was possible.

Public relations is a unique place to be a designer. We're not a known quantity the way a studio is in an ad agency, and it's not why a client comes to a PR firm as if it were a proper design firm. But the big mission statement of PR is "get people talking," and within that is an unrecognized opportunity for design.

I started as an unpaid intern without a desk—landscaping three days a week so I could afford the train ride to the city. I did nothing but trim and file.

Before the summer ended, however, I had a new art director who wanted to push things. Following her lead, we did. Design became part of how Handler did PR. We became a proper studio that won business and won awards. We built portfolios in an industry where it shouldn't have been possible.

I was proud of my part in that. It was a long road from cold-calling art directors and inventing an internship to the graphics bullpen with a wall full of awards. It was a long road indeed.

But it felt at its end.

"Wait? Now you're hooking up with a girl from jury duty?" Mark said with surprise.

"Well, yeah, I guess," I answered back into my phone, as I rotated my living-room chair and caught a glimpse of my superhero shipper—compounding my sense of pride.

"And the last girl…you met her on the JFK Air Train? I thought you were bad at this!"

"Government infrastructure, it seems, is my sweet spot."

"Unbelievable."

"Your tax dollars at work."

"I thought what I was about to tell you would cheer you up, but doesn't sound like you need it."

"I could always be happier. What's up?"

"A project came up at Lisa's work, so she can't make it to Jackson Hole. Want to take her place? Four days of skiing and eating game meat—leave Thursday night, come back Monday. It's already paid for."

A free trip to the Rockies…that sounded pretty great. And lord knew I could use a vacation. But man…I'd spent a lot of time out of the office. The perception was that I'd had a month of half days. Asking for time off this soon after wouldn't go over well, especially with short notice.

Listen to me. A group of people used the phrase "pulling a Cicirelli," but the real Dave Cicirelli was worried about taking a long weekend? Screw it. I was expecting an offer from LiveWired anyway.

"Yeah," I said. "Sounds great."

The whole flight over, we were calling it a "bro-cation." This, we decided, was like a normal vacation, but with a lot more high-fiving. The trip was off to a good start. But during the lulls in conversation on the flight there, I began to write.

I was in a different place than at any other point of Fakebook. The end no longer felt a long way off, but almost imminent. If Fakebook crashed now, so be it. I was comfortable with my life, with its opportunities and its challenges. I felt capable, more sure-footed than I had been when I started this. I felt like I had some clarity.

So when I wrote the long-awaited explanation of how Fake Dave ended up in Mexico, I wrote it uninhibitedly. It was long; it was insane; it was highly implausible.

But it was more than that. It was an expression of all I'd done. It felt personal and, in its own way, completely honest. A couple hours after touchdown, from a hotel lobby in Jackson Hole, Wyoming, I sent out the note that sent Fakebook toward its final, absurd conclusion.

MARCH 6: I'M FREE...FREE FALLING

I've always loved my country, but I've never had the opportunity to miss it. I miss it now, living in its shadow.

I was so vulnerable when the Center recruited me. I was empty, desperate, and in pain. I was physically weak from the hospital, emotionally drained from Kate, and spiritually drained from the failures of my travel.

I went to the Center with outward skepticism and arrogance, but deep down yearned for what they promised—belonging. But while they promised a path towards acceptance, they withheld its fruition—creating a sick dependency which controlled me.

We were allowed to look no further than the Center. How could they build a paradise without quarantine from the wicked? We were told that outside influence created dissent, and dissent created conflict, which is what pushes us towards imbalance.

But somewhere deep down I couldn't quite commit to the idea, and I was caught posting to Facebook and the outside world.

I only have a vague sense of what happened after that. I know there was isolation and sleep deprivation. Dream and reality meshed together, and the impossible things I saw looked and felt so real. During this time I had...almost a vision.

I was back in my old life, walking down the street in New York. I realize I'm caught on something. It's a web...no, more like a fabric that all of humanity is woven into, and it's suddenly visible to me. Once I have this glimpse, I'm overcome with the urge to unlock its secrets. I begin to pull at the thread that holds me.

As I loosen the stitching, I begin to float above the world, seeing more and more, gaining a deeper and deeper understanding of life, as I become less a part of it. Soon only a single, hair-width thread anchors me. I can see almost everything. I'm so close to the epiphany that I yearned for, that clarity that I seek…to finally know the world and how it works…to finally understand…

When I free myself of that final thread, for a moment, I float above the world and see everything.

But then, like a bolt of lightning, I realize that I'm not floating. I never was. I'm falling. I am falling without any control, and the entire world is spiraling above me, spiraling out of reach. Finally, after an eternity of free fall, I see something far away, but falling with me.

It is Kate.

I yell for her, and she yells for me. But we continue to fall separately but together.

She was just like me. We both sacrificed the lives we had for an empty promise. We were the only two people that could possibly ever relate to each other, and I pushed her away.

***

When I woke up, I was in Mexico.

Whatever the Center did to me was meant to break me down—turn me into a blank slate for the Center to write over. It sort of worked. I was purged, but purged of the Center.

I feel clear. I'm in a bad spot, but it's going to get better. I befriended people in the temple who got me in touch with a network of border crossers. If all goes well, I'll soon be back in the States.

I'm not sure what happens next, but for the first time in a long time, I feel prepared for it.

Jay Patterson This sh!t is unreal man.

less than a minute ago via mobile · Like

Greg Cicchelli You need to write a book.

less than a minute ago via mobile · Like

Elliott Askew Am I the only person following this that thinks Dave's story is bullshit? I mean…this stuff just doesn't happen…

just now · Like

Uh oh.

11 | places

Last night, I created a post that could destroy Fakebook—but I didn't know it yet. Instead I had breakfast on my mind.

"I'll have the duck sausage," Mark said to the waitress, "and the bison bacon."

"Two sides?" the waitress at the Snake Creek Lodge asked.

"Oh right. I guess eggs and toast as well," Mark said.

My brother's gluttony is one of his most endearing qualities…if only because he enjoys it so damn much. He approaches each meal with such an unbridled, child-like sense of wonder and enthusiasm—like a kid who realizes he can have sprinkles on his ice cream.

"I'll just have the oatmeal," I said, looking at the prices.

"That's ridiculous," Mark said.

"No, I'm all right," I said. "That's all I want."

"You got it," the waitress said, and began walking away.

"Actually…" my brother called to her, "can you swap the eggs with…elk sausage?"

Mark and I are very similar in a lot of ways, but we're still separated by the lifestyle distance you can achieve between your midtwenties and your midthirties, and with an Ivy League MBA versus a state-school art degree. And more often than I'm comfortable with, when we get food together, he'll pick up the bill.

"Bro," Mark said to me while I was scraping the last bit of oatmeal from my bowl. "Listen, I know some of these meals are expensive. But I got it. I won't enjoy the trip as much if you just eat oatmeal."

"Yeah," I said. "But Mark, I don't know…It's like when I order something, I'm appealing to your generosity. I don't want to assume things, you know?"

"Of course not," Mark said. "And the moment you act that way is the moment it ends."

"Ha. Fair enough," I said, "but still. I don't feel right about it."

Mark cut a slice of elk sausage and put it on my plate.

"You pick up the beer," he said, "and I'll pick up the game meat. Take a bite."

So I did. "*Holy shit!*" I exclaimed. That was a rather inappropriate thing to yell out in a crowded family restaurant, but I stand by it. My god...why don't we have more elk in the world?

"Holy shit," I whispered, looking somewhat sheepishly around the restaurant and eventually at my laughing brother.

I'm a novice skier. This trip was just my third trip ever. But I'm halfway decent, considering. I spent the morning on my own, going down a few of the less challenging slopes. I felt pretty good.

As early afternoon came around, I thought it time to join my brother on a more challenging trail, so I hopped on the gondola. It wasn't a ski lift like the others, where your feet dangle. It was an enclosed tram car and I felt a little cheated of the open-air views. Still, even through the window I could appreciate the sheer aesthetic of Grand Teton looming over us and the skiers below.

There's just something about the scale of mountains that moves me.

I've spent my whole life going through seven-foot doorways into rooms with eight-foot ceilings. Even living in New York, a city built for a staggering volume of people but still scaled for people. It's a dense sea of doorways and chairs and windows and taxi cabs. And for all the chaos of a city, it's still an environment that has you and me in mind.

Not true of mountains. Mountains are indescribably big. And riding a gondola to the top of one is a great reminder of our place. Looking out the window, I just marveled at it. How the ski lodge that I and a thousand other people were staying in looked small and pathetic from there. How the canopy of towering trees and gigantic boulders were suddenly small—nothing more than a texture that carpeted the landscape, made with total indifference toward our convenience.

Just then, it dawned on me…I'd been on this gondola way too long. I was supposed to ski all the way down? That was insane. It was a fucking mountain!

I felt my phone vibrate as we finally approached the top. I took a quick look—it was Ted calling. I lifted my gaze from my phone and noticed the curvature of the earth falling away below me.

If this is the last chance I ever have to talk to another human being, I thought, I didn't want it to be Ted.

I put my phone back in my pocket and took my first cautious, terrified push down the mountain, trying to ignore the flock of birds flying below.

When I finally got back to the ski village at the base of the mountain, I was exhausted and relieved. I wobble-walked back through the ski lodge's impressive entrance—something that had looked so small from that mountaintop—and headed toward my room. I tossed my clothes off into a lump and took a shower.

Only after I fished my phone out of the pockets of my terror-sweat-soaked pants did I see the real reason to be alarmed. I had five missed calls from Ted. Something was up.

I give Ted a ring—still too relieved to be back on earth for the implications of his frantic calling to really register.

"Where were you?" Ted exclaimed. "I've been trying to call you all afternoon!"

"I'm sorry, Ted," I said. "I had more pressing concerns." Like fast-approaching cliffsides.

"Have you been on Facebook today?"

"Nah. Hey, you ever wonder why no one invented skis with brakes yet?"

"Look. Now."

So I did.

Elliott Askew
Am I the only person following this that thinks Dave's story is bullshit? I mean…this stuff just doesn't happen…
Like · Comment

Ted Kaiser Who knows, Elliott. It is a mystery of our time like Big Foot or the Loch Ness Monster. What is there to say about Dave? He has been delusional for a while now. He could be in Mexico or just laying in a gutter somewhere in Arizona and just thinks he's in Mexico. I gave up trying to help him. Dave wanted to see this through, real or not.
39 minutes ago via mobile · Like

"I see," I said.

Elliott's accusation scared me and surprised me a little. It even excited me a little. Was this it? Was this the moment I had both dreaded and courted for all these past months: the moment I would finally be called out as a phony for the whole world to see?

"Well, Ted, I like what you wrote."

And I did. It was a perfect response. Ted's ability to never challenge anyone's suspicions but instead deflect their curiosity had been really effective in getting people to accept the uncertainty of Fakebook with a shrug of their shoulders.

And suggesting that I may not be a reliable narrator was a stroke of genius. It was savvy and clever and something I frankly wish I'd thought of. It compounded the mystery rather than dismissing it—suggesting that there might be a complex alternative to the whole thing falling apart. It's like when your mom tells you that the mall Santa works for the real Santa.

I left the room and went in search of my brother, who was sitting at a table in the outdoor deck under a heat lamp. He'd ordered lunch—we were splitting a gourmet bison burger and each having a glass of wine. I couldn't wait to take a bite.

"This is it," I told him. "Someone called Fakebook out. I think I'm at the end of the road."

"What are you going to do now?" Mark asked.

"What else can I do? Confess."

Elliott Askew
Am I the only person following this that thinks Dave's story is bullshit? I mean…this stuff just doesn't happen…
Like · Comment

Ted Kaiser Who knows, Elliott. It is a mystery of our time like Big Foot or the Loch Ness Monster. What is there to say about Dave? He has been delusional for a while now. He could be in Mexico or just laying in a gutter somewhere in Arizona and just thinks he's in Mexico. I gave up trying to help him. Dave wanted to see this through, real or not.
46 minutes ago via mobile · Like

Dave Cicirelli You caught me. I'm actually enjoying a long ski weekend in Jackson Hole. Last night I had a $46 cut of free range Elk steak after a first course of duck sausage. Currently I'm taking a break from the slopes with a glass of Malbec wine at the Four Seasons.

Cheers.
just now via mobile · Like

Mark and I let out an evil laugh and toasted my moment of honesty. We even took a photo commemorating the occasion. It was so perfect. It captured my smug look of satisfaction. I was even tempted to post it—to have this image of my shit-eating grin be the definitive end of Fakebook.

But I resisted.

And before I had a chance to finish my Four Seasons bison burger with wild boar bacon and crumbled blue cheese that had been aged eight months in an oak cask, Elliott responded.

Elliott Askew

Am I the only person following this that thinks Dave's story is bullshit? I mean…this stuff just doesn't happen…

Like · Comment

Ted Kaiser Who knows, Elliott. It is a mystery of our time like Big Foot or the Loch Ness Monster. What is there to say about Dave? He has been delusional for a while now. He could be in Mexico or just laying in a gutter somewhere in Arizona and just thinks he's in Mexico. I gave up trying to help him. Dave wanted to see this through, real or not.

an hour ago via mobile · Like

Dave Cicirelli You caught me. I'm actually enjoying a long ski weekend in Jackson Hole. Last night I had a $46 cut of free range Elk steak after a first course of duck sausage. Currently I'm taking a break from the slopes with a glass of Malbec wine at the Four Seasons.

Cheers.

12 minutes ago via mobile · Like

Elliott Askew I called the tattoo shop. They never even heard of Dave Cicirelli.

just now · Like

"*What?*" I blurted out.

"What's the matter?" Mark asked facetiously. "They didn't try to pass off a 2008 Malbec as a 2007, did they?"

"No…Elliott called Tatooine, and they denied I worked there. Chris was supposed to have me covered!"

"Wait, Elliott? Elliott Askew? I think I used to babysit him."

I ignored him as I frantically dialed Tatooine.

"Hi, this is Dave Cicirelli. Is Chris Bailey there?"

"Speaking."

"What happened?" I asked.

"Wait? Is this about that guy from Facebook? I'm sorry, dude. My partner picked up when your friend called. He didn't know."

"All right…" I said, somewhat deflated.

"Good luck, dude."

I put my phone down and took a gulp of wine.

I don't know why I underestimated Elliott when I posted my wise-ass truthful response. To be honest, I don't know if I was even thinking about him when I did it. It was just such an opportunity to get away with yet another thing. Through all this, I clearly still can't resist the temptation.

If I'd been thinking clearly, I could have followed Ted's lead and deflected Elliott's questions. I could have raised the stakes on him tugging on the thread—after all, he took a risk and called me a liar. If he was wrong and I was actually peso-less, struggling to get back to America after narrowly avoiding total brainwashing by a nefarious cult leader…well, he'd really look like a twat.

It was checkmate.

"You all right, Bro?" Mark asked.

"Yeah…I guess this is it," I said. "It's funny. I almost feel relieved. I mean…I've been simultaneously courting and deferring this moment for half a year. Part of me…part of me thinks, 'Let this be it.'"

I glanced over my shoulder at the mountain. I could see the gondola that we took up that morning go all the way to the peak. My phone was vibrating on the tabletop. The incoming call was from a New Jersey area code. I knew exactly who it was.

"Hello, Elliott."

Elliott Askew was exactly who Fakebook was all about. He was the perfect Facebook friend—an out-of-sight, out-of-mind acquaintance whom Facebook never allowed to stay out of sight.

Prior to Facebook, we would have had an entirely different and thinner relationship. He'd be a fading memory—someone I knew within a context that long ago expired.

But the image in my mind of who Elliott is remains sharp—it's constantly updating on my news feed. Photos remind me what he looks like; posts reflect his sensibility; details give me a bullet-point list of what he is doing, where he is living, who he hangs out with.

The version of Elliott who inhabits my perception of the world—that character on my personal stage—is a new type of relationship. He's a memory rooted in real life, in real interactions, in real shared experiences he and I had a long time ago, but that memory has been updated and largely replaced by content offered through his own discretion.

So rather than fade, Elliott Askew, the memory, has been digitally fossilized, as bit by bit of what was real has been replaced by the 0s and 1s of information—until Elliott Askew has become a digital projection.

Figuring out what that meant—that's what Fakebook was originally all about. It was a reaction to this new type of relationship. It was born out of the disconnect between people and the images they broadcast. But right now, Elliott, not his profile, was on the other end.

"Is this Dave?" His voice was energized. I recognized the reaction from my own—from the surreal moments of Fakebook, like texting my secret foil on the Williamsburg Bridge three months ago. It sounded as if Elliott couldn't believe any of this was happening. I'd had almost six months to prepare for this, and part of me couldn't believe it, either.

"Yep," I said with a fair amount of fear. "So…you caught me, huh?"

"So it is all bullshit? You're still in New York?"

"Well…my last post was true, actually. I'm in Wyoming, skiing. Heh."

"You son of a bitch!"

I wasn't sure how serious his anger was. He sounded angry, but not exclusively. Like he couldn't decide what he thought of it all. His entire context of me was shifting. He was bridging the gap between what he'd experienced on Facebook and what was happening in real life.

"And Ted's in on it too, isn't he?"

"Some people are in on it, but I'll leave it up to them if they want to be revealed or not."

"Ted's definitely in on it.'"

I laughed a bit. His anger seemed to subside a little, giving way to amusement. He was solving a mystery, uncovering the twist of this story he'd been following daily. And this conversation—the satisfaction of uncovering the truth—was a payoff.

"I mean—listen," I said. "I just want to apologize if this caused you any trouble...That was never my intention. Just the idea for doing this...well, it just seemed inevitable. It just felt like someone was going to do it, and I thought I'd make it funny. I didn't expect this to be anything more than harmless entertainment."

"Oh, it was entertaining. It was so damn amusing. I checked it every day, just to see what was happening next," he said. "And you're right. People took it seriously. You were a hero—people would say, 'Man...work was rough. I want to pull a Cicirelli.' And I'd be like...'*He almost just died!*'"

"Hahaha...I'm sorry. But things like that, I love hearing that. I'm sorry, though."

We talk for a while longer. I could hear in his voice how he was wrapping his head around it. He told me that he'd been pacing around his apartment all day, trying to reconcile my dream quest and the cult and all the oddities with the reality he was clinging to. He told me that he found himself explaining away any discrepancies he noticed. And to my immense satisfaction, he compared himself to a kid who was trying to still believe in Santa Claus.

I told him that I wouldn't have doubted a thing if our roles were reversed. It was true.

"Listen, man," I said. "I was going to end this thing on April 1 no matter what. I was really cautious at first. To be totally honest, I was scared shitless of getting caught. But I'm past that point now...This thing is coming to an end. I wasn't going to be able to do it forever, and I'm not willing to dovetail it back into my real life...That feels too dishonest."

"Have to draw a line somewhere..." Elliott said.

"Well, yeah," I replied. "I mean, that's what's interesting to me—the complete separation of real life and Facebook. Otherwise it's just a pointless hoax."

"Yeah, I can see that."

"So, I guess what I'm getting at is…thank you. You helped make this ride so interesting. You, Joe Lennon, Matt Campbell—the whole gang who followed from the beginning." I look at the mountain again and the trail heading down it. "A bunch of individual posts kind of added up into something, didn't they? We did something pretty cool, I think."

"Yeah…" he said. I could almost hear a sense of loss in his voice. Fakebook was ending. And he was losing it—first he was losing the adventure he'd followed, and now he was losing the adventure he took in unraveling it.

The conversation ended. I leaned against the faux rustic wood fence and stared out at the landscape. I could feel my legs ache a little from the morning's excursion. I took a breath of mountain air. The biggest project of my life was ending. But I was glad it had happened here, two thousand miles from my criminally expensive 250 square feet under the Williamsburg Bridge.

My brother and I went out for a couple of beers. We toasted the end of Fakebook and the return of my life—whatever that was going to be.

Even though I was mostly at peace with it ending, enough of me was too reluctant to watch it break down. I turned off my phone and retreated to reality. After all, even though Fakebook was essentially over, real life kept going. Tomorrow was Monday, and I'd fly back to the city and go back to my old life. But it wasn't really my old life. The week ahead was going to give me an answer about a new job. I had dinner plans with a new girl. Chapters close, but the story goes on.

A bit later, with a few beers giving me courage, I turned on my phone to see the end of Fakebook.

Elliott Askew
Am I the only person following this that thinks Dave's story is bullshit? I mean…this stuff just doesn't happen…
Like · Comment

Ted Kaiser Who knows, Elliott. It is a mystery of our time like Big Foot or the Loch Ness Monster. What is there to say about Dave? He has been delusional for a while now. He could be in Mexico or just laying in a gutter somewhere in Arizona and just thinks he's in Mexico. I gave up trying to help him. Dave wanted to see this through, real or not.
3 hours ago via mobile · Like

Dave Cicirelli You caught me. I'm actually enjoying a long ski weekend in Jackson Hole. Last night I had a $46 cut of free range Elk steak after a first course of duck sausage. Currently I'm taking a break from the slopes with a glass of Malbec wine at the Four Seasons.

Cheers.
2 hours ago via mobile · Like

Elliott Askew I called the tattoo shop. They never even heard of Dave Cicirelli.
2 hours ago · Like

Elliott Askew Actually the tattoo parlor owner just called me back…he was concerned about you. I guess you didn't cash your last pay check. Not that impoverished I guess.
2 hours ago · Like

Joe Lennon So we have real life confirmation on our side of the veil that he worked there?
about an hour ago via mobile · Like

Elliott Askew Yeah. I was really surprised by the call back…more horrified really though that this is actually happening.
about an hour ago · Like

What? Apparently, Fakebook wasn't over just yet.

On Monday morning, I looked over at Mark sitting in the waiting area of the Jackson Hole airport. He looked a little insane, gnawing at a piece of duty-free elk jerky in a futile attempt to wean himself off elk steak.

It seemed a good time to begin the next chapter of Fakebook—one last big push into absurd character assassination.

Dave Cicirelli

The kindness and spirit of my fellow border crossers is really inspiring. I'm simply attempting to go home after my own self indulging run from responsibility. These men and women are enduring great risk as a first step down a difficult and uncertain path to a better life for their families. And still, they share all they have with me.

Like · Comment · Share

Dave Cicirelli

Everywhere around the world

They're coming to America...

Like · Comment · Share

Dave Cicirelli
Maybe I'll be a journalist after I return to the real world. I seem to have a great skill in emerging myself into different communities. Maybe one day I can get back in touch with my new hermanos and see where their new lives have taken them. I'm in a great position to tell their story, now that I am so close to them.
Like · Comment

This was, of course, all set up for the horrible twist. The second chance to continue this story made me go at it with reckless abandon. Every weird, cruel, and humiliating idea that I found funny but unacceptable to implement was now back on the table. I was living my fake life on borrowed time. And, I figured, if Elliott was willing to throw Joe Lennon under the bus, I should be willing to throw Fake Dave under the bus headfirst.

So a few hours later, as I touched down in Dallas for a connecting flight, I did.

Dave Cicirelli
I panicked. Yelling out "I FOUND THEM!!!" when the Minutemen approached is unquestionably the worst thing I've ever done in my life.

Like · Comment · Share

Claire Burke Dude.
less than a minute ago via mobile · Like

Ray Chan You're like a modern day Benedict Arnold!
less than a minute ago via mobile · Like

Kevin Conway Real scummy move Dave…I don't get you anymore…
less than a minute ago via mobile · Like

Ted Kaiser I've been judging you since you started walking across the George Washington Bridge.
less than a minute ago via mobile · Like

Erin Brennan Hanson boooooo
less than a minute ago via mobile · Like

Dave Cicirelli We were all boned. I didn't cause that. I thought if I passed myself off as a camper or something I'd at least have a chance. How dare you people judge me.
just now via mobile · Like

It was one of the more messed-up posts of Fakebook. Hell, it even gave me pause. But damn it, it made me laugh. It had taken nearly all of these six months for me to get comfortable enough with myself to completely destroy my reputation, and I felt…okay about it.

After all, that was the plan. I'd started Fakebook to be a self-deprecating, absurdist adventure that would court people's voyeurism and get people to question what they saw on Facebook. And if Elliott was my audience, then that's exactly what had happened. I held his interest for nearly six months. I kept pushing Fakebook into stranger places until he couldn't bury his doubts anymore. I rode it off the rails to where he finally stopped believing it and called me out right on my wall—just like it was supposed to happen.

But then he surprised me. He changed his mind. When he held the fate of Fakebook in his hands…he undid its destruction. He protected it. There was something powerful about that.

For so much of Fakebook's history, it was about pushing things until they became undone. But now that it had happened, it felt so hollow. The story of Fake Dave felt real to me now, despite the strange places it continued to go.

Looking back at Fakebook as an almost completed whole, I could see there were accidental themes. I actually wasn't writing a series of unrelated events and Photoshop gags—I was drawn to certain story beats, to certain conflicts. Even when I tried to subvert a belief, I was still guided by what resonated—and what resonated to me also spoke to my audience. I didn't set out to write a Facebook novel, but it seems I couldn't avoid doing so. Just like everyone else, I was choosing what to post, and my life and my anxieties couldn't help but be a part of those decisions.

And that's why there was a connection strong enough to make a guy like Elliott pace around his apartment, gathering the courage to find out for sure. That's why he gave me the opportunity to write a real ending. I just had to figure out what it would be.

Somewhere between responding to people's judgments and an unsuccessful search for airport elk burgers, the real world chimed in. A job offer arrived from LiveWired. It was exciting—validating even.

This was something I wanted, but suddenly I became nostalgic for Handler before I even quit. I wasn't sure I wanted to take the LiveWired job. I didn't want to jump at the first new job presented to me…but I didn't want to pass on it because I was scared of something new, either. I wasn't sure what to do.

I looked over at a big sign just outside the food court. "Welcome to Texas." Funny, for the first time since Fakebook began, Fake Dave and I were in the same state. Too bad for him, I had the passport.

Dave Cicirelli

I'm being taken in for questioning, if that makes people feel any better. They think I'm a coyote.

Like · Comment

Dave Cicirelli Oh god…They couldn't possibly put me in the same cell as these people…could they?
3 hours ago via mobile · Like

Matt Campbell Whoah man. I think it is time to get some legal help. You could do some serious time for this.
3 hours ago via mobile · Like

Ted Kaiser Putting you in the same cell would be eerily ironic.
3 hours ago via mobile · Like

Jay Patterson your adventure is un-real. But I believe it. Too bad the publishing rights will barely cover your upcoming legal fees.
2 hours ago via mobile · Like

Matt Campbell Due to the lack of communication, I would assume that this questioning is not going well.
45 minutes ago via mobile · Like

Steve Cuchinello Perhaps they will also discover the warrant out for his arrest in Pennsylvania for kidnapping.
36 minutes ago via mobile · Like

Matt Campbell Kidnapping? Can you get in trouble with a willing participant who is of age? I was worried that Jonathon may have pursued the hate crime threat…
less than a minute ago via mobile · Like

The long ride on the J line wasn't as exciting as last time with Dhara, so I just sort of meditated while watching the outer boroughs of Brooklyn and Queens pass by through the window. I had a job offer and a dinner planned with Juror 10, and I had just publicly assassinated my own character. It was a productive trip.

When I got home, I threw my bag down, kicked off my shoes, and lay on top of my covers with the lights off. I couldn't help but wonder what Fakebook must look like to someone who was just getting to know me.

So I sent Juror 10 a text: "I hope you like jury-based humor. Keep an eye on Facebook."

I was going to do a post that was meant for her—an attempt to build a relationship out of Washington Square Park.

I put the phone down on my chest. I was tired and had work in the morning, but my mind was too active for sleep. I looked ahead at my bedroom wall. The ambient light of the building to the north came in through the curtainless window, as the heavy bass of the nightclub on my east permeated through our shared wall as a low-register beat. A house-music lullaby.

LiveWired offered me the opportunity to build an art department, to build a brand, and to make real things. I'd finally break free of being in service to a service industry. But the job at Handler wasn't without its merits.

Balanced on the dresser that didn't quite close was my superhero shipper. If I left Handler, this was what I'd be giving up. For a guy who grew up drawing superheroes in the margins of every notebook I ever owned and idolizing Jack Kirby, projects like these were really special.

While most people know of Stan Lee, Kirby, in my mind, was the truer genius. He was the artist that co-created almost every superhero you can name—dozens of characters and whole worlds that have continued to endure for well over fifty years. Captain America, The Hulk, the X-Men, Thor, Fantastic Four, and Iron Man—to name just a few. It's amazing how prolific and enduring his legacy in popular culture has been. Each one of these characters has outlived him and spawned billions of dollars and hundreds of millions of fans.

His illustrations have a pop-art quality, with their unapologetic grandeur and powerful dynamism. But the brilliance isn't easily accessible—it's out of step with modern, naturalistic sensibilities. I mean, his drawings mock the very notion of nuance—but there is a deep humanity to them. How else could all the crazy, ridiculous concepts he came up with manage to endure?

Take the Silver Surfer, for example. That one still astonishes me. A surfer…who is silver. What a dumb idea. I mean, if the thought of a shiny spaceman on a surfboard crossed my mind, I'd dismiss it immediately. It's outlandish. But the way Kirby drew him…it was like the Surfer was sculpted out of cosmic marble, evoking all the nobility and grandeur of Greek myth. In Kirby's hands, the Surfer was a god who, to soar through the universe, simply needed a place to stand.

And within that weird, cool image he infused a tragic irony. For despite how much the Silver Surfer's flight evoked freedom, he himself was a slave—forever in search of new worlds to be sacrificed for the appeasement of his creator. That is, until he arrived on Earth and was forced out of the sky. Here, he walked among those whose doom he heralded, and discovered his humanity. He turned on his master and saved Earth. His punishment was to become exiled to it. He regained his soul, but it cost him the sky.

It's so elegant and grand. A beautiful and bold tale of compromise and rediscovery wrapped up in a cosmic adventure that's captured imaginations for fifty years and counting. The Silver Surfer. Such an inspiring, exciting, enduring, beautiful, tragic story that Kirby created out of such an incredibly dumb idea.

And to think—he grew up here on Delancey Street, where I live now. I lay on my bed—eighty feet and eighty years away from where a young Jack Kirby had lain on his—and looked into the eyes I had drawn on a face he imagined.

Kirby was a guy like me. He had bills to pay; he had deadlines; he had a boss. He was a guy working for a wage. He made a living and not much more. Hell, he made less than the lawyer who approved my version of his creation.

But he built a legacy out of nothing but pencil lead and imagination—a legacy of original ideas and restless creativity that continues to grow. So far, my legacy was a drawing unoriginal enough to please three legal departments.

Jack Kirby was a hero of mine, and working at Handler allowed me to contribute to his legacy. This project had been special—the most Handler could offer me—and it was no longer enough. Because I realized then that I was still in service to other people's ideas—even if the idea belonged to Jack Kirby. And what truer tribute to Kirby could there be than to imagine something new?

I still loved the piece. But it was a tribute to what can come out of dreaming on Delancey Street, nothing more.

I decided then to take the job at LiveWired. It was time to create new things.

I felt my phone vibrate on my chest. It was Juror 10, responding to me teasing her about courtroom humor. "It's my favorite kind," she wrote with a little winky face.

I smiled a little. I didn't even know how Fake Dave's trial was going to turn out. I still had to write the Fakebook ending I'd never planned on—all because this story had earned an audience that deserved one.

More than anything I've ever done, Fakebook made people laugh and feel inspired and excited, and it captured imaginations. It did everything I ever wanted art to do. It was worth the frustrations and the labor that had come with doing it. But it wasn't done yet. I opened the front pocket of my suitcase and pulled out the weekly planner I plotted out Fakebook in. And from atop my covers, in my apartment on Delancey Street, I started to map out the ending I wanted to tell.

It came naturally and surprisingly easily. It felt like the only ending Facebook could ever have—a twisted, funny, slightly mean-spirited mess of Fake Dave's own making. But it was upbeat and optimistic and ultimately satisfying. It felt like the only way Fake Dave's journey ever could have ended. Heh. Lying on Facebook. What a dumb idea. But I'm a believer in dumb ideas.

12 sign-off

"Hey, Dave," Christine said, as she popped her head into the graphics bullpen. "Did you get my email?"

"The one you sent"—I took a look at the time stamp—"seventy-four seconds ago?" I replied with a smirk. I actually enjoyed this ritual, now that it was ending.

At LiveWired, there'd be no client and no client demands. It'd be predictable and ownable. I even had some ideas about creating downloadable wallpapers to match the cases we would sell, and maybe rolling some of what I'd learned working at a PR firm into creating buzz.

It was a job where I was going to create new things. I was going to be building an art department and a product line. I was going to be building a look and feel for an entire company. It was exciting.

"Haha," Christine said. "Yeah, you know how it is. But I just want to make sure this is on your radar. The event is in six weeks," she said as she put her hand on my arm.

"You'll still let me go to the party, right?" I asked.

"Why wouldn't I?" she asked.

"Well…" I almost whispered, "I just put in my notice. My last day is in two weeks."

"What!" Her hand on my arm quickly turned into a fist.

"Ouch!"

"Is this another one of your little lies, David Cicirelli?"

"No, no, I swear it!" I said. "And my lies aren't that little!"

Dave Cicirelli

Just got out of my Grand Jury hearing…

FREEDOM!!!!!!! Case is dismissed!!!!!!! The vindictive nature of a grand jury full of Texans is greatly exaggerated!!!!

Like · Comment

Dave Cicirelli Oh my god…I'm the guy who updates his Facebook page from court. How did this happen? Screw it. Can I get a USA chant going…?

USA!!!!!!!!!!!USA!!!!!!!!!!USA!!!!!!!!!!

7 hours ago via mobile · Like

Ted Kaiser if the jury knew any better they woulda sent u back to Mexico

7 hours ago via mobile · Like

Mike Grassano DC for president 2024

4 hours ago via mobile · Like

Dave Cicirelli Ted, I'm speechless.

4 hours ago via mobile · Like

Dave Cicirelli Grassano!!!! You're right! If I became a felon, I couldn't run! NOW I STILL CAN!!!!!!!

I've got the looks, the sense of responsibility, the magnetic personality and charisma, and am only mildly corrupt. I can win this!

4 hours ago via mobile · Like

Mike Grassano Dave, f#!+ that. Make a run for the border. Get yourself a couple tacos, mingle with the locals. Get into the local drug trade. Work your way up the ladder. Become a drug lord and overdose on some high grade street level meth. That's how I always saw you going out, man.

2 hours ago · Like

Steve Cuchinello Ironic that the person who poisoned you when he brought you into the world saved your ass. You got work to do if you come back to NJ.

2 hours ago via mobile · Like

Mike Grassano You know what, second thought, I was thinking that's how Paco would turn out. Come back to Jersey

2 hours ago via mobile · Like

Curtis Fischer I checked out your profile and your other updates—wow. Lol.

about an hour ago via mobile · Like

Mariko Nakatani Congratulations, Dave! What are you going to do with your newfound freedom?

about an hour ago via mobile · Like

Dave Cicirelli I think I'm gonna take it easy a little while, Alyssa. Haha.

about an hour ago via mobile · Like

Mariko Nakatani That sounds like a good idea :)

about an hour ago via mobile · Like

Brian Hennessy Welcome back, Dave.

about an hour ago via mobile · Like

Dave Cicirelli

The warden let me look at my mug shot yesterday. Apparently it got a lot of laughs. I really hesitated to post it, but I know I'm not the only person who is crying in their mug shot. I can't be, right?

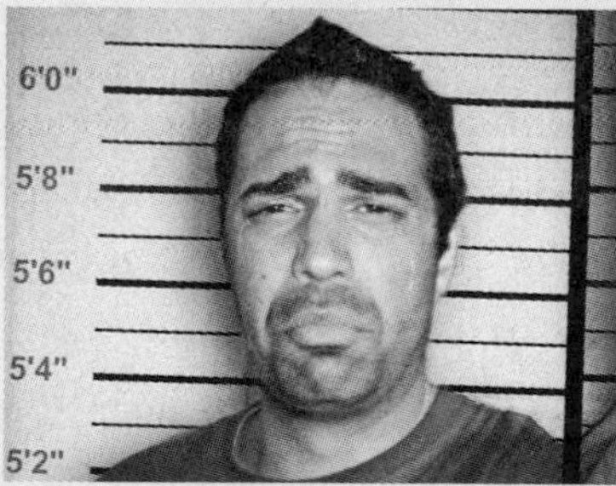

Like · Comment · Share

Sara Whipple no worries, Lindsay Lohan was crying in hers too.

12 minutes ago via mobile · Like

Dave Cicirelli That's good company!
less than a minute ago via mobile · Like

John Peluso I considered smiling in mine, but figured they wouldn't allow it.
just now via mobile · Like

The rest of March would be about wrapping things up—I'd already begun wrapping up six years at Handler. And at the end of the month, I'd wrap up being twenty-six. Most important to me was wrapping up the six months of Fakebook. Prior to the discussion with Elliott, I would have thought that falling apart was the only way for it to end. Now I wanted it to hold together—and I feared that a nonsensical ending that failed to turn a half-year of random thoughts into a story would make the entire enterprise silly and forgettable.

I wanted to stick the landing. Of course, for his story to end, Fake Dave needed to go back to its beginning. I was going to send him back to New Jersey and give him a chance to reconnect to our father before he finally connected with himself.

"All this food for ten dollars!" my dad told me over the phone from Florida. "You'd have to be an idiot to eat after six!"

My parents had rented a house for a month in a fifty-and-over community outside Naples. It was a trial run before they committed to the tried-and-true model of getting old and migrating south.

"Your father's obsessed," my mom chimed in. "We're spending all our time at the Players' Club."

"Wait…where?" I said with a laugh.

"The community has a club," Ralph explained, "with a beautiful pool, a gym, and a restaurant that has a great early-bird special."

"…called the Players' Club," I said, unable to hold back the laughter as I pictured the "players" popping the collars of their finest Tommy Bahama shirts and diamond-studded hearing aids.

"It's where the players go to play," Ralph said, making himself laugh, too.

There's something inspirational about it. I mean, I've never seen someone take to being an old man quite like my father. The man loves getting discounts and having nothing to do.

I've got to admit that after I visited my parents in Florida, they sold me on it. You wake up early, take a walk around a lake, feed some ducks...and before you know it, it's time for an affordable 4:00 p.m. dinner. Life's pretty sweet when you're a player.

At the time of his retirement, however, I didn't know any of this. I was worried that he'd just sit at home all day watching cable news and getting angry at whatever outrage they were manufacturing that week. So to start things off in the right direction, he and I went on a road trip down to the Blue Ridge Mountains in Virginia.

It was a pretty good time—and it gave me a great batch of pictures to use in Fakebook, as Ralph and Fake Dave spent the second week of March driving back from Texas and mending their relationship.

Dave Cicirelli

It's a special day when a father picks up his son from court. I'm genuinely moved right now. I just want people to know I'm ok.

Like · Comment

Ralph Cicirelli For all who have been following this crazy misadventure, I want to say I think Dave has finally seen the light. At least I hope so.

Hopefully the long drive home together will give us a chance to reconnect, sort things out and help Dave decompress.

3 days ago via mobile · Like

Dave Cicirelli
Buddy Road Trip!!!!

Let's see how far this senior discount card can take us!... wait, I'm driving how far with a senior?!?!? This may be the most dangerous leg of my journey.

Like · Comment · Share

Mariko Nakatani Have a safe trip!
2 days ago via mobile · Like

Mary Corrigan LOL good thing for the card because your dad does not look old enough for those discounts!
2 days ago via mobile · Like

Dave Cicirelli oh jeeze. Mary you have no idea what you just started, haha.
2 days ago via mobile · Like

Stephen DiSclafani I hope he doesn't drive like his father!!!
2 days ago via mobile · Like

Gabe Harris At least he has a newer card than my dad LOL.
2 days ago via mobile · Like

Dave Cicirelli I haven't heard him bust out Grandpa's classic line "who gives a shit about the guy behind me" yet, haha.
2 days ago via mobile · Like

Matt Riggio Hope you're heading out of the southern portions of the US.
2 days ago via mobile · Like

Dave Cicirelli Yeah, the south isn't safe with Jeff Shaw on the prowl.
2 days ago via mobile · Like

Matt Riggio Truer words were never spoken.
2 days ago via mobile · Like

Dave Cicirelli
Officially crossed state lines. I'm in NJ for the first time in what seems like a much longer time. Starting to feel a sense of dread…like I've lost.

I can't breathe…and it's not just NJ air quality.

Like · Comment · Share

Ted Kaiser Let's meet up when you get settled. We can bury the hatchet.
less than a minute ago via mobile · Like

Dave Cicirelli Yeah, Ted. You're my top priority.
less than a minute ago via mobile · Like

Ted Kaiser Go back to Mexico
just now via mobile · Like

It's funny…the whole point of Ralph's retirement trip was to develop a taste for the outdoors—to make sure retirement didn't meant watching more TV. Yet, without question, the highlight of the trip was from a hotel room in Virginia, watching some fool lose a half million dollars on *Deal or No Deal*.

For those not familiar, *Deal or No Deal* is a show where there are twenty-six numbered briefcases—each with a dollar value ranging from one to one million. The contestant picks a case and spends the next hour second-guessing himself or herself. One by one, the cases the contestant didn't pick gets opened—narrowing the range of what his case is worth. As the range narrows, the contestant is offered a dollar amount to stop playing—usually close to the average of whatever prize amounts are left. There is no skill involved at all. Only good and bad judgment—of knowing when to take the deal.

And while my father and I occasionally judge each other's decisions too harshly, we're usually on the same page when it comes to judging strangers. Especially when a contestant has two values left—one dollar and one million dollars—and a $450,000 offer to walk away now.

"If this guy bets a half million dollars on a coin toss," Ralph said, "then he's an idiot."

"Yeah," I said. "He's not thinking of the 450K as his money."

The camera panned to a close-up of a guy who didn't comprehend that he was risking a decade worth of his salary.

"We have your family here," said Howie Mandell, the '80s comedian known for putting a glove on his head and present-day *Deal or No Deal* host. "Let's see what they have to say."

They panned to his sister. "I think you should go for it. You're such a special person. You deserve this!"

"Yeah," my dad said sarcastically. "You deserve to win a million dollars on a game show."

"That briefcase," I said in near rage, "isn't capable of judging your character!"

My father laughed.

"I believe in you!" said another sibling.

"It doesn't matter if you believe in him!" Ralph yelled at the screen. As a family, Cicirellis get very emotional about logic.

And then finally the host walked to this fool's poor mother. "It's a lot of money you're risking," she said. "Don't be greedy. Be sensible."

And suddenly you just felt…awful. This poor woman, who'd raised three stupid and greedy children, was watching them gamble away possibly the biggest break that family had ever had. Sadly, her voice of reason was drowned out by the cheering of the crowd and the encouragement of her misguided children.

He jumped up, waved his arms in the air like a home-plate umpire, and yelled out, "NO DEAL!"

He should have taken the deal. A minute later he would be gone from the stage with nothing but a buck in his pocket and a lifetime of regrets. His "this is my moment" fantasy was over, and it came with a $450,000 price tag. Meanwhile, my father and I jumped up out of our motel beds and high-fived. That moment of schadenfreude-driven unity far eclipsed any heartfelt chat that long weekend could have offered.

But looking back at the photos from that trip, I had a slight bit of sympathy for the contestant.

"I can handle the pressure!" he yelled to the crowd at one point, receiving thunderous applause.

But he couldn't handle the pressure—not even close. He was completely controlled by the cheers. Since the beginning of Fakebook I had felt like that. I was hearing two sets of applause—my unknowing audience's cheers for what I claimed to do, and my knowing audience's cheers for me claiming to have done it. One I loved, the other I hated. Yet, I realized the knowing audience's influence was clearly stronger than that of my unknowing viewers—after all, I kept doing it. The support from the people I fooled bothered me when I thought about it. I didn't have to think about it, though, so I often didn't.

The people I saw, however, were the ones in on it. I could actually hear the laughter from Joe, or the encouragement from

Elizabeth or Ted...and especially my father. Their support was tangible and immediate.

In truth, when I was probably ready to hang up Fakebook months ago, my collaborators had encouraged me to continue. I wasn't overtly pressured, but I was fueled by the continued surprise and delight at what they added. This was social media storytelling, which meant it was participatory. My audience was part of the cast, and they played their parts around every post. They made the story better by being part of it.

So I had Fake Dave and Fake Ralph recycle our trip through the Blue Ridge Mountains—and their trip was the one on which we bonded most.

That Friday night, I took Juror 10 to a themed cover-band night at Bowery Ballroom. It was a mistake.

Apparently the only thing more depressing than the first time you see KISS without makeup is seeing Mini KISS without makeup. Watching those poor dwarfs out of costume and loading their tiny instruments into some van between sets—it's a glimpse into a side of life you don't want to see.

It was supposed to be a fun Friday night full of tribute bands, including the top-billed Tragedy, a heavy-metal tribute to the Bee Gees. Joe Moscone and I had seen them before, and they are unbelievably entertaining. It's such an absurd spectacle, full of backup singers in angel wings and some guy dancing around with a feather boa. It had been a really fun night full of weird, unexpected highlights—including a surprise cameo by Moby.

So when Joe was pulling a group of my favorite Handler people together—a group I knew I'd be seeing a whole lot less of—I thought it'd be a knowingly silly and fun thing to take Juror 10 to.

Unfortunately, this glimpse into the sad visage of life on the road as a dwarf cover act was not quite the aphrodisiac I had hoped. Even before we were confronted with the moral issues of watching a band whose main selling point was their disability, I could just tell we didn't have the same sensibility. She was reluctant to jump into the absurd spirit of the night and not especially interested in mixing with my friends. I felt a little too self-aware to really melt into the heavy takes on the Bee Gees' tasty grooves.

Juror 10 and I—we had a really nice moment in Washington Square Park exactly when I needed a moment most. But "just a moment" seemed increasingly like all it would be. I was okay with that. Fakebook was about to end; I was about to start a new job; and my whole life was about to expand again.

So without feeling like there was much keeping me in the city, the next day I took a train to New Jersey, and spent a rainy Saturday and Sunday in my parents' empty house.

On the train ride down, I looked at my calendar. It was March 16. I wanted to end Fake Dave's story in the middle of the next week. From there I'd not post for one week—giving people time to discover the ending. Then, on April 1, I'd confess.

In between would be my last day at Handler and my first day at LiveWired. And on April 2, I'd turn twenty-seven. I had to keep reminding myself of this. It was the first year I wasn't throwing a party. I really didn't know if I'd have enough friends left to throw one.

I'd felt like I needed the comforts of home. It was an hour away, and I hadn't been there since Thanksgiving. But this weekend, that's exactly where I was supposed to be.

Dave Cicirelli

20 minutes until Jeopardy.

The $500 answer is "this jackass f'd his life and career so he could spend six months smelling like piss with nothing to show for it but a bow tie tattoo." God, I feel the walls closing in...

Like · Comment

Bryan Cassidy Who is David Cicirelli!
yesterday · Like

Dave Cicirelli Thanks.
yesterday via mobile · Like

Kristin Boros Williamson i dont even know you but IM proud of u!!! takes a lot of balls to do what you did!!!!!!!!! most people would have stayed where u were and STAYED miserable!! you live and learn right?? :O) xo
yesterday · Like

Dave Cicirelli My dad said "he's glad I'm finally ready to grow up." Night went down hill from there. Screw this. I was fine living on the road.
yesterday via mobile · Like

Dave Cicirelli
Nasty fight with the folks last night, and was shown a letter that…I need to deal with.

At Sandy Hook…thinking.

Like · Comment · Share

Steve Cuchinello Dave, you were a matter of feet from my apartment. You need to come by. I want to see the tattoo.
less than a minute ago · Like

It was the first time in nearly half a year that I had posted a photo that was undoctored and in the moment. I was actually there—at Sandy Hook on March 17—thinking. I was thinking how funny it was to post an honest message that applied to both my lives. How strange it was that Fake Dave and I were crossing paths—him about to end his adventure, and me about to start one of my own. It felt strange to be in the same place at the same time, as strange as it had when I first watched my online persona cross the George Washington Bridge without me.

Now, six months later, I was used to seeing my image as someone else. It felt invasive, almost intimate, to take a picture of our shared shadow. I kicked off my shoes and walked out onto the sand, still cold and wet from last night's rain. The wind was kicking up and pushing against my lightweight jacket. I carefully stepped into the frigid March ocean water, barely able to tolerate the lapping waves as they soaked the bottom of my dark denim jeans.

I looked south, away from the Manhattan skyline, and did the game I always do: look at just the right angle so the entire horizon fills my vision—with nothing to focus on but the vast ocean meeting the vast sky.

Around my ankles, I felt the waves recede—and with it, the grains of sand flooded out from under my heels, causing me to sink slightly into the ocean floor. It was a sensation I'd felt on those summer nights with the friends I grew up with, and those fall afternoons without them.

And it was a feeling we were feeling now—Fake Dave and I—separately and together. But who was the person I was sharing this moment with? Who exactly was Fake Dave?

Fake Dave was deeply flawed, I concluded. He was a guy who ran away from things. He was a guy who was fleeing the narrowing of his future. So he'd jump into a new possibility. Yet each new adventure soon became old routine, and the disappointment would crush him. Because what he was really after was a happy ending. Don't I feel that way? Doesn't everyone? But in real life, there are no endings. Life simply goes on.

Fortunately for Fake Dave, this moment wasn't real life. It was fiction. After all we'd been through, it was time to give him his happy ending. It was time for him to overcome his flaw and become the man deserving of the attention and goodwill he'd received. I wanted to give him something worth the trials I'd put him through.

So after all his running away, I gave him something to finally run toward. I gave him a strange, complicated, rewarding mess of his own making.

Dave Cicirelli
So I found out that Jonathon contacted my family. Kate came back home and she's pregnant.

BTW. Now that I want a DNA test, she's Amish again. The only thing that could make today any worse is if the Irish were somehow more drunk than usual. Happy St. Patrick's Day, everyone.

Like · Comment

Matt Campbell Wow. Is this in addition to the letter you have to deal with? Or is the letter you had to deal with from Jonathon re: his prego daughter? You never really specified...And what the hell do you do with your Census form?

3 days ago · Like

Matt Riggio is this your fucking kid Dave? When will we know?!

3 days ago · Like

Joe Moscone I'll start by saying that I'm VERY glad to hear you're home. However this Kate news...get a paternity test. I'm not trying to be a dick, but we both know that it's quite possibly (read: likely) that her time with you might have triggered some "questionable behavior" since she's left you. It's what girls like her do.

3 days ago · Like

Elizabeth Lee O.M.G. David...is it yours?
3 days ago via mobile · Like

Elizabeth Lee Joe, I usually don't agree with you...but in this case, I do. You should def. get a paternity test.
3 days ago via mobile · Like

Mary Carroll Cuz maybe you should get some drinks tonight...
3 days ago via mobile · Like

Dave Cicirelli Is there ANY chance that Jonathon will allow his Amish grand son to get a DNA test?
3 days ago via mobile · Like

Kevin Conway Well at least all your Maury Povich experience will finally come in handy...
3 days ago via mobile · Like

Ted Kaiser So many questions...I had given up feeling bad for you, but now there's a kid involved. I hope for his/her sake that you get your life together man.
3 days ago via mobile · Like

Dave Cicirelli I don't know if its mine. She did cheat on me at least once. But what are my options? I mean, can I leave her to raise a bastard child that may be mine in a community that is NOT cool with the single mother thing...? I mean, I still care about her. Can I abandon her if she's in need? Am I a sucker? What a spectacular mess.
2 days ago via mobile · Like

Erin Brennan Hanson O.M.G.
2 days ago · Like

Lauren Shockey maybe you can write up your adventures and pitch it as a lifetime movie.
2 days ago via mobile · Like

Erin Brennan Hanson "Confessions of an Amish Baby Daddy"?
2 days ago via mobile · Like

Dave Cicirelli I've racked my brain, and there doesn't even seem to be a Morrissey song that perfectly encapsulates this situation. Perhaps I should write my story. Like Jim White once sang "what wonderful fiction I will craft from this terrible pain."

2 days ago via mobile · Like

Steve Cuchinello Dave, its time to man up. If this isn't a slap in the face of reality I don't know what is. Your self destruction is one thing but now you are talking about a kid's life and that has to teach you to grow up. If its yours it's time to be a man.

2 days ago via mobile · Like

Dave Cicirelli It must be hard to read type this small from atop your high horse, Steve.

2 days ago via mobile · Like

Steve Cuchinello Oh yes I forgot the last 6 months has constantly reminded me of your excellent choices in judgement. What was I thinking.

2 days ago via mobile · Like

Dave Cicirelli

Ok, let's get to it. Names that will ruin (possibly) my baby's life. Go!

Like · Comment

Ara Arnn David Cicirelli, Jr.

yesterday via mobile · Like

Annette Pandolfo De Luca Sue, but only if it is a boy.

yesterday · Like

Chris Mitarotondo sapphire

yesterday via mobile · Like

Kristen Scalia Sissy Cicirelli

yesterday via mobile · Like

Stephen Ortez Ismael

yesterday via mobile · Like

Aaron Summers Aaron Summers

yesterday · Like

Ted Kaiser Mark Messier Cicirelli

yesterday via mobile · Like

Howard Tsu Hettoit Cicirelli

yesterday via mobile · Like

Dave Cicirelli Good suggestions.

Let's remember, this kid'll be going to an Amish school. Can we think of anything for that specific breed of school yard bully?

Combustible Engine Cicirelli?

yesterday via mobile · Like

Dave Cicirelli I've reviewed the entries and have decided Ara showed the most wit. Well done.

Regardless, I'm naming my son Sparkles, and if it's a daughter I'll name her George Foreman Jr.

yesterday via mobile · Like

MARCH 29: END OF THE ROAD.

When it all began...

I've been through a lot. An awful lot. So, so much. I think I've reached the end of the road.

I'm writing this from a coffee shop in Intercourse Pennsylvania. The same coffee shop where I wrote a post leading to my first visit to the Amish. I'm about to return.

It reminds me of the classic philosophical question that asks "can a man step into the same river twice?"

It feels an appropriate thing to ponder just before my return…and my reunion with Kate. I'm a different man than the inspirational figure who thought freedom meant walking over the GW Bridge and across three states to find a niche religious community just to toilet paper their horse and buggy.

When I was last here, I was a vandal, an unrepentant hate criminal who indignantly left with one of their daughters, whom I'd taken as a lover.

When I rejoin them, as I step into that same river twice, I know the waters will be choppy. But as the river changes, so has the man. I'm stronger now, strengthened by the confidence that only a fashionable tattoo can provide.

I started this journey running from responsibility, now I run towards one. It's come so full circle, it almost feels scripted.

Although Kate being pregnant with (probably) my child is the unplanned driving force for me to adopt the Amish way of life, I'm at peace with this. I'm not running away any more.

I used to feel so compelled to have more and more. I was an experience glutton, discarding all that I had because I was seduced by the abstract "thing that I'm missing." Now I see that only thing I was missing was maturity. The maturity to know that my friends and family weren't obstacles keeping me from the world, they were protection from its cruelty and danger. I always knew how important it was for them to look up to me, but I didn't realize how important it is to me to look down on them. To all my friends, I'm sorry for taking you for granted.

This will likely be my last post. I'm leaving the world of Facebook with a heart full of sadness for what I'm leaving behind...but also full of hope for the future I'm committed to build, and the roots I hope to grow.

I almost lost everything in my inspirational search for more. Now I'm ready for a simple, honest life in a community that I always hated, to win back the woman I think I love, so I can raise what is quite possibly my child. Father hood with a twist.

Finally, a wacky adventure I'm excited to settle down with. Even though I'm no longer a citizen of the road, I still encourage us all to march into the future with no destination other than to court the many possibilities that lie just around the next bend.

Look how well it worked for me!

Thank you for all your support over these past six months. I'm happy to have traveled with you.

Tara B. It's been one hell of a ride (and we're just readers). I mean it with all of my heart when I say: Good luck!

about an hour ago · Like

Pete Garra Amazing. Seriously kudos.

about an hour ago via mobile · Like

Elizabeth Lee Good luck david

about an hour ago via mobile · Like

Matt Campbell Wow
32 minutes ago via mobile · Like

Jay Patterson For what its worth man, you may have deterred some of us in the same "wanderlust vs rut" mentality of taking the same crooked travels. And even tho i barely know you its been good reading about your adventures, good luck with Fatherhood man!
29 minutes ago via mobile · Like

Peter Glass Hey Dave, haven't really seen you since high school, but just wanted to wish you all the best, good luck man.
5 minutes ago via mobile · Like

Greg Cicchelli "Sometimes your whole life boils down to one insane move"
less than a minute ago via mobile · Like

With Fake Dave's story over, and my confession still on the horizon, I could focus on my last two days at Handler PR.

Or at least I tried to. My voice mail was full of messages from Freddy and LiveWired, trying to get me to come in early or do assignments at night. It wasn't an option—I'd already agreed to start that upcoming Monday, skipping out on any sort of downtime between jobs. I wasn't willing to now have these jobs overlap.

The guy's demeanor changed once I took the job. He was demanding, but I still kind of liked him. And I took him up on his offer of talking frankly by affirming I wasn't available until the last week of March. I owed Handler my two weeks' notice, and I was going to make sure they got it.

There are plenty of stories about horrible bosses and horrible jobs and the types of skewed versions of lifelong dreams that a job offered. This was never one of them.

On a professional and artistic level, I was completely at peace with my decision to leave. On a personal level, I was devastated. I was saying good-bye to a lot of friends—friends who, over the last six months, had been especially important to me.

And as the last two days wrapped up—with me putting the contents of my desk into one of my completed superhero shippers—and as I stacked dozens of collaborative projects into this 20-inch cube, each press kit or invitation or stupid-awesome bobblehead was a memory. Feeling none of the day-to-day pressure of approaching deadlines and client demands, it was hard not to feel nostalgic.

That feeling was only compounded by the happy hour my boss threw for me on my last day. It was a great time, and it kept going well past the original venue. Christine and Joe were there until the very end and even bought me the greatest slice of pizza a dollar has ever been spent on.

Come Saturday morning, it was over—with Friday only lingering as vague memories and a sharp headache. It occurred to me, as I took some aspirin and tried to salvage what I could of my two-day stretch of unemployment, that it really was over in more than one way.

Both PR and fictional profiles were behind me. I was officially out of the business of creating public faces.

In my life before and after Fakebook, I've had a lot of bosses. And in my experience, there's usually a line or a moment within the first few days that speaks volumes of the relationship that's about to unfold. I once had a creative director who welcomed me into his office. He had the classic album *In the City* by The Jam playing out of his speakers and an autographed photo of legendary New Jersey Devils goaltender Martin Brodeur on his desk.

"This," I thought to myself, "is a good sign."

His replacement, however, canceled our initial meeting because she had to deal with her "au pair quitting via text message."

"This," I thought to myself, "is a bad sign."

But as far as red flags go, little compares to "Where's your computer?"

"I'm not sure, Freddy..." I said somewhat confused, as I got up from the couch in reception of LiveWired to greet him. "Where did you set it up?"

"You mean you didn't bring yours?"

"I'm sorry," I said, completely dumbfounded. "Were you expecting me to donate the use of my personal computer?"

"Donate? I'm paying you! What happened to the one you brought on your interview?"

"It's at home...with the shirt I wore that day, too..."

"Just bring it tomorrow. Come on, I'll show you to your desk."

I follow him in a bit of a daze, trying to process what I'd just learned—attempting to figure out how this fit into the vision of building an art department that I was sold on.

We walked past the large conference room I was interviewed in and past a dozen cubicles in the quiet, early morning office. We turned a corner and walked down a small hallway.

"Welcome," Freddy said, "to LiveWired."

"Is this storage?" I asked.

"What? No."

I couldn't believe what I saw—it was like I'd stepped into an office-themed episode of *Hoarders*.

The room was cramped and overflowing with boxed and unboxed crap—every kind of cheap garbage merchandise you could imagine—from pocket knives to fake leather wallets to those computer mice that drew me to the gig. Mounds and mounds of inventory were piled onto shelves, in bins, in freestanding drawers, on desks, and on the floor. It was less an office than a Dumpster.

"This is the office?" I asked again. "Then what did we just walk through?"

"That's another company. We rent this space from them."

It was four days until my Facebook confession, but I suddenly began to question if my real life should be public again.

"I didn't realize..."

"It's fine. Here's your desk." Freddy waved his arms toward a precariously stacked pile of LiveWired-brand iPad "armor" cases. I carefully walked toward it, afraid too hard a step would cause an avalanche of accessories. I took a deep breath and began to stack them in some semblance of order and structural integrity.

After careful excavation, I found the tabletop and sat down at my chair—promptly banging my knees and causing an empty armor case to fall three and a half feet onto the floor, cracking on impact with the soft carpet.

"Careful!" Freddy blurted out. "I can't have you breaking all of our samples!"

"Sorry! I banged my knees on something." I looked under my desk to discover it wasn't a desk at all. It was a bookshelf. And I banged my knees because bookshelves have shelves.

Soon after I removed a bunch of LiveWired keyboards to give myself a small cavity in which to place my legs, one of my new coworkers arrived. He was setting up a laptop on the bookshelf next to mine.

"Hi, I'm Dave," I said, still clinging to my "first day at camp" enthusiasm. "The new designer."

"Hi, I'm James," he responded somewhat meekly. We reached over a pile of computer mice stacked between our shelves and shook hands. "Head of product development."

"Oh great!" I said. "We'll probably be doing a lot of work together."

"Let's hope so," he said. He hands me the power cord to his Dell. "Do you mind plugging this in?"

"Sure," I said. "Is that a PC? I was hoping we'd be on Macs. That's what I'm used to."

"I'll be on a Mac soon," he said. "I'm saving up."

It was Thursday night, and my first week at LiveWired was almost over.

I decided to walk home after our product review meeting—the full forty blocks and eight avenues. It didn't feel sufficient to decompress from that crystallization of my new company.

How to explain it…

You know how, near the checkout line at a T. J. Maxx, you'll see the world's crappiest pocket knife packaged with the world's crappiest binoculars and, like, a carabiner? And they'd call it something like "Extreme Outdoor Adventure Kit," and they'd sell it for $7.99, and your grandma would buy it for you, and it'd ruin your birthday?

These were the people responsible for that product.

It was a knock-off firm. They'd buy something that exists, send it to a factory in China, and make a lower-quality version of it. It was the opposite of creativity. It was theft.

And the whole thing wasn't just disheartening but degrading.

During the meeting, Freddy began clapping his fingers into his palm. It was only after he increased in speed that I realized it was the "gimmie" motion of an infant. I got up, walked a few steps toward him, and nudged a flashlight a few inches toward his flapping fingers.

You just felt…humiliated.

Somewhere around Thompson Square Park, the weight of my personal laptop began to pinch my shoulder.

"We'll discuss it next week," Freddy had said to me today when I told him I wouldn't bring my computer in indefinitely. "But if we buy you the computer, you can provide your own software, right? I don't care if you steal it."

Freddy and I had a lot to discuss—including a ten-thousand-dollar salary discrepancy.

This whole thing was an epic disaster. It wasn't like I could be happy just to have a job—I'd had a job. And I quit it because Freddy convinced me this was a better opportunity.

And now I realized that the qualities I'd found so endearing when I was interviewing—that he was so quick to tell people that he "never tells a lie," and why he could so proudly handle people calling him "a piece of shit"—had a simple explanation. Practice. He'd had lots and lots of practice.

I tried to briefly forget about it. Tomorrow was Friday. And Friday was my birthday.

And tonight...well, tonight was April Fools' Day. And that meant I had something important to do.

With a sore shoulder and a coffee shop across the street, I decide this was as good a spot as any to confess the Fakebook fraud. So I grabbed a coffee and sat down at a table. I pulled out my laptop. Lifting the screen woke it from sleep mode and presented me with the LiveWired files I'd been working on. An intense frustration swelled up in me. I closed my eyes tightly and inhaled.

So this is it, I thought to myself. This is my penance.

I'd fooled my friends and family into believing I was on the move—and at the end of it, I was fooled into moving. Like Fake Dave, I even ended up in a place without computers.

I closed the window with LiveWired work and opened the Word doc I've been preparing for the past week.

This was the moment I'd been dreading for half a year, but also one I'd been looking forward to. This was the moment when I could finally rejoin my community—when I could rejoin the world and reclaim my reputation. This was where I no longer had to pretend my life was this "leap-before-you-look" disaster.

Except now it actually was.

Served me right for believing something I read on the Internet.

APRIL 1: IT WAS ALL A DREAM...

What a crazy dream I just had...

...April Fools...?

So all that crazy stuff that's been going on in my life...none of it is true. It's all been a six-month social experiment, a hoax.

I never faced hate-crime charges in Pennsylvania Dutch Country, nor did I sway a young, beautiful Amish girl into joining me on my journey. I never wandered nude through the desert while suffering from extreme dehydration and rabies-induced hallucinations. I did not fall victim to the sly-tongued, brainwashing ways of a cult's recruiters. And there is certainly no baby on the way.

So why did I spend so much time destroying my reputation?

I think most of us share a collective anxiety about how Facebook has changed the social paradigm. There is no such thing as falling out of touch anymore. Over time our relationships just devolve into newsfeeds that nurture both voyeurism and narcissism. We select a version of ourselves and present it to an audience with every new post. I find this fascinating, and wanted to exploit and subvert this phenomenon.

But to try and say that what I did was completely out of intellectual curiosity or artistic impulse is not true. To be honest (for once), my motivation was mostly a love of mischief. There is nothing to stop someone from simply making stuff up.

I hope people realize that I meant no ill will. People enjoyed reading it, right?

Against a backdrop of boring nonsense in all of our news feeds, I think there's a place for a page where anything can happen. I don't think we even scratched the surface of Facebook's potential as a new storytelling medium, but I think we are among the first to discover that it exists at all.

Who could have guessed that a reaction to Farmville would blossom into the first attempt at real-time, social media storytelling? And it was social. We all played a part in making this thing something special. It wasn't just the knowing collaborators who drove the plot forward in the message section, but also everyone who didn't know this was a hoax. If you read the page, if you left comments, or if you did good old fashioned gossip about "what's going on with Dave," you were a part of it.

It's rare to be part of something that breaks ground, and flips an experience that hundreds of millions of people share. Now that it's been done once, it can never again be done for the first time.

So...April Fools. This profile is once again a real one. I'm done with tricks. You have my word, and you know what that's worth.

Also, tomorrow is my birthday. I love you.

But I didn't post it…not yet. I sat there, looking out the window toward Thompson Square Park at dusk, with my cursor hovering over the Submit button and my index finger over the Enter key.

It was a feeling I was familiar with but still not quite used to. This confession was floating in limbo—it both had already happened and was still to come. But this time, the feelings of nervousness and embarrassment and fear of judgment from my audience—my friends, my Facebook friends, my family, my old colleagues—faded into something else.

Six months ago, when my finger first lingered over the Enter key, and just before I gave the first words of Fakebook life and allowed them to broadcast to the news feeds of an unsuspecting audience, I'd had no notion of the consequences of what I was about to do. I didn't think about the people I'd have to avoid or the feelings I'd hurt. I didn't consider the places I couldn't go and the events I couldn't take part in. I didn't consider the many hours a week I would be devoting to my second life, or how I'd have to be ever vigilant of exposure.

I was also completely ignorant to how intertwined my real life and my online persona were—of how much of what was on that screen was actually a part of me. I underestimated how impactful our separation would be and didn't consider what it meant to be estranged from my community—a community which would make me into an undeserving folk hero. I didn't realize how it would complicate old relationships, and what an obstacle it would be in trying to form new ones.

And I certainly never imagined it would change lives.

But now I had experienced it. I had told Elliott that what makes Fakebook interesting is the total separation of real and fake life. I was wrong. That's impossible to do. In truth, that was me up on people's walls. It was the side of me that likes to push things—that challenges authority and assumptions. Fake Dave was a compilation of various sides of me, many of which I thought I had discarded for the sake of growing up.

But in truth, those sides of me were just an Enter key away. Pressing down would end this and reconnect my selves on both sides of the screen. We'd both blindly leaped into a disaster, and not for the first time. But for all Fake Dave's flaws, he's always had the guts to leap again. And that was a quality I needed again.

So I pushed Enter.

John Muscari How do we know that this note is not the real April Fools' joke and you are using it to disguise how you are once again running away from reality by abandoning your unborn child?
4 hours ago via mobile · Like

Erin Brennan Hanson I'm with John. I call bull$hit.
4 hours ago via mobile · Like

David Thomas whichever version is true i've enjoyed it maybe as much as you have. As people we both cherish the opportunity to be connected and protected from others and ourselves. it is a true jewel to be able to create our own destiny. Got fired? Just call it artistic differences:) Got dumped? You're looking for new opportunities:)
4 hours ago via mobile · Like

David Thomas Also...Rabbit Rabbit.
4 hours ago via mobile · Like

Greg Cicchelli Wow. You put an absurd amount of work into this joke. You got me, I still think you should submit the script as a sequel to Into The Wild.
4 hours ago via mobile · Like

Elizabeth Lee I think this was and is awesome. And thank you for giving me the Fakebook fairytale happy ending (as odd as it was, it satisfied the hopeful girl in me).
4 hours ago via mobile · Like

Joe Moscone Dave, if it's okay with you, I'd like to continue writing disapproving, cantankerous comments on your wall? I've come to enjoy it. And to everyone that bought into your story/lies...well, let's just say that I feel bad for stupid people.
4 hours ago via mobile · Like

Brian Eckhoff Fine, Dave, let's put all our cards on the table. My family isn't Amish, and I came to the conclusion that Ben Franklin was nothing but an Illuminati stooge a couple years back. But mutual deception has taken us this far…All the best to you, Kate and baby Zipper.
3 hours ago via mobile · Like

Aaron Summers The Bob Newhart ending. Classic. Thumbs way up.
3 hours ago via mobile · Like

Kristin Boros Williamson Holy crap…
3 hours ago via mobile · Like

George Gross I think I'm just sad that it had to end.
3 hours ago via mobile · Like

Peter Glass well played sir, feeling very used here :)
2 hours ago via mobile · Like

Michèle Malejki Awesome! Congrats on the creativity, sir.
2 hours ago via mobile · Like

Ralph Cicirelli Happy birthday for real! Thanks for letting me be a part of the adventure.
2 hours ago via mobile · Like

Jamie McAllister So were you in NYC the whole time? I admit I believed the whole thing and defended the truth of it to people who were dubious. Good job.
about an hour ago via mobile · Like

Dave Cicirelli Jamie…your personal message to me gave me an anxiety attack, haha.
about an hour ago via mobile · Like

Jamie McAllister haha—no worries. I was just in a bad place at the time and after I quit I started getting nervous that I'd done something stupid, and fake or not reading your story made me feel sane. It turned out it

was 100% the right decision (whether it was a sane one or not).

about an hour ago via mobile · Like

Matt Riggio You sack of shit!

just now via mobile · Like

13 fakebook friends

It's 9:00 p.m. on a perfect, spring Saturday night. Clear skies, seventy degrees, and the whole of New York has that energy that comes from that first nice day after a long winter. It's obvious. I can even see it from New Jersey.

In town for a visit, I'm spending my night on my parents' couch with the television on in the background and my new iPad on my lap. I scroll through Facebook posts and posts on the half-dozen other mainstream social media platforms that have emerged since I ended my fictional journey.

People are checking into the newest bars on FourSquare. I'm reading celebratory tweets with hashtag-based humor. I'm looking at their Instagram photos of overgarnished cocktails and fancy desserts. I recognize some of their outfits—all pinned on Pinterest a week in advance. I parrot to myself a sentiment I've heard over and over in the hundreds of articles, editorials, and films I've absorbed since this became one of the focuses of my life.

"We've never been more connected, yet never more isolated."

It's a clean statement that reveals irony. It has a nice symmetry—a simplicity of concept that has all the affectations of being profound. It sounds right. And when the only thing illuminating the room is the ambient light of social media posts from a Saturday night I'm not a part of, it almost feels true.

Then I take another look at the posts. People are out drinking and dancing. They are meeting, breaking up, having fun, being miserable. They are making mistakes, taking chances, backing down, and stepping up. They are getting into messes. People continue to live their lives.

I realize what a fool's errand it is to try to sum up the social media experience in a single, universal statement. Facebook hasn't built walls between us; it's built roads. Social media is driven by people, and people are complex. And that complexity only grows when we cross one another's paths. The landscape we cross has clearly changed, and new rules and new behaviors are emerging out of it—but these new roads still lead us to one another.

I pick up my iPad and look at my list of Facebook friends. My eyes linger on those who were such a big part of that strange six-month experience but have since faded from my life. I know that Dhara moved out of New York and is dating someone new. I know that Juror 10 had a creme brulee at a nice restaurant with her sister. I know that Elliott likes to post open-ended musings, and that Kate Moulton just went to a costume party—not as an Amish girl.

And I'm still struck by how much emotion these images and a handful of short statements can stir in me. Sure, it's minutiae—but those little details do matter. Community is a mosaic of branching out lives—and your news feed is a reminder that other people's stories don't end just because we stopped sharing a stage.

But it's just a hint—an unreliable, easily manipulated, heavily spun posting from an author with an agenda. We'll only know as much as their protagonist tells us and what we can infer. In some ways that's so little; in some ways that's so much.

I scroll down a little farther and come across the profile picture of someone who learned this lesson well. In the picture he's walking away, while his one-year-old son on his shoulders looks back toward the camera with a little smirk. As an image, it has right amount of mystery and mischief that I'd expect from Matt Campbell—my secret foil.

It's appropriate that his back is to me. I can never know what struggles and triumphs exist behind his profile—the depth of the things he doesn't care to share. And ten years ago, I never could. But a post is just one click away from becoming a conversation.

It's still early. I'll see if he's around.

I park my parents' Saturn between an Italian sports car and a pickup truck and cut through the back entrance to the Dublin House, that inimitable bar within a house. I pass through the Saturday-night crowd at the main bar and take a quick look in the adjacent living room, with its leather chairs around the big fireplace. I walk past the main staircase to the second floor and out the front door.

Sitting on the brick patio out front, I see someone who for months had the better of me.

"Matt Campbell," I say.

"What's good, buddy?"

He stands up, and we do the classic "dude hug."

"How've you been?" I say. "How are Kristen and the baby?"

"Yeah man, things are great. Kristen is doing well," he says. "And Shane's getting big. It's crazy how it goes."

"I know. I saw the pics on Facebook. It's nuts…"

"Speaking of pics on Facebook," Matt says, "…did you really meet Springstein?"

Dave Cicirelli

yep

Like · Comment · Share

Amanda Brokaw Schweitzer For real?
yesterday via mobile · Like

Daniel Timek wow, cool look alike.
yesterday via mobile · Like

Stanley Shih Don't you have a habit of photoshopping FB posts?
yesterday via mobile · Like

Ted Kaiser is this real or more Fakebook?
yesterday via mobile · Like

Erin Brennan Hanson It's not so much that you're standing next to the Boss, but that you're in a Blockbuster that is blowing my mind.
yesterday via mobile · Like

"*Yes!*" I say with a laugh. "It's killer! My credibility is completely shot."

I make light of my credibility, but it's more than a little bit true. Fakebook has become my identity—for its audacity and for people's personal relationship with it. People are eager to share their experience—when they first saw it, what they thought of me as it was happening, whether they thought it was funny or if it made them angry.

To my relief, Elliott's arc was fairly common—people went from disbelief to anger to appreciation in a quick span of time. Sure, I got a handful of "fuck you's" like I'd expected, but mostly people were more interested in why they'd believe it than why I'd do it.

"At least you didn't photoshop highlights into Bruce's hair," Matt says with a laugh.

"I've learned my lesson," I joke back. "That still cracks me up...Of all the ridiculous things I posted, it was the peroxide in Amish Kate's hair that did me in."

"Credit goes to my wife for spotting that," he says. We both laugh at the sheer dude-ness of my oversight. Apparently Amish girls don't do highlights.

We order a round and begin the enjoyable process of catching up. It's a gutsy thing he's doing—leaving his steady job as a CT technologist in New Jersey and moving to Ohio to be near his wife's family and opening an artisanal coffee-roasting company.

I ask him about the kind of place he wants to open, and he tells me all about his vision for Branch Street. He speaks passionately about his philosophy on roasting and the history he's eager to be part of. He tells me about the experiences when he first discovered the nuances and flavor notes of good coffee, and speaks about regions and climates with the passion and expertise of a good sommelier discussing great wine cellars. He talks about the type of place he wants to create, how it will be unpretentious and inviting. How it'll feel like it's always been part of the community. In short, he tells me his dream with the energy of a man who's pursuing it.

"You know what's crazy," Matt says.

"What's that?"

"It was really Fakebook that got the ball rolling on all of this," he says.

"*What!*" I cry. "But…you *knew* it was fake. With the flowers, and the copy of *Million Little Pieces*, the ironic mix tape…my god, even the anonymous text messages…you tortured me because you knew it was fake."

"Yeah," he says, "but the whole time I had to reflect on why watching you—or him—or whatever…watching you pretend to walk out on your career—I started thinking about why that meant so much to me. So yeah, Branch Street exists because of Fakebook."

"Please don't put that on me…" I say. "I already have to live with Jamie quitting her job."

"You quit your job, too," he reminds me.

"Yeah," I say. "A couple of them, ha. The best is still LiveWired."

"What happened there?"

"I called them up and said, 'Yesterday was my last day.'"

We both laugh.

"So you quit a job without notice," Matt says. "Sounds familiar."

"Yeah...Fake Dave rubbed off on me too, I guess," I admit.

I smile a little and think of the journey I've been on since Fakebook ended. Of how I hustled to get out of the LiveWired mess—waking up early and staying up late, calling in every favor I had until I got a new job at another PR firm. It wasn't the move I'd originally envisioned, but it stopped the bleeding, and came with a computer and a desk.

From there, I kept pushing forward in perfect Fake Dave style—with unearned confidence and a complete lack of planning. I chased what was interesting and ultimately landed a really creative gig in a field I never knew existed. I'm a senior art director at an experiential design firm called Mirrorball. We create live experiences—sponsor concerts, throw big events, put on shows—all over the country. We're tasked with creating new and different things and sending them out into the world—all with that wonderful open-ended mission to "get people talking." I'm done making up fake events. I now make up real ones.

But beyond my day job, I feel like my whole life has been reinfused with a proactive spirit—a "why not?" attitude. I spend my time working on personal art and projects with a newfound energy. When I began, I felt like the future was narrowing for me. Now it feels wide open, and my scope of what's possible is much broader than it ever was. I'm more willing than ever to walk forward without a plan and let life surprise me.

"It all worked out," I say to Matt. It did for him too, actually.

"So I'm opening a coffee roaster, Jamie is living in Portland, and you've become an art director," Matt says. "A lot happened, out of, you know, nothing happening."

"That's the power of art," I say.

"Oh jeez," Matt snarks. "What do you say, arteest, care for another round?"

"Sure." I laugh.

Over two years ago, when I sat on this patio that Labor Day weekend, Matt Campbell was a Facebook friend. That is to say, not really a friend at all. Almost three years later, I'm raising my glass in the town I was exiled from, with a friend I wouldn't have had, in the bar where it all started.

We've never been more connected, yet never more isolated, I think.

What a crock of shit. The truth is so much more complex and so much more compelling.

We've never been so connected.

acknowledgments

It's hard to even know where to begin thanking people for all their efforts in this unplanned experiment in social media storytelling.

This book truly is a social story. In many ways, this is a story about my relationship with my community, and my community had a starring role. It wasn't just the knowing collaborators who turned Fakebook from an idle thought into a strange adventure, but also everyone who didn't know this was a hoax. Anyone who read the page, left a comment, or simply gossiped about "what's going on with Dave" made Fakebook what it is.

Thank you, Ted Kaiser, Steve Cucinelli, Joe Moscone, Elizabeth Lee, Matt Campbell, Elliott Askew, Kate Moulton, Jeff Shaw, Matt Riggio, Rolando Alvarado, Suzanne Pagliorola, Alula Medhen, Christine Reardon, Chris Bailey, Joe Lennon, and everyone else whose contributions are visible both on my wall and in the pages of this book.

But where the fake story ended is where the real work began. There were countless people who made this book possible.

My father, Ralph, gets a lot of deserving attention in this book, but none of it would be possible without the enthusiasm and support of my entire family. So thank you, Ralph, Mark, Jeff, Lisa, Elisha, and especially my mother, Phyllis. She was an invaluable sounding board as I wrote and a patient set of ears when I was feeling overwhelmed.

I'd also like to thank the entire Sourcebooks team—in particular my two editors, Peter Lynch and Stephanie Bowen.

Peter, my original editor, first purchased *Fakebook*. His enthusiasm helped me believe in my own crazy idea.

I cannot thank my editor Stephanie Bowen enough for joining this project mid-stride and never skipping a beat. Upon meeting her, it was immediately clear that she understood what I hoped to accomplish, and together we worked toward it. This book is better because she became a part of it.

In addition: With a book requiring as many production logistics as this, pulling *Fakebook* off would have been almost impossible without the patient organizational efforts of Heather Hall, Chris Norton, Jenna Skwarek, and Abby Saul.

And of course there is my agent, Stephen Barr. He saw the potential in *Fakebook* as a story and me as an author. More than anyone else, this book exists because he believed I could write it. I truly cannot thank him enough.

None of this would have happened if not for Maya Rock, who thought enough of *Fakebook* to put me on Stephen's radar. Or Mariko Nagataki, who was the "friend" when Maya and I were just friends of friends. Or Brian Morrison, who got me to join the coed hipster hockey league where Mariko and I met. And on and on backward through the many crazy interlocking and complicated webs of personal and professional connections that make up the social network of humanity—going all the way back to when Adam first met Eve.

about the author

Dave Cicirelli is a New York–based writer and art director with extensive experience serving iconic consumer and entertainment brands across all print, digital, and experiential media. His work has won a number of awards, including a Silver Anvil and honors from *HOW* magazine, *GDUSA*, and *Creativity* 38.

In the eight years he's been in the marketing industry, he's witnessed the impact social media has had on how brands talk to consumers. In the sixteen years since he got an AOL screen name, he's witnessed the impact social media has had on how people talk to one another.

Fakebook is his first book, and that's why there are so many pictures in it.

Photo Credit: Stephen Papageorge